Show Barn Blues

Natalie Keller Reinert

One

Of all the types of boarders I could have had, the woman in my office right now was by far the worst sort.

Believe me, by this point in my life, I knew all about boarders. After twelve years of running a successful A-circuit show barn with forty stalls, a covered arena, a jumping course, dressage arena, and a dozen paddocks, I knew way more about boarders than I could ever want. I knew the good. I knew the bad… and I knew the bad easily outweighed the good. You try to make forty different horse owners happy sometime. I just dare you to try.

"This is no kind of a way to make a living," I'd tell my working students as they came and went, and some of them would believe me and go back to college, and some of them wouldn't and would go into the business themselves, and then they'd see me at horse shows and commiserate and say things like "Grace, you were right all along."

I'd just nod while they unloaded their troubles, secure in the knowledge that I was usually right, and I was used to people not believing me until it was too late. I was like a mother that way, I supposed, although I didn't have any children of my own. Just a barn full of adult children — the aforementioned boarders — and four-legged children — the horses. It was hard to tell which were more trouble on any given day, but most days, I'd give the top score to the humans.

Still, they were the ones that paid the ever-mounting bills, and there were fewer and fewer of them these days. I sighed and ran a hand through my short-cropped hair, (once dirty blonde, now dirty grayish-brown, emphasis on the grayish) then fastened on a quick smile so that the young woman sitting across from me didn't think anything was wrong. I was a businesswoman, after all. It wouldn't be fair of me to make her feel uncomfortable while I judged her application. For the thousandth time (or millionth) I thought how much easier life would be if I just got the horses, without the boarders.

The horses had their own quirks, but they were the reason we went into the horse business in the first place. It was the people that owned the horses, bought the horses, paid you to train and care for the horses — they were the problem. In their various archetypes, they made life as a trainer and barn manager impossible, each in their own special ways.

For example, you had your Precious Pony type boarder — the controlling, doting horse mother, who thought nothing of phoning up a barn manager at eleven o'clock at night after a bad thunderstorm so that she could make sure her darling love was able to sleep all right after all that nasty noise. Precious Pony's mummy would not hesitate to drag one of the already-overworked grooms off to embark on some private stall-betterment scheme, and was always buying horse-toys that had to be drilled into barn walls (by the grooms, again) or putting up a stall guard so that Precious Pony could stick his head out into the barn aisle, despite the fact that this was strictly forbidden to prevent bites and barn aisle battles between passing horses. Precious Pony was above the rules because Precious Pony's mummy and her four-footed offspring were *special*.

Precious Pony types had lost me more good grooms and put more holes into my stall walls than I would care to recount.

Then you had your Poor-But-Proud Go-Getter, always trying to work off riding lessons and to convince other boarders that she's their gal for any extra riding or schooling that their horses might need. All talent, no money — and not just teenagers, either. Some women hang on to their trainer dreams for surprisingly long, lean years before they realize it just isn't going to happen, or they finally sell all their belongings and move to Germany to take a dressage apprenticeship just like they had wanted to do, when they were seventeen but had chosen to go to college like their mothers wanted instead. The Go-Getters were a problem that I usually flushed out pretty quickly. It wasn't a lack of respect for these perpetual working students, don't get me wrong — we all had to start somewhere and I'd done my share of begging for rides — but there were simply too many of them, and if *they* were schooling a fellow boarder's problem horse, then, simply, *I* wasn't.

The Go-Getters were welcome to pursue their dreams and I wasn't above throwing them a lesson now and again in exchange for the occasional pulled mane or mucked stall, but they were not permitted to infringe upon my cash flow. The minute they started riding horses previously on my schedule, they were out on their ears. I had my own working student already, whom I had vetted and interviewed and sank plenty of time and money into, and one way to lose a good working student was to hand over their jobs to someone else. Working students could be very prickly.

The complete opposite of the Go-Getter and the Precious Pony boarder was the Absent Mother. She drops her horse off, rather like a child at boarding school, and then simply disappears. As long as the checks arrive regularly and the horse is in training, I really don't mind Absent Mothers — most of the time. All is well until suddenly Absent Mother remembers she has a horse, checks the stable show calendar, and arrives on a show morning decked out in a new jacket with the tags still attached and a pair of never-worn custom boots, wanting to know why I didn't put her name on the entry forms, *of course* she wanted to go to the show. This usually was followed by a disagreement that ended with the Absent Mother heading off to a new farm, with a new trainer to charm, pay, and then irritate beyond all sense.

Those boarders were just the tip of the iceberg. Believe me, there were plenty more, each with their own brand of insanity.

For all of that, I loved running a boarding stable — really, I did! But you got a real cross-section of crazy moving through your barn year after year. You saw too much money, not enough money, and the bad effects of both. You saw good horses with bad owners, bad horses with good owners, and everything in between. You tried *really* hard not to be a therapist. You tried *really* hard not to admit to yourself that if you could afford it, you'd be in therapy yourself. You got through your days on caffeine and the relentless ticking of the clock, as you worked through your schedule, horses to ride, lessons to teach, fires to put out, tempers to soothe.

It was... fun? Maybe that wasn't the right word. It had been exciting once. My own barn! My own students! No one else telling me what to do! I'd worked for years for this right.

I wouldn't give it up for anything — mad boarders or otherwise.

Mounting costs or otherwise.

Empty stalls with cobwebs in the corner or otherwise...

Kennedy Phillips, the young woman who was sitting opposite my desk and making me stifle a sigh of regret, crossed and recrossed her legs. My silence was making her nervous. I glanced up from her application, smiled tentatively, looked back down through the papers as if I was checking them most thoroughly. Of course it was all here: the Coggins test showing her horse had a negative blood test for Equine Infectious Anemia, the proof of standard equine vaccinations within the past six months from a veterinarian's office, the application with billing and horse information. All printed out from my website, all done in advance, all very promising if the only things that I were looking for in a new boarder was meticulous record-keeping, responsible horsemanship, and organizational skills. It was the Riding Discipline and Riding Goals entries that disappointed me.

She had written "Pleasure Riding" and "trail riding and

fun" under those headings.

Which was very nice for Kennedy, but it put her at the very bottom of my list of Most Wanted Boarders.

"Pleasure riding" and "trail riding and fun" meant no horse shows for Kennedy and her horse, and no lofty training goals, either. It meant no riding lessons, no training sessions, and none of the assorted fees that came with showing — the braiding fee, the shipping fee, the coaching fee, the extra training and lessons afterwards when she didn't bring home the color ribbons she wanted. Kennedy described herself as an excellent rider, with a history of big jumps and shiny ribbons, and all she wanted to do now was goof around with her horse (which was perplexing in and of itself — the horse was sound, she was in good health, what on earth was wrong with this picture?)

According to the application, Kennedy didn't need *me* for anything at all, other than to make sure that her horse had a roof over his head, a clean stall to sleep in, and a paddock to relax in. She didn't even mind that the unused horse trails adjacent to the farm were overgrown and needed clearing, or so she had assured me when I explained, uncertainly, that I wasn't sure how my farm was the right fit for her needs.

"I just really love your property, and your standard of care is well-known," Kennedy now told me earnestly, leaning forward in her chair, clearly anxious to break the silence. "I'm used to caring for him myself, but now that I work full-time, I can't do it all anymore. If it can't be me… then it has to be someplace like this. The very best."

We were in the second-floor barn office, a cluttered place wallpapered with rosettes and horse show photos. Above her left ear I could see myself, ten years ago, jumping a picket fence in a Working Hunter class. My face was serious, my horse's face was serious, the faces of the people watching in the background were serious. Showing was serious business. A show barn was a serious place.

"And of course the location matters a lot. But I don't want to show or anything. I just want to have fun."

I nodded. I had six empty stalls, and two boarders making rumblings of moving to another state. Six was too many — one more and I might have to let a groom go — eight was unthinkable.

I couldn't afford to turn this one away, as much as I wanted to. But I felt compelled to explain that she was about to be the odd man out — a lonely position to be in at a bustling boarding stable. "No one else here trail rides," I warned her. "You'd be on your own."

"Not even once in a while? For a treat?" Kennedy's voice was wheedling, and I could imagine her using that on impressionable boarders, worn out with training for the winter season through what seemed like an unending Florida summer. *Just cancel your lesson, just skip that schooling session, come out on the trail and relax with me!* Sounded charming, until you considered their actual practical knowledge. More than a few of them hadn't ridden outside of an arena since their childhood, some never at all. There would be problems. There would be accidents. There would be ambulances and vet calls.

I gave Kennedy a sympathetic smile, spreading my hands to show her that things weren't going to end in her favor, and I was sorry, but it just couldn't be helped. "Take a look out here," I invited, standing up and heading over to the observation window behind my desk. Kennedy followed uncertainly, and together we looked out over the scene below.

From way up here on the high-ceilinged second floor, we could look down on the horses in their stalls, the grooms in the wash-stalls and cross-ties, and the boarders leading their tacked and wrapped horses to the covered arena. We could even see into part of the adjacent covered arena, where a few boarders were walking together, reins loose, after a hard ride. Their horses were dark with sweat, white foam on their necks — it was a hot day in October, another Florida autumn that felt like other people's summers. Everything about the scene said *hard work, dedication, ambition.* I needed Kennedy to understand the vibe around the barn before she got any ideas about changing it.

"This is a show barn, Kennedy. Everyone here is concentrating on their show season coming up. They have big goals and I help them get there. We work hard." I sat back down and waved her back to the guest chair. "I don't think you'll find any trail buddies here."

She nodded ruefully, settling back in the chair, folding her leg over again. Her jeans were threadbare in one knee, and were stained dark around her calves. I knew that pattern. She rode in them, without chaps. Another strike — we weren't casual around here. My boarders rode in breeches and half-chaps, or field boots. There was an expectation of classiness when people paid what I charged for a box for the sole purpose of putting a pooping horse inside. The unspoken dress code was part of that class. If Kennedy had understood what kind of barn this was, she wouldn't have shown up in ragged jeans at all. Still, she persisted. "I guess if I want a full-service barn, having a lot of really serious riders around probably comes with the territory. I wouldn't feel comfortable with anything less than a barn like this, though. I looked at the place down the road. Rodney's barn..." She trailed off, but her face said it all.

"Rodney's barn is a little rough," I agreed. Rough, hell — it didn't even have full walls to keep the rain out. Rodney's place was essentially a long lean-to with partitions to separate the horses at feeding time each evening. It wasn't an atypical Florida barn, though. My fancy show stable was the new kid on the block. "But he's a nice guy. He's been here his whole life — knew my grandfather when this was just a little breeding farm —"

"Your grandfather bred horses?"

"Right here. His real business was oranges, but he had a couple mares all the time, Thoroughbreds, mostly. A few Standardbreds, back when they still trained in Orlando."

"I didn't know there was a Standardbred track there! It's not still open?"

"Long gone." I sighed. "Still some horses there, though. A nice therapeutic riding center. But horses aren't front and center here anymore." I paused. "How long have you been here?"

"Oh, I've been in Orlando a few years," Kennedy said. "I finished school here. But I'm from Indiana."

I absorbed this information without interest. Nearly everyone in Florida was from somewhere else.

"And maybe someone *will* want to come trail-riding sometime," Kennedy suggested hopefully as she slid the papers back to my side of the desk. "I mean, it's fun, right? I'm sure I can find a buddy."

I didn't *want* her to find a buddy. Still, with the threat of eight empty stalls... I looked at the boarding application again, searching for reasons to tell her take her business elsewhere, but all the reasons that came to mind didn't exist on paper. I didn't have anything but my own disappointment that she wouldn't bring me any training or showing fees. I looked down the neatly typed pages and noticed she'd put the horse's breed and age, but not his name. "What's your horse's name?"

"Sailor."

I felt a momentary twinge deep in my gut, a lump in my throat, a bitter taste in my mouth. I bit my lip, forced a smile, and remarked as brightly as I could: "What a nice name."

My first show pony had been named Sailor. He hadn't been called that at shows, of course. At shows he was Maplewood's Sailing Weather, a title as far from an eight-year-old girl's dream pony name as one could get, but such was the world of show ponies. At least I could call him Sailor at home.

Instead of bursting out with all those childhood memories, I just closed the binder I'd laid out on the desk when Kennedy had first come into the office, its pages listing my various boarding options and training packages. I put it back on the shelf next to my horse show catalogs and training logs and lesson plans, which were usually of great interest to prospective boarders, but which today had not been disturbed. "And he's a Quarter Horse!" I went on encouragingly, busying my hands with straightening the binders, which always toppled over when you moved one little thing. "We don't have any other Quarter Horses here. I think we did a few years ago, but the owner moved to Chicago." At a barn like mine, Quarter Horses were as old-fashioned as rust-colored breeches in the hunter/jumper ring, but without the trendy vintage respect the breeches could command. "Then again, he might have been a half-Dutch Warmblood," I added upon further reflection.

Maybe she'd take the hint.

"He's not fancy, but he's my pal," Kennedy said, a little defensively. "We aren't here to set trends. Just living life to the fullest. We don't need ribbons to define us. We just want to have fun. Isn't that what life's all about?"

"Of course," I agreed, and took a sip of coffee to hide the twist of my lips. What an optimist. What a hippie. What a pain. I wished she'd just go away. I wished she'd see that this barn was not at all a good fit for her. I needed to fill stalls, but I needed paying clients who wanted my expertise and coaching more than anything.

But of course she didn't go away. There was nowhere for her to go. There weren't any other farms like mine within an hour's drive, and we both knew it. Subdivisions and condos and resort communities were snapping up every inch of land, wet or dry, as fast as their bulldozers could roll over old scrub and pristine pasture, as fast as their diggers could dredge out canals and drain the swamps. I was the last one left. I was the only game in town. Everyone else had sold out, gone to Ocala or Georgia or out west, anywhere land and grass were as plentiful as tourists were rare.

I was the last of the dinosaurs, and Kennedy was an endangered species herself, a dinosaur enthusiast.

While Kennedy signed the boarding contracts, smiling away as she dotted the *i*'s in her last name, I mentally worked out the new language I'd be sending my attorney as soon as possible, maybe as soon as Kennedy left my office, that required all boarders to engage in a training/coaching program. "Seabreeze Equestrian is for serious training and competitive riders only," something to that effect. This casual pleasure stuff was no damn good.

"And maybe someone *will* want to come trail-riding sometime," she suggested hopefully as she slid the papers back to my side of the desk. "I mean, it's fun, right? I'm sure I can find a buddy."

I nodded and smiled and sent her on her way, waving as she walked down the landing that overlooked the Grand Prix arena, then I went silently back to the office to look down at her as she strode along the barn aisle, turning her head from side to side, taking in the horses as they gazed out from behind the bars of their stalls. "You better not," I said aloud. "No poaching my students, girl."

I wasn't going to make much having her here. I certainly couldn't start losing income from other clients because she wanted to go play in the woods with her pony.

Which, in my experience, didn't always turn out well anyway. I glanced at the little photo of Sailor, leaning drunkenly in its cracked frame against a row of riding manuals, and sighed.

I added the new Sailor's name to the boarder list and asked Tom to prep a stall for the day after tomorrow. He nodded, his white-blond hair falling untidily over his tan forehead, and then asked if he could leave early that day. He mumbled something about a friend's manatee expedition to some canal on the East Coast. Tom was a marine mammal enthusiast; for him, horses seemed to be a land-version of whales, and he found both were preferable to humans. "If Anna can take over for you in the evening feeding, sure," I told him, and went off on a tour of inspection through the barn, leaving him to go find my working student and try to convince her to give up an evening off.

Walking my barn made me happy. It was a grand barn, the stuff of dreams, and I loved it. Two paved aisles, with twenty stalls each, connected by a central bank of wash-stalls that doubled as cross-ties for students, owners, and grooms to tack up horses and have them ready for lessons. A soaring roof and open rafters to eliminate hot, stale air. A small apartment for the working student over the tack room at one end, my office up a narrow flight of stairs at the other. The central aisle led to the crown jewel of my success: the huge, shady covered arena, comfortably situated alongside the barn and always buzzing with riding lessons, schooling sessions, boarders idly chatting while they walked their sweaty horses on long reins after hard rides. The riders who moved to Florida from Up North (a designation that meant everything on the map above Jacksonville) took one look at the covered arena and signed on the dotted line as fast as their fingers could fly. The shade was the only thing that stood between them and giving up riding for nine months out of the year.

Hell, *I* loved riding in my covered arena, and I had grown up riding under that unrelenting Florida sun.

I leaned on the rail and watched a thin woman on a striking dapple gray warmblood trotting in big, irregular figure-8s. Colleen was better over fences than on the flat, probably because her Trakehner gelding, Bailey, was an auto-pilot jumping machine who could cart anyone around a High Amateur-Owner course without any real direction. But she put in her time on the flatwork anyway, and dutifully attended the fall dressage show I inflicted on all of my advanced students as a preparation for the winter jumping season, so I really couldn't fault her for any lack of trying.

Sometimes it was just hard to get back what had come so easily in girlhood, when you took off twenty years for career and husband and family.

"A bit more leg, Colleen," I called as Bailey jogged by with his nose in the dirt and a bored expression on his big face, and she grimaced and picked up her heels a bit, digging into Bailey's dappled sides with the harmless little nubs of spurs I allowed the riders with less-than-enthusiastic horses. Bailey grunted, lifted his head, and gave me a side-eyed look of disgust, but at least his trot picked up some momentum.

"Very nice," I congratulated Colleen, watching them continue down the rail, and I tried to ignore the way she twisted a little to the right with every rise from the saddle. It really wasn't important, not worth the misery it would take to try to fix. Some things like that, tricks of an aging body, you couldn't fix. Hell, did I post straight anymore? Probably not. Things hurt that didn't used to. Things stopped working. You got on and rode anyway, because that was what mattered.

I walked back through the barn to the other side, and looked out at the paddocks. Sandy and small, they weren't much to look at if you were used to green fields that stretched to the horizon, but for the suburban equestrian, they were certainly good enough. A cloud of dust rose from the nearest paddock, and four legs waved in the air. I sighed. Lying in the middle of that mess would be the one and only Ivor.

"Get up, you awful beast!" I shouted, and a head that might have been white once, but which was now coated with black sand, popped up from the dirt to look at me. Ivor nickered, and I smiled despite myself. He was a lovely clown.

"We have to ride, you know," I told him, putting a foot up on the fence-rail and leaning over the top. He clambered up from the ground with an alarming lack of grace and jogged over, rumbling nickers from deep in his chest. He was talkative and desperate for attention, like a few other stallions I had known. It was endearing, and almost made up for the hard labor induced by having a glowing white coat beneath his habitual cloak of dirt. Unlike Bailey's dark, steely dapples, Ivor fancied himself a unicorn, and the only dark hairs left in his maturity were wisps at his knees, fetlocks, and around the boney bits of his head. Otherwise, he was one big stain-magnet, a whitening-shampoo commercial, an argument for the selective breeding of dark bays.

Now he tried to rub his filth onto my face and my spotless blue polo shirt. "Get off, get off," I snapped, jumping back from the fence just as he shoved his head over, fluttering his nostrils in greeting. "I'm going to have to hire a groom just for you this winter, now that you're going to do some Grand Prixs and need to look fancy." Ivor flung his head up and down and brought a huge fore-hoof crashing down on the fence's lowest rail. I leapt at him and clapped my hands like a child scaring a pigeon and he squealed and took off running around the paddock, creating a minor dust storm in the process.

"Jackass," I muttered, but I was smiling when I went back into the barn. Ivor always raised my spirits. We'd been together for a good six years now, and it was becoming the deepest relationship I'd had with a horse. Well, since childhood. Since Sailor.

Still, no matter how much I loved that horse, it was nice to have someone else to clean him up.

"Ah, Anna," I said cheerfully, leaning into the spotless feed room, where Anna was sitting on a bucket and measuring out feed supplements. "How would you like to tack up a horse for me?"

Anna looked at the dirt on my face and grinned. "I'm on it. Give me about a half an hour, though. Judging by how dirty you are."

I grimaced, to let her know that Ivor was exactly as filthy as she thought, and watched her put away the supplements and bags before she skipped away down the barn aisle. More of a rider than a groom, Anna would always try to wheedle her way out of the more tedious cleaning and management work that kept the barn ticking over, in favor of anything hands-on with the horses — grooming, warming-up, bathing, schooling a lesson horse who needed a tune-up. She was either going to have to learn to like the nuts and bolts work, or marry rich, I'd told her more than once. Horses were fun, but the care and keeping of them was never-ending work.

The people were no picnic either, I thought, as I heard raised voices in the boarder's tack room. I poked my head in cautiously and saw, amongst the enamel-covered tack trunks and slipcovered saddles, the ever-contentious Stacy Hummel throwing up her hands, a poisonous expression on her ferrety face. "And then the sneaky bitch thinks she can just borrow my padded bridle, like I won't notice, and lets out the throat-latch to the very end and now the leather won't stay down in the keeper because her horse has such a fat face —"

"Ladies?" I cut in, my voice solicitous. "Problem?"

Gayle, round-figured and round-eyed and ready to run from the room, gazed at me in horror, her cheeks pink. Stacy flung back her blonde ponytail and faced me defiantly, looking every inch the cheerleader captain her small daughter would doubtlessly become. "Just Melanie taking Fallon's padded bridle without permission! Nothing special!"

I pointedly looked over at the neatly wrapped bridles hanging along the east wall of the tack room. Each one was labeled with a horse's name in neat black letters on white tape. Every boarder got one bridle hook, and they were encouraged to keep spare or show bridles in their tack trunks. I noticed that Fallon's hook was bursting with three bridles, hanging untidily one atop the other, and remembered seeing a bridle on the floor the other day. It was a rare enough incident that it stuck in my mind. I ran a tight ship. "Ah, I think I know what happened. I asked Anna to pick up the bridle on the floor and hang it up on an empty peg. She must have put it on Rowan's hook by accident."

"And why would Melanie think Rowan's plain old bridle magically became a self-padded bridle with brass fittings, ordering specially from England?" Stacy crossed her arms under her chest.

"Because Melanie asked for an extra schooling session for Rowan yesterday and I had Anna ride him?"

Stacy's face fell just a little, possibly as much as it could, since I couldn't imagine Stacy ever going so far as to admit she had been wrong.

"Honest mistake, I think," I went on soothingly. "I'll ask Melanie what she did with Rowan's bridle. Maybe she took it for repairs and forgot to tell me. In the meantime," I looked meaningfully at the heap of leather hanging from Fallon's peg, "you may want to put your extra bridles in your trunk, so they don't fall down anymore."

Gayle smiled tentatively, always ready for peace. I wondered how she'd ended up cornered by the angry, brittle Stacy in the first place. Bad luck, I guessed. She'd never have voluntarily walked into the tack room if she'd known Stacy was in there. Gayle was afraid of most things, but she was terrified of mean people, and Stacy definitely fell under that heading. "Guess that's alright then!" she burst out. Without another look at either of us, she tucked her saddle firmly against her side and raced out of the tack room.

I beamed at Stacy, who gave me an unwilling quiver of the lips in return. "Always best to ask about these things, rather than to make accusations," I said. "And show the leather to Tom and he'll make the keeper fit again."

Stacy nodded tightly. "Thank you." There was a pause. "I'm sorry."

I paused and waited, but the sky didn't fall and no pigs went flying by. Maybe I had misjudged Stacy. More likely I hadn't and she was just having an uncharacteristically weak moment since her expensive bridle had been slightly damaged. "It could happen to anyone," I said brightly, and went on down the aisle before I could accidentally say something honest and tell her what a nasty piece of work I thought she was.

Speaking my mind would be terrible for business.

Two

Rain moved in that late that night, and the next morning I slept through my alarm, lulled into uncertain dreams by the watery gray light drifting through my blinds. I woke at seven thirty when the orange sun finally pierced through the mist and glinted on my face. I sat up, looked at the clock, and sighed. Thank goodness I wasn't feeding the horses this morning.

I picked up my phone, checked for messages from the barn, and when there was nothing, decided to take it easy for the morning. Boss's prerogative. I padded out to the kitchen, the old wooden floors of the bungalow creaking beneath my bare feet, and made coffee and toast. My avocado-colored refrigerator hummed furiously, and when I leaned against the door so that I could peer up into a high cabinet for a new pack of coffee filters, it felt hot against my back. "Don't die, fridge," I told it, but I figured a trip to

Lowe's was in my near future. The appliances, which had come with the old house, were older than I was, and they'd been dying one by one. I still ran my hand adoringly over my new stove; the old one, with burners which refused to light when the kitchen was too humid for its liking, was not missed.

But a green fridge was to be mourned. They didn't make things that shade of Kermit anymore. My grandfather had loved it.

I had just settled down at the kitchen table with coffee and my tablet, ready to read the morning paper, when there was a mechanical sound aside like the death rattle of a dragon. I put down the tablet with a sigh. Rodney had stopped by. I liked Rodney just fine — he was the last hold-out, along with me, of the old riding community that had once thrived here. I just wasn't in the mood to chat this morning. Or most mornings, really. But what could you do? He was my only ally at zoning board meetings and community rallies. I got up and opened the door just as his cowboy boots hit the splintering boards of my sagging front porch.

He smiled and touched the brim of his cap, old-fashioned and Southern to the bone. "Miss Grace," he greeted me, weathered face splitting into a grin. He'd missed a few spots shaving, and the bristles on his tanned cheeks were white now. But the unkempt hair curling from beneath the feed-store cap was still a boyish dirty blonde, and there was no hint of age in his bright blue eyes. Which was impressive, because if I stopped and did the numbers, I'd probably find that Rodney Blake had already been receiving his AARP magazine every month when I'd moved back here more than a decade ago. The farm life would either age you young or keep you living forever, I guessed. I wondered which one it was doing to me.

"Rodney," I replied with real warmth, suddenly pleased to see him. "Come in and have some coffee."

Rodney wiped his boots carefully, leaving behind at least some of the morning's mud on my mat, and stepped into the little bungalow, looking around appreciatively as he always did. "You sure have a fine house here," he said, nodding at the living rooms walls. They were bedecked with framed horse show posters and a vintage Aer Lingus print advertising the Dublin Horse Show. The little room was centered around the sagging couch covered with a horse-racing throw. "I always did like this house. Your grandpa built it real solid."

"He sure did," I agreed, my voice slipping back into a long-abandoned country cadence. "I love it so." I adored my house — a 1920's cracker bungalow, with all the termites and raccoons under the porch to prove it, dark and cool in summer and dark and drafty in winter. "Couldn't be more different than those candy-shell pink mansions they're building now, right?" I fetched coffee from the galley kitchen and set it down on the table, then thought and grabbed milk from the growling fridge. Rodney settled down in a creaking thrift-store chair and started in on the coffee. I sat back down at the other side of the table and waited for him to get around to his reason for stopping by. We were not social people, given to leaving our farm and our work just to drop by and say hello. He had something on his mind.

"You thinking about selling?" he asked after a few sips.

"I'm sorry?" I nearly choked. Although I got printed letters in the mail every few weeks, announcing that this realty company or that developer was looking for properties in the area and was ready to buy, I always threw them straight into the recycling. There couldn't possibly be a rumor in the neighborhood that I'd been considering selling up.

"I heard the Roth boys were coming after you pretty hard. Heard you might be giving in."

"The Roth… I don't even know who that is." I tried to picture the most recent of the thin paper envelopes. Nothing came to mind. "Who told you that?"

"Dean Roth." Rodney sighed. "I'm selling to him."

I put down my coffee mug with a clink on the wooden table. The porcelain cow decorating the table's center wobbled dangerously. "*What* now? Rodney, you can't be selling. You're all I have left." Rodney and his twenty acres a few miles north on the highway, Rodney and his little lesson barn, ramshackle with age and losing a section of roofing every now and then when a big storm rolled through, Rodney and his collection of mutt ponies and horses, teaching kids how to ride in a big muddy ring for the past forty years, give or take — Rodney was a fixture in this community, much more so than me.

If he left, there wouldn't even be a community, I realized. Two barns left out of twenty was sad. One barn was a woman in denial.

"I'm sorry," Rodney said, shaking his head and looking into his coffee mug. The bill of his cap covered his face, but I could see his hands were shaking a little. Worry? Or age? I bit my lip. "I'm sorry, Grace, but it's time. Taxes are already killing me, and now they want to run sewer and city water out there and it's going to be a fortune. Something about protected swamps, filtering water. I don't know."

I knew — the land behind Rodney's farm had been rezoned. We'd both been at that meeting, and neither of us had really grasped the technical details, but I'd understood more of it than he did. That's how I knew that the new golf club that was going in across the highway from him had managed to change their zoning from agricultural to residential, and that the land behind him had been changed from agricultural to protected wetland. Mitigation, making up for the loss of habitat where the golf club would be. Now his twenty acres would be next — maybe a shopping center with a new Publix, a Subway, a dentist, and a hair salon, a carbon copy of the one five miles down the road. Or maybe it would be two hundred new houses, painted shell-pink and peach, crammed in one on top of the other, surrounded with St. Augustine lawns and sprinklers that kicked on every morning at 6:15, rainy season and dry. Or perhaps a resort, its manicured grounds peppered with ostentatious date palms that were more at home in the Arabian Peninsula than in Florida.

It was enough to make a farm girl sick.

What could any of us do, though, against all the millions of dollars being thrown at these projects? We couldn't pay lobbyists to stand up for us, the last two farmers in a countryside converted into vacation-land. We were expected to go where we were wanted — north Florida, presumably. Rodney had seen this coming for a long time, and so had I. It just hurt so damn bad now that the time had finally arrived.

"I understand," I managed to croak. I needed to be upbeat, to ease the defeated slump of his shoulders. It wasn't his fault that the world had changed. "Of course I do. It's just a shock, is all. Where are you going?"

"Altoona." Rodney looked up and smiled, already looking more cheerful at the prospect. "Up in horse country. I bought five acres. There's a doublewide, and a barn for Misty and Patch. I'm going in the spring. Perfect retirement for an old cowboy like me."

"It sounds wonderful." I smiled more brightly, tamping down the slight panic within. "Misty and Patch will be happy to leave behind all those other horses and get a little peace and quiet. What are you going to do with them?" The one big pasture at Rodney's place had twelve other horses in it, lesson and trail horses of uncertain breeding and probably uncertain futures. Misty and Patch were two leftovers from Rodney's old life as a Paint breeder, the last two babies he'd bred out of his favorite mare. They were both in their teens now.

"Well," Rodney tipped his head a little coquettishly. "I was hoping you might want a few."

I took a big gulp of coffee to hide my uncertain expression. Was there a nice way to say his horses weren't exactly what my clientele were looking for?

"And some of my students," he went on. "Some of the local kids. There are some real budding champs in the group. Winning at the 4-H shows. I bet they could do real good at the bigger shows."

"But I don't teach children. I don't even know much about the junior divisions." Or ponies. Or the children themselves. I had built a business around adult amateurs and selling imported horses, and I was happy to be a specialist.

"Oh, they're easier than adults," Rodney said airily. "You just tell them what to do and they do it. No answering back or telling you they can't. And you can always tell them they have to get off the horse if they sass you. Straightens 'em right up. But my kids are good. No one'll give you any trouble." He watched my face, saw that I was still skeptical, and his tone turned wheedling. "Come on now, Grace. The neighborhood kids will have to go all the way to Skip's, and that's nearly an hour away. Some of them will have to stop riding."

I doubted that — when Rodney said "neighborhood kids" he talked like they were poor kids riding their bikes to the barn and working off lessons, when in truth they were all from the new subdivisions and country clubs. Their parents could find the time or get the nanny to drive them out to Skip's or one of the other equestrian centers north of town if they really, really wanted to ride.

Probably.

Maybe.

"I can think about it," I promised him, but Rodney wasn't finished.

"I have a few trail horses."

"Mmhmm." I busied myself getting more coffee from the kitchen.

"Really quiet, really easy keepers. They wouldn't be any trouble."

"And what would I do with them? I don't think that would be a good fit."

"You could do trail rides," Rodney suggested. "You have all that land out back going to waste, and if you're not going to sell... They *really* haven't been pushing you to sell?"

"Nothing out of the ordinary. But I can't do trail rides." I shook my head briskly. The idea was out of the question. "Where would I find the time?"

"Oh, you could hire someone to take them out. You'd just be providing the spot for them. It's easy money, trail rides. I've been doing it here and there, working with the hotels when they have big groups. You put helmets on them, you have them sign a waiver, you take them out and show them a gator. It's nothing."

My phone buzzed on the table and I glanced down. Anna wanting to know if she could have an early riding lesson. As good an excuse as any. "I'll think about it," I promised again, typing a quick *yes* to Anna. "I have a lesson to get ready for now, though. Sorry I can't visit with you longer."

"Oh, that's okay," Rodney said affably, getting up from the table. "I know it's early and you have the day ahead of you. No hurry on the horses. I was just driving by and saw the sign and thought I'd check in."

"What sign?"

"That's a big sign, all right."

Tom nodded sadly. He hunched a little over the Gator's steering wheel, as if he wanted to hide from the impending doom, the construction crew's arrival, the downward spiral of the farm, and, finally, the loss of his job. I hopped out of the Gator and walked over to read the fine print more closely. I wasn't quite so ready to give up on my farm.

Hannity & Roth Realty and Investments. It was smaller than the rest of the letters on the sign, a big piece of plywood with a poster plastered over it, set up on two-by-fours in front of the plot of land next to the farm. The big letters said *Coming Soon: Tuscan Hills Resort and Country Club*. Then the usual suspects, a line-up of meaningless descriptors that vaguely indicated what sort of atrocities would be on offer. *Elegant resort-style living. Fine homesites available now. The very best Florida has to offer.*

There was an illustration, too: Italian Revival columns and arches, exposed brick and faux-crumbling plaster, twisting non-native pine trees and sparkling blue lakes between green fairways, a cypress dome humping in the distance like some primitive monument kept whole only out of legislative requirement. "The very best Florida has to offer," if only Florida was an artistic rendering of Tuscany.

I sniffed derisively and then, struck by some old-fashioned sense of the evil eye, spat on the ground. I picked my way through the sand-spurs and tiny cactus sprouting along the sandy verge and climbed back into the Gator. "Let's go back," I told the despondent Tom, pretending nothing had happened. "Anna probably has her horse warmed up now. I'll get her lesson taught and then I'll have her strip those two stalls for you." Every now and then we gave Anna some of the hard physical work, the Tom-Work, to remind her that the horse business required big muscles and a strong stomach. Stripping the ammonia-soaked underbelly of two recently emptied stalls was just the thing.

Tom nodded and did a quick u-turn, sending us the few hundred feet down the highway's shoulder to the entrance to the farm, and we motored through the gateway and the glade of live oaks that sheltered my house before we started passing the paddocks, already occupied with horses for the morning, and came around the back of the barn to the parking lot. He cut the motor by the barn aisle and looked at me with melancholy eyes. I just couldn't take it.

"What?"

"Are you going to sell?" Tom asked.

"What, are you crazy? This is my home. This was my grandfather's farm. I'd never give this place up. You know that." We'd had this conversation a hundred times before. Every time someone else sold, every time someone else closed their barn and moved north to the hill country around Ocala, or south to the tiny ranches on the outskirts of the Everglades. Every time another subdivision, or resort, or strip mall went in where horses and cattle had once grazed — every time, I promised once more that I would keep my stable intact. Tom didn't know that Grove Pointe, the subdivision across the highway, had once been my grandfather's orange grove, or he would have had a conniption. That part wasn't important. The *stable*, I always emphasized, was safe from the developer's touch.

I'd developed this land myself, in the image I had always wanted. From empty pastures had risen an equestrian center. The truth was, I had laid my share of concrete here on my grandfather's farm, I had paved my bit of Florida. I shook my head a little, trying to rid myself of the thought. At least his house and live oaks were preserved, and to museum-quality, if I said so myself. So I'd built up the pastures, so what? The scrubland out back, I'd never touch.

"When that over there is all houses, you won't sell?" He pointed at the tangle of pine and scrub to our right, the southern border of the property, the future Tuscan Hills Resort.

"I'll never sell," I repeated. Firmly, like I meant it. Just as I had every other time he had asked.

I hopped out of the Gator, leaving Tom to sit and worry over the future of the farm. I had my own worries on that count.

I walked down the wide south aisle of the barn and stopped in front of the newest empty stalls, eyeing them glumly. They were part of a growing trend.

Two horses had left over the weekend. Three more might be gone by the end of the month, while their owners waited to finalize home sales and moves. The dreaded eight empty stalls was just a matter of time, and my wait-list was a thing of the past.

For a long time, development around here had been good for the riding lesson and boarding business — subdivisions meant families, and families meant clients of all ages. For years, I had a full barn. I had a waiting list. I had a full eight-horse rig and several private trailers unloading show horses and ponies at every A-circuit show from Venice to Jacksonville. I'd given up my first love, dressage, and devoted myself to hunter/jumpers, because that was what my clients wanted. I'd shaped my life and my business around teaching and training adult amateurs.

Then, things changed. Slowly, and then all at once.

First, it was the hurricanes. People from up north didn't like hurricanes, and they *really* didn't like four in one season. You could tell folks it was a fluke, a hundred-year-season that wouldn't be repeated in their lifetimes, but losing their roofs once was enough for a lot of them. Then it was the local government — failing schools, not enough money to fix them, taxes voted down time and time again. White-collar families, my bread-and-butter, voted with their moving vans. They rented out their houses when the houses wouldn't sell, and suddenly the neighboring subdivisions were playing host to a revolving door of international families renting vacation homes.

After that, things changed very quickly. The developers changed their plans, bought more woodland and farms, and got to work.

They built the water park. They built the luxury mall. Then the resorts began popping up. Vacation homes, villas, towering hotels, grand and classy and seemingly all echoing some collective unconscious memory of Tuscany, of all places — I shook my head, I still couldn't figure out how they had landed on *Tuscany* as the ideal Florida image. Either way, my little corner of central Florida had somehow became a new epicenter of every sort of accommodation and amusement a tourist could want for a week or two of sun and fun.

Not exactly a source of long-term clients, the students who bought horses and boarded them here and showed with me, the ones who had been the backbone of my business for so long. Hell, *all* of my business.

I shoved my bangs from my eyes, pushing them behind my ears, and determined that I would think positive. I would figure this out. I would fill my empty stalls. I would adapt, I would evolve, I would prosper. I might be closer to fifty than forty, but I wasn't a dinosaur yet.

A horse next to the newest empty stall nickered to me, pushing his nose through the stall bars and wiggling his upper lip along the steel. "Hey, Poppy," I told the horse, and gave him my fingers to play with. A big bay warmblood with a white spot on his nose, Rebel was one of my favorites — one of the first horses I'd imported from Europe to sell to a student ready for her own jumper. He was the beginning of an era. The Golden Age of Grace Carter's Seabreeze Equestrian Center.

Rebel wiggled his long upper lip against my fingers,

trying to pull them into his mouth. I tickled the damp flesh under his lip and he jumped back, eyes widening with surprise, then he was back for more immediately. Rebel would play grab-the-fingers all day long. He'd never bite anyone, either. All he wanted to do was catch things in his lips. Anything — reins, pony-tails, shirt collars. Rebel wasn't picky about what went into his mouth.

"You're the cutest," I told him, retrieving my fingers. He pricked his ears as I walked away, disappointed that I wasn't going to stay and play. As I turned the corner into the center aisle, I heard him nicker encouragingly, hoping to convince me to come back. But work always beckoned. I went on a morning tour of inspection, savoring every shadow and angle of my barn.

I peeked into the wash-stalls in the center of the barn and saw Margaret, my grim senior groom, solemnly brushing the tangles from a school horse's tail. She looked over the horse's shining chestnut hindquarters and gave me a stiff nod. I nodded gravely in return and Margaret bent her gray curls over the horse's tail again, applying a generous measure of detangling spray to the witch's locks. Skeeter, a stout little Dutch Warmblood, liked to rub his tail against the tree in his paddock, and if the brambles weren't kept down, he brought a shrub of sticks and thorns back inside with him every morning.

"He only has two lessons today, Margaret," I called, and she nodded again without looking up from her task.

"Lotta work for two rides," Margaret grumbled. "Oughta put it up in a bag."

"You know we can't do that," I reminded her. "The clients won't like that look. Or the noise." Tail-bags were pretty loud when a horse swished a tail at a fly and thumped their side with a big old nylon bag. And it wasn't a look I thought my clients, who were mainly fairly well-heeled career women, would relish in their beautiful steeds. They wanted the fantasy — there was a reason so many of the sales horses I brought in were dapple gray or flashy chestnuts with plenty of chrome.

"Any rides on Skeeter today?"

I thought, picturing my calendar, open on my desk upstairs in the office. "No," I said after a moment. "He can go back outside today. Same for Splash."

"Slow day," Margaret observed. She lifted her eyebrows and regarded me over her plastic-rimmed glasses.

"Guess so," I said lightly, but I was thinking *slow week, slow month, slow year.*

Why weren't the locals riding anymore? Not everyone had moved, but still, my lesson books weren't full anymore. Either riding was going out of fashion, or the heat was finally keeping the northern transplants confined to air-conditioned pursuits.

Or maybe they just plain couldn't afford me any longer. My monthly board for one horse was higher than some downtown studio apartments. My riding lessons were just as expensive as lessons in tennis, or golf, or a host of other sports more manageable and less dangerous than riding. I wasn't even price gouging — it was just so expensive to keep horses this close to a metropolitan area, with taxes shooting up year after year, with supplies growing so scarce that I had to pay to have everything from feed to shavings to horse shampoo delivered from a farm supply store way up the turnpike. I couldn't cut my rates, either — if anything, I was going to have to raise prices in the next year just to make ends meet.

Things were getting tight. Cleared land and construction next door were going to make it tighter.

But I wasn't ready to give up on this yet.

I turned into the northern barn aisle, past a few more empty stalls, past a few more nickering horses, to the end of the barn. I gazed out across the parking lot. Ahead of me was a decent chunk of the last wilderness in the area — hundreds of acres of scrub and savannah and swamp. I had spent my childhood wandering this land on horseback. Now it sat silently, its trails overgrown or lost, for all I knew.

I hadn't ridden out there in years. I hadn't kept all my promises in life, but I'd kept the one I'd made to myself, to keep out of the woods and stay in the arena where I belonged.

And, I'd kept the promise to my grandfather to keep this land untouched. So far, so good.

I lifted my eyes above the dense thicket of palmettos, their fronds rattling in a gentle seabreeze from the distant ocean. Sixty feet up, the stark, sparse branches of the longleaf pines swayed gently against a clean blue sky, scattered with tiny white cotton balls of clouds. It looked like an impenetrable wilderness, but it wasn't.

There was still one little trail that could have led riders through the scrub and deposited them onto a wide white road, a sandy path through the palmettos, that led to rich treasures of old Florida. First, an ancient shell-mound, crowned with oak trees and carpeted with leaves, a shady oasis on a hot day. Further along, a cypress swamp humped up in a dome, its centurion trees protecting a tiny blue spring. As kids, we'd called it that white path the Indian Road. My grandfather had said his father called it the

Timucuan Trail.

I wondered if the road still went all the way to the cypress swamp, or if the scrub had taken back its sandy ruts. Somehow, I doubted that the wilderness would ever really take it back. That old road had been clear for decades, maybe centuries, despite hardly ever getting touched by anything more destructive than horses' hooves. It was a natural element of the scrub, not a scar on the landscape but a shining jewel, bright white in the sunlight, ghostly gray beneath a full moon. I remembered those nights, my pony glowing in the moonlight, Grandpa sitting up above me on his big chestnut mare, smiling down at me from beneath a wide-brimmed Stetson.

"Are you ready for a little midnight ride?" I heard his voice as clearly as if he was truly beside me, and for a moment the bright world dimmed and it was full dark, a whip-poor-will singing somewhere in the oak trees behind us, the horses' bits jingling as they yearned to be turned loose on that wild white road —

"I'm all tacked up!"

I spun around, heart pounding, the vision splintering around me. He'd been so close to me, I'd almost reached up to touch his calloused hand.

Anna was standing in the aisle, holding the reins of her bay warmblood, Mason. She had on her hard hat and breeches, her half-chaps and boots, and her usual big smile plastered across her tan face. Her blonde hair was scooped up under her hat, nearly invisible. Just the way I liked her turned out — show-ring ready. Mason wore black polo wraps, gleaming brown tack, and his usual sleepy expression. "Is now a good time?" she asked, beaming.

I turned my back on the Florida scrub, on my

grandfather's trails, on a past that I didn't have time to rehash. It was time for the barn, time for business as usual. "Let's do it!"

We marched together down the aisle, turning at the center for the walkway to the covered arena. I immediately felt more comfortable with groomed clay beneath my feet. After all, in this business, what relevance did the woods and wilderness still have? Under cover from the blazing white sun, on safe footing, and with a comforting white PVC rail delineating our work space, we'd get down to the business of training show horses.

I'd figure out the future later.

Good feelings only last so long. Late that evening, as I was flipping out the barn lights, the construction company's sign invaded my thoughts again. I walked down the paved driveway towards my house, wishing I had a dog to keep me company. It was seven thirty and dark out, the long summer evenings already a thing of the past despite the lingering heat. It would be hot until mid-October, I knew, and then we might get a cold front or two, a cool night or two. It would be a rare thing, brought by wind and storm, and everyone would be just as bad-tempered about the cold as they were about the heat.

I took it all in stride. This was my home. Florida's weather was unpredictable to some, but for me, the next day's weather was always written in the clouds the night before. You just had to know what to look for.

Tonight the night sky was clear as spring water, but the stars were more dim than they had been in years past. Light pollution had invaded my farm. When I was a kid, begging to go ride at Grandpa's farm, the nearest street lights had been on the interstate, nearly fifteen miles away. That was before the interstate was joined by a toll road. That had been the enabler — the houses, and then the tourists, had come in a flood once the roads were improved.

It had happened so fast, but life went in a blur, didn't it? Look at me: one day I'd been riding with my grandfather, the next day I was installed at a show barn and perfecting my hunter rounds, and then suddenly I had been showing professionally for my entire adult life and students were asking me to start my own barn and settle down in one place.

By the time I'd come back from the show circuit, lean and tanned and twenty years older, the farms had already started to disappear. But the tack shop was still downtown in its dilapidated brick storefront, right next to the Wagon Wheel Restaurant *(Family Cooking with a Smile!)*, and the feed store was still a collection of rotting wood outbuildings sprawled alongside the railroad tracks. Now the feed store had made way for a home design store and nursery, and the tack shop had been renovated into a clothing boutique, part of a pretty, antique-laden downtown beloved by day-trippers. I didn't bother going into town much anymore. The village had been reborn, but I had kind of liked it the way it was. The cost for a revitalized downtown was very high, for the farmers who had frequented the old one.

Grandpa hadn't had to see it change. He was gone by then.

I crossed the grass under the live oaks and went up the sagging wooden steps of my little house. A new roof, a half-rotted front porch, and flaking paint — it was my favorite place in the world. My grandfather's house, left for me, the black sheep of the Carter family. The only one who loved horses as he had done, the only one who would never give it up.

I flicked at the green paint curling from the doorframe. Paint would be the fall project, now that the dry season had come. The porch... I hopped experimentally, listening to the creaking wood, feeling the sponginess in the boards beneath my boots. The porch could probably wait until spring, if no one too heavy did any jumping jacks on it. The roof and the floors had already been redone. I had been working from the inside out, a project at a time, to restore the bungalow. It would outlast me now, if a big hurricane didn't blow through and knock one of my gorgeous oaks on top of it.

Selling to the developers would have meant more than giving up the business. It would mean giving up this house, and I couldn't imagine living anywhere else, now that it was mine and mine alone. Too many sweet memories here, of staying with my Grandpa on the weekends, playing with his couple of Thoroughbred broodmares and any foals that might happen to be hanging around the place, crossing the two-lane county highway, which had been less-frequented then, to the orange grove stand he ran in the picking season. Stealing oranges from the big bins he set out for the tourists, sharing them with Sailor when I was allowed to keep him here, when we weren't off at shows, before I made the mistake, before the accident.

The grove was two dozen luxury homes and a clubhouse with pool now, hidden behind a brick wall and Queen Anne palms. The old wooden fruit stand had burned down long before my return, victim of a midnight lightning strike. I'd been in Virginia, at a horse show. My parents told me after I won the finals and came home flushed with triumph and exhausted from nerves. That fire was the beginning of the end of the orange grove; by the time I came back to take over the farm, the trees had died in a freeze and the homesites were being sold. The pastures and the scrubland where Grandpa rode with his buddies, and with me, was all that was left.

That, and this lovely little house. Thank God it had been built on *this* side of the street.

The front door whined open and old floorboards creaked beneath my feet, sloping in places like rolling hills. The wood had warped as the house slowly sank into the soft Florida ground. But wood was flexible, and adapted more readily than concrete to the shifting sands. Things were built better in my grandfather's day, and houses made more sense. This low-slung bungalow was dark and cool in summer, with a broad front porch made for capturing breezes. The shade from the overhanging live oak trees came with a price, since those lovely trees housed entirely too many spiders for my comfort. Other pests I could handle: I fed a few feral cats outside to keep the mouse population down, and reluctantly sprayed for bugs. Someone had suggested chickens, to keep down the palmetto bugs (that's what Floridians call massive flying cockroaches) but I hadn't been willing to commit to the birds yet, in case they required more maintenance work than folks were letting on.

On the other hand, I really liked eggs, and I had an idea that if I had a couple of chickens there would be eggs all over the place, so that was a temptation.

My stomach grumbled.

"Speaking of food…" I said aloud, slipping off my boots and setting them neatly next to the door. In breeches and boot socks I went down the hall to the little kitchen, hoping I still had some food in the freezer from my last expedition into town.

I peered into the tiny freezer of my ancient fridge and was rewarded with a bag of frozen pasta and shrimp. "I am Italian tonight," I announced, pulling the bag out with a triumphant smile. "I dine on sea-bugs and noodles."

I ripped the bag open, dumping the contents into a pan. "A little olive oil…" I usually had a dog, but I'd been alone for a few months now, and in the quiet of my house, I hadn't gotten out of the habit of narrating my life to the dog, who would be watching me right now, sitting on the linoleum floor maybe, wagging a bristly tail, or a wavy one, or maybe just a little stump, hoping for a bit of shrimp as a treat. It was a break from the silence of the house, even if it was only my own voice.

"And don't forget to turn the gas on," I finished, because it wouldn't be the first time I had waltzed out of the kitchen, thinking with pleasure of the gourmet stove-top dinner awaiting me, and realized twenty minutes later that I had never flipped on the burner. The flame burst into life under the pan. I looked at the floor next to me, where the dog should have been, watching me hopefully. "Lord, I need a dog," I told the empty spot, and took my wine into the living room.

I sank into the sagging couch, sighing as its upholstery took me in. A tired old couch, like me, I thought, but charming in its own way, faded plush covered with a brocade throw decorated with prancing racehorses, their nineteenth-century tack and long willowy legs the relics of another age and another way of looking at the horse, and sipped at my wine. There was a thump somewhere beneath my feet, but it didn't bother me — just a cat under the house, stalking mice, doing its cat job. I liked animals to have jobs. I considered chickens once more. I didn't love the roaches, after all, but they were part of life in Florida. Roaches had no job, but I could employ chickens. "I think I'll get chickens," I told the living room, and no one answered. "And a dog," I added. A big dog, maybe, that barked all night. Tourists loved that.

Three

A good manager smooths over silly fights, and, as promised, I made sure that Stacy's bridle was fixed. She accepted it with a lack of grace that didn't surprise me, but at least the fight was over and everyone was happy again. Briefly, I supposed. The week ticked by quietly. I rode, I taught lessons, I tried not to worry about the impending development next door. Rodney didn't call back about the trail horses, which I hoped meant that he'd found a better solution for them — some place a bit more appropriate for them than my equestrian center. Sailor arrived without fanfare, walking quietly into his stall and eating his hay as if he had always lived there.

Then, turmoil.

Stacy canceled her riding lesson.

It doesn't sound that dramatic, even though the lesson was prime Saturday afternoon spot that Stacy had been hanging on to with grim determination for the past four years, refusing all comers when they sought to barter time slots, armed with sob stories about soccer games, band trips, and lunches with in-laws. Stacy Hummel knew what she had and wasn't letting anyone else have a sniff. Still, anyone might have to cancel a lesson. Kids got sick, cars had to go to the shop, mothers-in-law dropped by and the house had to be cleaned. If it had been any of those reasons, the world might have kept on turning.

As it was, I saw everything begin to tilt dangerously.

I was standing in the barn aisle, observing the grooms as they threw lunch hay to the thirty-odd hungry equines of impeccable European lineage, and also to Sailor. The barn was echoing with horses and their shouting — big bold whinnies, throaty nickers, high-pitched neighs. Everyone went gaga for lunch hay — it broke up the monotony of the day. Breakfast hay had been so long ago. Dinner hay was so far in the future, it was barely worth contemplating. A grooming and a ride? Didn't have the same ring as a big old pile of dried grass. Stall doors were rattled, teeth were run up steel stall bars with eye-watering results. Feeding time at the zoo.

My phone rang and I walked outside to get out of the cacophony, a little relieved at the excuse.

"Hello, this is Grace," I said, holding the phone to my ear. The sun was hot on the parking lot asphalt and I tilted my face up into its rays, closing my eyes. The light was red through my eyelids. "Stacy? Hello, what's up?"

"I just need to cancel today's lesson," Stacy said. She sounded out of breath. I wondered if she was running away from something — a fire, a burglar, an alligator.

"Is everything all right?"

"Oh, yeah. Can we just reschedule for midweek?"

"I can check the calendar and call you back." I bit the inside of my cheek to stop a gusty sigh from letting her know how annoying I found a late cancellation. An empty hour in my Saturday afternoon was a chunk of money lost. I paced along the barn wall, kicking at stones that had escaped the edging. A toad hopped under a hedge and peered out at me resentfully. "Want me to ride Fallon for you this afternoon, then? You have that show next weekend. I'd hate for him to get an unauthorized day off!" I forced a laugh.

"Oh, no thanks," Stacy said lightly. "I'm going to go trail riding with Kennedy this afternoon."

There it was — the ground tilting beneath my feet. I stopped pacing and stood still, too surprised to reply. The toad blinked at me and hopped away to safety.

The grooms went driving by on the Gator, and I let the roar of the motor serve as a convenient excuse for my radio silence, but in reality I was reeling from those few simple words. No one on the farm went trail riding. Their beautiful show horses were just that — beautiful show horses. They were not accustomed to the rigors of the natural world, and they would surely get themselves into trouble out there.

I certainly did not trail ride, not since the accident. I hadn't been out there since I was a kid, and I had impressed upon my students that the arena way was the proper way to ride. We were all much safer in the arena, with rails and groomed footing, *and* lovely shade if we were in the covered arena, than we could ever be out there in the swamps and scrubland, where anything might happen.

The grooms parked the Gator in the hay and

equipment shed on the other side of the parking lot, switched off the roaring motor, and quiet returned to the farm. My window of acceptable silence had closed. I gathered my wits about me and tried to remind Stacy that she had goals. "Are you sure you want to skip a lesson for a trail ride, right before a show? Surely there's a better time down the road. You don't want to give up any training time, do you?"

"There's *always* a show coming up, though," Stacy said, aggrieved, (and since it was October and the beginning of the winter season, she was right). "And I know I've never taken Fallon trail-riding, but I'm sure he'll like it. Kennedy says he's very stiff in the top-line and a nice trail ride will relax him and help him move forward more naturally. And she says Sailor is the perfect babysitter for a green trail horse — Fallon can just scoot up against him and feel perfectly safe —"

She prattled on a little bit longer in a similar vein, her sentences peppered with "Kennedy said..." By the end of the call, I was ready to call the sheriff to have Kennedy Phillips and her perfect Quarter Horse removed from the property. If her "live life to the fullest/just have fun/YOLO" spirit infected my performance-minded students, I'd lose half my business.

And, more immediately, despite her bad temper, Stacy was a pretty rider with a talented horse. They could always be depended upon to bring home a few blues. We were going to a dressage show next weekend, to make sure our show jumpers were paying attention and ready for the upcoming season, and I was looking forward to seeing some excellent scores from Fallon. And from Stacy, of course. She sat very prettily, always in the perfect pose, and Fallon did his thing. They were a good team, and I was always proud of them, happy to show them off in front of rival trainers.

Despite all that, it didn't seem there was much I could say on the phone to convince her that she was making a mistake. *Someone* had gotten her all jazzed up over this trail riding business. I could probably get her back in the show-ring state of my mind, but my power over my students' decisions was best conveyed in person, standing before them with the convincing uniform of custom riding boots and German riding breeches, with tapping riding crop in one hand, and the reins of a 17.2 hand Oldenburg stallion with a rebellious streak in the other. I was pretty hard to argue with, then. I was a queen.

Stacy finished carrying on about seeing the natural side of Florida from the back of her darling horse and hung up, and I pocketed the cell phone and looked across the heat waves shimmering up from the parking lot. Beyond the asphalt, wilderness reigned, and the thirsty pine trees cast their thin shade on the sharp-edged palmettos. The natural side of Florida looked about as appealing as the Sahara right now.

The grooms came out of the hay-shed and headed across the parking lot for the barn, their normally quick gait slowing to a languid stroll in the blazing sunshine, ready for their lunch and a break from endless chores. They saw me watching them, and the older two wisely affected careful nonchalance.

Anna, being the working student, was the one to foolishly make eye contact with me, and so she was the first to reluctantly veer from her intended trajectory, the shady oasis of the picnic area behind the barn, and head my way instead to see what the boss wanted. Margaret and Tom, older and wiser and more irritable, brought up the rear, casting disgusted glares at their youthful colleague. They could have made it all the way to their break area without ever acknowledging my presence, as they had proven on more than one occasion. Trust Anna to get them into extra work, they were thinking. I knew. I'd been a working student, and then a groom. I'd done my share of avoiding the boss.

"Hey guys," I called as they drew near, and Anna smiled, genuinely, the way very young working students still do, and Margaret and Tom nodded, warily, the way older and wiser grooms do for the rest of their careers. "Has anyone used the trails recently, that you know of?"

"The new boarder has," Anna volunteered brightly. "She went out there the first — no, the second day her horse was here. Then she went out the next day with a machete."

"A machete?" This was unwelcome news. We didn't have a farm where swords were encouraged, of course, but it had never occurred to me to specifically ban *machetes* from my property. Cigarettes, yes. Dogs, obviously. Weaponry? The subject had never even come up.

"For chopping overgrown palmetto, branches, crap like that," Margaret drawled. She ran a hand through gray-streaked hair, sweaty from a morning of hard work, and pulled it back up in an untidy bun without much thought. "My old boss always cut trails with 'em. They'll hack right through brush."

"I should think so." Margaret's old boss had been a competitive trail rider of some repute. Of course, that had been twenty years ago, and I would have thought trail-blazing might have progressed beyond swinging swords from the saddle, but this was the horse biz, after all. Change came slowly out here. "So the trail out to the sandy road is open again?"

"Guess so," Margaret shrugged. She didn't care.

"Everyone's been taking about trail riding," Tom said. He still cared a little. "The new girl has been talking it up. Says horses need the down-time."

"She talks it up while I'm out in the ring and can't hear," I guessed, and Tom nodded, brushing back his white-blonde locks.

"She's going to get someone hurt," I said testily. "These ladies aren't used to trail-riding, to say nothing of their horses. Let me know when some of them are planning on sneaking out there, will ya? And try to discourage it. Discreetly. Mention the shows coming up, that sort of thing. They won't want to throw away all their hard work if you remind them of how important their training is to a successful season." After all, that's why they were here, every single one of them, paying top dollar — to *win* on the A-circuit. Not to goof around in the woods with a priceless show horse.

There was a trio of nods, from weary and uncaring (Margaret) to brisk and can-do (Anna), with Tom somewhere in between. I released them for lunch with a nod of my own, and walked back to my office, climbing the stairs slowly, aware of every step as my kneecaps protested the hard labor, reminding me of all the years I'd been training, all the successful and not-so-successful seasons I had had.

These ladies with their Mercedes and their BMWs and their imported horses had it easy, but they still rode hard and aimed high. I wasn't about to let them fritter it all away.

Four

The new worries about the trail riding joined the older worries about the development next door, plus some old favorites that came up when the electric bill arrived in the mail, and they were all eating away at me. I tried to put in a training session on Gayle's silly mare, but I couldn't concentrate on walk-canter transitions anymore than Maxine could. I gave it up, handed the sweaty mare over to Anna, and tacked up Ivor.

Riding my big gray stallion often seemed like the answer to all life's problems. I could forget about everything — bickering boarders, mystery lamenesses, overdue balances, unpleasant bank statements — and just sink into his spirit, moving with him as easily as an eagle soaring on the thermals. We had been together long enough to know each other on the sort of deep level that made self-help-equestrian mash-up books such a success. Everyone wanted what Ivor and I had. I happened to know that it was rare. I'd ridden a lot of horses in my time, and only had this kind of connection twice.

Whatever we had — one person's psychic-bond scenario was another person's practical explanation that we had just been riding together for a very long time, and I tended towards the practical side of things at all times — it was enough to knock my old boarder's defection and my new boarder's dismal lack of ambition and the presence of that damn sign next door quite out of my head. I was granted forty-five minutes of happiness and peace, worrying only over finding the right stride and cadence in Ivor's big ebullient canter.

Once we had bounced through a jumping school, me relishing the way he bunny-hopped through gymnastics, he swapping his leads for fun as we circled after each course of fences, I handed him off to Anna to cool out and got down to the business of teaching. I was thankful for the further distraction, especially as it would last right through the evening. Friday evening was a busy time for riding lessons, especially with the clients who worked all week in air-conditioned offices, and sweated through their evening rides every night before hurrying home to heat up dinner for their families. They showed up in breeches and boots despite the late-afternoon heat and grew red-faced as they labored through figure-eights, lead changes, and triple combinations. Huffing and puffing, one by one, my students toddled out of the arena leading their sweating, blowing horses, and I felt I could pat myself on the back for another job well done. Miserable work in summer would be a delight in winter, and they'd ride like champions in the show ring.

Most days, we had just a little small talk before lessons — how were the kids, how was work, of course I'd be delighted to ride your horse on Tuesday, so sorry you can't make it — but today, everyone I hadn't seen all week only wanted to talk about The Sign, and what it would mean for the barn.

"Do you think the construction will be noisy?"

"It's going to be so weird to lose those trees. It's going to change the whole character of the farm."

"Sad to see another piece of woodland get mowed down."

"I guess this place will be next."

I heard this last one from every single student, and I marveled that they could all think I'd just up and sell. "Why would you think that?" I asked my last student, mystified. Did they have so little faith in my commitment to Seabreeze, and to them? Did they not understand this was my life's work, and I was doing everything that I could to preserve it? Sometimes I wondered why I bothered, if this was all the respect my struggles had gained me.

"No one would blame you," Melanie said matter-of-factly, rubbing Rowan's forehead. She had him in his flat bridle, the one that Anna hadn't seen the day she used Fallon's new bridle and stretched out the throat-latch. Rowan *did* have a huge head, I noticed. Stacy had been right about that, anyway. The flat hunting bridle really complemented his massive noggin. "Everyone else has sold. Even two years ago there were at least four more barns on this road. Now there's just you."

"Well, don't forget — this is my home. I couldn't possibly sell it." If anyone thought for a second I'd sell the property, they'd all be barn-shopping and I'd have an empty barn and a bankrupt business in no time.

"Even when you're the last one here?"

"Especially then. I'll have a lock on the market!" I grinned. "Now let's get rolling. We have a dressage show coming up soon."

Melanie groaned and led Rowan up to the mounting block. I smiled. You wanted to do the Winter Equestrian Festival, you did the little dressage show, that was the deal. *And* you brought home a good score, if not a ribbon. "Walk him on a loose rein for a few minutes, then pick him up, put him together, and give us a few nice walk-trot transitions!" I bellowed, in full teacher-mode, and managed to forget about the construction company next door for another half an hour.

Five

Saturday arrived hot and dry, a September sizzler without a cloud in the sky. The logical person would have savored a free hour in the schedule and spent it lolling in the air conditioning. However, I was not logical, I was a horsewoman.

I decided to fill in the extra hour in my day that Stacy had gifted me with a bonus afternoon ride on Ivor. After six years with Ivor, I was about as close to him as I could get to a horse, but every day Ivor pushed me a little further into respecting him in a very human way. He was aloof and prickly with most people, respectful and patient with me, and athletic enough to jump a barn.

Despite his natural talent for jumping, however, Ivor was the horse who had convinced me that every show jumper needed dressage, and plenty of it. His difficult youthful years were legendary amongst the handful of boarders who had been with me as long as I'd had him. They used to drop whatever they were doing when they saw me tacking him up, just so that they could rush out to the arena and form a little peanut gallery, gasping and oohing and aaahing over Ivor's spectacular leaps, crashes, dead stops, and back-breaking bucks.

"Look at you now, Ivor," I told him, and his ears flicked back to listen. We were turning around a corner of the covered arena at a beautiful working trot, his neck arched and his mouth soft on the bit, his back bending around the curve from poll to tail. "You were a pill, you know that? And now you're a pleasure."

He was still difficult from time to time — he had occasional aversions to the requests that I made, which manifested themselves in tail-wringing, rearing, even squealing like a toddler throwing a tantrum. But he was a stallion, I reasoned. You'd have that. I had high hopes that after this show season, I'd be justified in my decision to keep Ivor intact. Balls weren't usually my thing on a show horse, too much trouble with the ladies in the boarding stable and on the trailer and at the show-grounds, too, for that matter. Ivor was different, though — his brain was so quick and his attitude was so interesting to work with, I couldn't bear the thought of changing him. If he won a few Grand Prix classes this winter, I was going to go into the stud-horse business with him.

I mulled over Stacy and Kennedy while we trotted through the arena. A lot of the work I'd done to fix Ivor's brain had been out on the trails, working alone, where he was the only horse, without the distractions of hormones and pheromones and studdish rivalries that had kept him from concentrating in the arena.

I hadn't liked doing it that way — it was risky, riding alone out there, and no one knew that better than I did. I liked my fences, I liked my closed gates, I liked a barn full of people or at least a groom or two nearby in case something went wrong and a horse got loose. But I couldn't deny the plain facts in this case. Isolation and the quiet woods had worked wonders for jittery, angry Ivor, as the smooth-moving horse beneath me was demonstrating with every lovely stride. Kennedy was right when she told the other boarders trail-riding could fix horses — I just disagreed with the premise that *my* boarders had any of the problems that necessitated trail work. Anyway, there was no reason for any of them to take the kind of risk riding out on the trails with their show horses entailed — or to mar their own show-perfect positions with more defensive poses.

I sat down and closed my fingers, stilling my motion, and Ivor settled easily into a walk. I glanced at my watch, and then out of the covered arena, wondering when the new pair of trail riders were headed out on their adventure. It was easy to keep an eye out for them — the covered arena was adjacent to the barn, separated by a little swath of green grass and palm trees, and this gap between buildings afforded a clear view of the parking lot, with the hay and machine sheds just beyond. Next to the shed, the trail-head beckoned, a slim gap in the trees and palmettos that lined the farm.

The trail wandered through a chunk of my own land before it met up with the old road through the scrub. The Timucuan Trail was white-sand, fairly straight, and virtually forgotten. I supposed it was a national treasure, or at least a state one, but no one outside of the local equestrians and ranchers had ever seemed to know about it, and I was the only one left.

What would they think, if they saw the riches out there? Would they see the beauty I saw, in the dark, still pools glimmering darkly beneath the cypress trees; in the rattling green fronds of the palmettos, lizards darting across the white sand and into their shadows; in the stark skinny longleaf pines that cast hardly any shade and roared like an ocean when a storm threatened?

It wasn't the Florida folks from up north expected.

All around my farm, the other ranches that had once dotted the countryside had disappeared, the pastures covered with concrete of every sort: concrete driveways, concrete hotels, concrete houses, concrete-bottomed drainage canals, concrete pools — artificial versions of the swimming holes and sparkling creeks which had once snaked through this land. People didn't come to central Florida to see what it actually looked like — they came to Florida for a fake version of some paradise in their own head, one which didn't include mud-bottomed lakes or tannin-stained lazy rivers, shimmering as the ripples from slow-moving alligators caught the sunlight.

It was certainly true of my clients — few of them had grown up in Florida, fewer of them had any sort of knowledge of local flora and fauna, or any interest in such things, besides what flowers looked nicest in their gardens and what those long-legged white birds were.

"Which ones?" I'd ask dryly when this question came up with the latest boarder to arrive from up north. "Could it have been the ibis, the great egret, the snowy egret, the wood stork?"

This usually invited a blank stare.

The new Floridians had never heard a great horned owl

break the silence of a still night, and they'd never backed away from a diamondback rattlesnake. They couldn't tell a blackjack oak from a live oak, and they didn't know that Spanish moss was as murderous to trees as it was beautiful. To them, none of that matter — the great outdoors wasn't part of their lives. They came from Up North and they lived in stucco Spanish-revival houses, they had a landscaping crew come once a week to mow and edge the lawns, and they kept their horses at my farm, with its covered arena, so they didn't have to ride in the hot sun.

People like this certainly had no business riding out in the Florida wilderness. Maybe on experienced horses, maybe on a guided trail ride, I would have let them go without worrying about them. But I ran a barn that catered to a group of wealthy women whose wild equestrian stories were all from their teenage years, or even before that. Twenty or thirty years of college, career, and kids finally loosened their grip enough for them to snatch a few hours of personal time a week, and now they were back in the saddle — which was great, but they weren't kids anymore, and they didn't bounce when they hit the ground anymore.

Heaven knew their horses were no better, used to groomed footing and guiding rails. They should have learned by now that show horses were show horses. I had learned that lesson young — how had they all missed it?

I lifted my hands and my calves and my pelvis and Ivor picked up a springing canter from the walk, the upwards motion and momentum flowing through my spine, and went bounding down the center line of the arena. It nearly took my mind off the situation back in the barn. There was no feeling like a good walk-canter transition. It was a controlled rocket launch, and I was the one controlling it. I adjusted my body and asked Ivor to change directions at the end of the arena.

Ivor skipped through his flying lead change with tremendous gravity and I gave him a quick pat on the neck for getting through such an exciting maneuver without throwing a crow-hop or a buck. He cantered obediently in a twenty-meter circle, then, just as I made to change reins and ask for him to swap leads again, he spooked hard to the left, away from the arena's railing, and broke into a rough gallop, his head high.

I wrestled him back down without too much fuss and swung him back around to the top of the arena, my gaze following his pricked ears, and saw Stacy and Kennedy heading out on their trail ride, which I hadn't been able to talk her out of after all, 17.2 hand high stallion, tapping whip, and custom breeches notwithstanding. Kennedy was sitting comfortably on Sailor the Wonder Horse, who was a rotund little apple-butt of a Quarter Horse and delightful in his way, but Stacy wasn't having such an easy time. Fallon, a tall, dark bay Hanoverian I'd had imported from Germany two years ago, was looking around the unfamiliar surroundings of the parking lot with alarm, his head high and his eyes wide. He spooked at the machine shed and went skittering into Sailor, a tangle of legs and mane and tail, and he might have turned back for the barn, but Kennedy reached out and snagged his reins, pulling his head close to Sailor's neck.

I let Ivor halt at the arena fence and we both watched the unlikely quartet of humans and horses as they disappeared into the woods, hoof by faltering hoof. Ivor was utterly astonished, his head as high as his neck could get it (which was pretty high) at the sight of seeing two horses foot-loose and fancy-free, beyond the familiar boundaries of the barn and the arena and the paddocks, in a realm usually known to only hold useful articles like the Gator, which always arrived at the barn full of delicious hay. I could imagine his thoughts: He wasn't allowed out there anymore, so why were they? He *was* the stallion, after all. Wasn't this *his* farm?

"Settle down," I told him, not unkindly, and gave the curb rein a little jiggle, just to remind him I was still there and still on top and still in charge. "They'll be back soon enough. Maybe not all together, but still."

Indeed, for a moment it looked like they'd be back sooner rather than later. Fallon, who was a solid show jumper, was less than reliable anywhere less secure than a nice fenced arena. He'd once run out from a jump and then just plain ran away at a show with a grassy, unfenced jumping field. But those sorts of courses were really few and far between in the show jumping circuit, and so it didn't matter if he had security issues outside of the nice safe railings of an arena. He was a show horse, not a trail horse. He was good at his job. I thought it was unfair of Kennedy and Stacy to expect anything more of him.

Sure, he had his sticky spots — every horse did. If now and then he got behind the bit and wasn't moving forward as well as we knew he could, that was something we could work on right here in the arena, where he was comfortable and happy. I didn't think blowing his mind out on the trail was the right thing to do at all, and as Stacy's trainer I *should* have had the last word in the argument, but she had insisted it was something she wanted to try. Now — well, look at them. They'd come to a halt halfway into the trail-head, and Fallon was throwing his head up while Kennedy was holding on as tightly as she could, and Stacy was kicking him so hard she was pulling her legs away from his sides like a kid on a tough pony. I had my doubts, but eventually the group effort worked and they dragged/shoved poor Fallon, all but kicking and screaming, into the forest.

"Sorry bud," I said, and Ivor twitched a muscle along his shoulder blade, as if he was nervous the same fate awaited him. Or perhaps jealous — maybe he *wanted* to go out there and goof around in the woods instead of preparing for his biggest show season yet. Well, we all had to work, and Ivor demonstrated constantly that he enjoyed his job, so there was no reason to mess with a good thing. "Nope, nothing for you but a few more lead changes and then a nice bath."

I picked up the rains again and gave him a poke with the spurs to remind him that Arena Time was My Time, and we trotted off down the rail, business as usual. When you gave a horse a job he was good at, he did it with pleasure, and asking anything more of him was really asking for the moon.

Six

Sunday's cancellation came from Colleen, who had decided
Bailey would benefit from Kennedy's Magical Trail Ride
Therapy. I was already furious, since Missy Ormond
showed up for her riding lesson in a pair of jeans, which
was strongly discouraged — I liked my students to have a
professional appearance at all times. I nearly spit nails
when, while wiping off her tack after her rescheduled riding
lesson, Stacy blithely suggested that we all have a group
trail ride in a few weeks.

I had been mulling over a new cancellation fee for all
riding lessons. "What's that?" I snapped, but Stacy didn't
pay me any mind.

"With a barbecue," she went on enthusiastically. "We
could use that old fire-pit, and roast marshmallows. Or
make s'mores. It'll be like we're kids again."

"*What* old fire-pit?" I knew exactly where my

grandfather's fire-pit had been dug and bricked, but nobody *else* knew about it. Rather, nobody else *had* known about it, and that was the way I liked it. Was Kennedy going to dig out all of my skeletons and parade them around in front of me? I put things deep into closets for a reason.

"It's out by the lake," Colleen explained. "We could all ride to the lake and maybe the grooms or anyone who doesn't want to ride can take out supplies and wait for us with the Gator. Kennedy and I rode out there yesterday. There's practically a *road*. Did *you* know there's a road out there?"

"It's an old Indian trail," I muttered, and everyone in the tack room started clamoring to see it, unable to believe I had denied them the opportunity to ride on a real live Indian trail. "That lake has gators in it," I added. "And water moccasins."

"So does all the water in Florida," Colleen said. I guessed she was feeling cocky after such a good ride. She'd gotten Bailey around a three-foot-nine course without any dirty stops at all, and Bailey was known for dropping his shoulder when he did not feel that his rider was paying sufficient attention, sending said rider tumbling into the fence while he went the other way. It was one of the things I liked about it. "I might not have lived here my whole life like *you*, but I know that. Have you ever been to Gatorland Zoo? I held a baby gator there. It had its mouth taped shut."

I had, but when I was ten or eleven, not when I was forty-four years old and the mother of three. "The gators out at the pond will not have their jaws taped shut," I reminded her. "And horses don't like them."

"Oh, they'll swim away when we come," Colleen

laughed derisively. "Little old gators! Kennedy says they're afraid of horses."

"Sometimes horses are afraid of gators," I said coldly. "Did you ever think of that?"

The tack room went silent, as if everyone sensed there was a story behind my warning. Well, they weren't going to get it. I went out and found Missy, who was warming up in the arena, and shouted at her for the next thirty minutes until I felt that she was satisfactorily punished for wearing jeans for her lesson.

It should have improved my mood, all that hollering, but I was still annoyed afterwards. Maybe it was the jeans, mocking me as I followed her into the barn. Donner's shoes rang on the concrete pathway, the sidewalk I'd had constructed over a perfectly good pathway of sand so that the boarders could keep their boots clean. I'd gone to insane lengths to provide affluent equestrians with a picture-perfect equine utopia, and now all they wanted to do was mess around in the woods and look at alligators. One had to wonder what the point of anything was.

I wanted to gather all of them together and give them the facts: that water moccasins do not swim away, unlike alligators — they were aggressive, venomous snakes, and my grandfather had shot them on sight — that horses see things before riders do, and react as they see fit, that sometimes that means injuries and death — but it just seemed like harping at this point. Everyone was getting the impression I was a total downer, the mom waving her finger and saying "no" when all the kids wanted to do was have a little fun, and I was going to have to let them work through this new obsession on their own.

Hopefully, no one would get hurt.

But there were still lines one had to draw… "Missy?"

She didn't turn her head. "Yeah?"

Rude. "Please don't wear jeans for your riding lesson next time. There is no point in training if you're not using the same equipment you'll be using at a show. The grip that you get in a pair of jeans is entirely different from the grip you get in breeches and boots."

She turned Donner into the nearest wash-stall and walked him around until he was facing the aisle. She looked at me then. "Jeans are more comfortable," she said flatly. "Won't we do a better job if we're comfortable?"

I shook my head. "So when you go to a show you're trying to perform the same movements, but now you're uncomfortable and in unfamiliar gear? That doesn't make much sense, does it? There's a reason we wear correct riding attire here, Missy. It's part of reaching our goals."

Missy busied herself unbuckling Donner's throat-latch and nose-bands. "I guess every now and then I'd just like to be comfy and have a little fun when I'm riding," she snapped, not facing me once again. It was probably easier to rebel against Mom when you weren't making eye-contact, I reflected.

"Are you not having fun?" I enquired, leaning against the wall as casually as possible. Because if you aren't, I'm in big trouble, I thought. "Aren't you looking forward to the show season?"

"Oh… I mean… yes…" Missy backpedaled rapidly. "I just meant… sometimes it seems like all hard work and no play."

That's *exactly* what it is, I thought. Very good, head of the class. "Well, if you want we can sit down and reassess your goals. If you want to take some showing off the schedule to allow for a little more fun time, we can do that. Of course, you won't be able to progress up the levels as quickly as you wanted to. But we can put Marshall & Sterling classes on hold for another year —"

"Oh no!" Missy had been talking about qualifying for the Marshall & Sterling classes since her first horse show, two years ago. She'd ridden as a child at a big hunter/jumper barn in Virginia, and still talked about the fabled Barn Nights at the Washington International Horse Show, when she and all her little friends had dressed up in their farm jackets and run around the convention center buying up horsey trinkets and watching the show-jumping from box seats. But Missy's parents hadn't been able to afford an A-circuit level horse when she was a kid. Missy's husband, twenty-five years later, *could*. Missy, like so many of my students, was just trying to capture her childhood dreams of showing and stardom. "No, I don't want to put it off — you said this year was going to be the year..."

"And I still think it is, if we stick to our training schedule," I said gently. "If you want to take Donner on a few gentle walks on the trail, maybe to cool him out, and you're going with someone else, and you feel totally confident that no one will spook or get hurt or run away in any way, shape, or form, that's one thing. You can *add* a tiny bit to your training, but you definitely can't take anything away, or you won't be ready. And you have to understand that there are risks to riding out there. If Donner gets hurt, that's going to be a big set-back for you, whether you meant to take some time off or not."

By now Missy had stopped untacking altogether and was just staring at me, Donner's reins in her hands, his bridle hanging loosely with all its straps undone. He shook his head and the throat-latch popped her in the ear. She jumped. "Ow!"

"You okay?" I didn't straighten from where I was leaning against the wall.

"I'm fine, fine." She went back to work, pulling the bridle over his ears and slipping his halter on in its place. The brass nameplate with his complicated German show name gleamed against the buttery leather. "I just never thought about Donner spooking or getting hurt. I guess he could, right? I guess he might get scared out there. I should have thought about that."

"It's okay," I said reassuringly. "It's my job to think about those things. That's what I'm here for."

"Have you had horses get hurt out on the trail? Is that why you don't ride out there?"

I closed my eyes briefly against the sting, then nodded. Would it ever stop hurting? "I have," I said without elaboration. "I have, yes."

"Was it at this barn?"

"No." I pushed off from the wall. This barn hadn't been built yet. "Different barn. But it was enough to teach me my lesson. I lost my pony."

Missy's eyes were round as platters. "Oh, Grace, sounds like it was awful."

"It was," I said, and headed down the aisle, leaving her to finish untacking her horse. "That was a good ride. Wear breeches next time."

I caught up with the Spirit of Adventure herself the following Thursday, as an endless fall rainstorm drummed industriously on the steel roof.

I was sitting on the mounting block in the center of the

covered arena, trying to recover from an evening of shouting myself hoarse over the din during riding lessons. The rains, though desperately needed after a strangely dry summer, made life more difficult than usual. Storms snarled rush hour traffic all over town, which in turn made everyone late to their riding lessons, and it was nearly eight o'clock when the last student finally led her horse back to the barn. I leaned my elbows on my knees and looked down at the hoof prints swirling through the orange clay, trying to summon the energy to go back into the barn and do night-check. If I went into the barn, the last student, Laura, would still be there, untacking her horse and wanting to chatter about her lesson and her hopes and her dreams. It was a conversation I wasn't up to tonight. Other people's dreams were very tiring after a long afternoon of teaching riding lessons, walking the tightrope between stroking egos and barking commands.

Maybe I'd just wait out here until Laura had finished putting up her horse and left for the night, I decided. Nights like this, I was just itching to flip out the lights and leave the horses to their own devices for the distressingly few hours until the grooms arrived for morning feeding, but that was impossible. Water buckets had to be checked, priceless horses had to be assessed for any signs of illness, stall door latches had to be jiggled for security. Skipping any of my evening routine was a recipe for disaster — the first time I did would be the one night a door wasn't completely closed and someone ended up on the highway or in the hay shed, working his way through an alfalfa bale and cruising for a colic. I'd go inside in a few minutes, get the job done, and finally make my wet way across the property to my little house and my large bottle of wine, which was waiting on top of the fridge for a hard day exactly like this.

I rubbed my forehead with my fingers and waited for Laura's car headlights to switch on and disappear into the darkness. It was too cool, with all the rain pouring down all evening, for her horse to need a shower. All she had to do was strip the tack, rub him with a towel, and put him away. I'd be out of here in ten minutes. The thought was soothing… I closed my eyes…

And then I heard the sound of horseshoes ringing on the walkway, coming towards the arena. I lifted my head and saw Kennedy Phillips for the first time all week. She'd been M.I.A. ever since the weekend before and her first round of guided trail rides, and all the while, I'd been waiting for her. I wasn't sure what the show-down was going to be, but I knew I wanted to have it out with her. I had to make her understand she was in the wrong, without actually telling her she was in the wrong. After all, there was no rule that said boarders couldn't go out on the trails. I was going to have to wait for something to actually go wrong before we had that particular confrontation.

There *was* a rule about being here after eight o'clock without a scheduled lesson, though. I tightened my jaw and waited for her to notice me.

Kennedy paused, flung the reins over Sailor's neck, mounted from the ground, and rode into the arena just as pretty as you please — never you mind it was ten minutes past the barn's posted closing time. When she noticed me sitting in the ring, she waved and pointed the Quarter Horse in my direction. He came striding over with the good-natured head-bob I associated with his breed. Just a nice horse, uncomplicated, undemanding. It had been a long time since I'd been on a horse like that.

I waited until she was close enough to hear me over the pounding rain. *"You're* here late," I announced, standing. I stalked over to meet her with my head up, my eyes narrowed, and my jaw jutting. Ready for battle.

Kennedy pulled up Sailor, her own eyes widening. She hadn't expected such a hostile welcome, huh? Well, *surprise!* She started to say hello, or something, but I interrupted her before she could get the words out.

"Is this why I haven't seen you all week? You come after closing time now?"

Kennedy's bright smile never wavered. "Oh, no, sometimes I come early," she said brightly. "Around five, before the grooms are even here! My job is kind of crazy but I wouldn't want to go a day without hopping on Sailor for at least a little walk. I couldn't make it early this morning so I just thought I'd pop out tonight. That's okay, isn't it?"

This was why I needed a dog, I thought. A dog would have barked when Miss Early Riser drove by at five o'clock in the morning, two hours before the grooms arrived. None of this sneaking around would be going on.

"It isn't okay. We have hours," I insisted. "The barn is closed from 8 PM to 7 AM. You signed off on this stuff with your boarding contract." I narrowed my eyes at her, suddenly suspicious. If she was breaking one rule, who was to say she wasn't breaking all the others? "Were you here Monday, too? The barn is closed on Monday. As you know."

"I never heard of a barn being closed one day a week," Kennedy said petulantly, her smile slipping. "I thought you just meant there were no riding lessons."

"It's plenty common in show barns," I snapped. It wasn't so much anymore — but there had been a time, back when half this countryside was horse farms and not subdivisions, when it had been the common practice, and trainers would get together for lunch and gossip about their students. I missed those days. Now I just sat on the couch with a book or ran errands. The community had dispersed, and I was the only one left to hold down the fort — and the old ways, maybe. "Mondays we are closed to give the horses a break after a busy show weekend." Me, too. Not to mention the grooms — one came in the morning to bring horses in and feed, two came back in the afternoon to feed, turn out, and clean the barn, all on a rotating schedule, so that every so often, someone got a full day off.

Kennedy looked cagey. "We don't show on weekends, so Sailor doesn't need a break. I don't bother anyone."

"That's because there's no one here!"

"Well, what's wrong with that? I'm riding my own horse, using my own tack, I clean up my own messes — I fail to see the problem." Her tone got snippier, which got my back even stiffer.

"That's because you don't pay my insurance premiums." I folded my arms over my chest, my *now-you-listen-to-me-young-lady* stance. "We have hours. We have rules. You signed off on them. You agreed to follow the barn rules in your boarding contract, which is legally binding. To find out you're breaking my rules on top of everything else —"

I shut up really fast then, but I couldn't unsay it.

"On top of *everything else?*" Kennedy cocked her head. "What *else* have I done?"

"Nothing," I said hastily. "Forget it. But you can't stay after hours. I'm tired and I want to go home." Thunder rumbled and the hammering rain picked up. It sounded like a crashing waterfall on the roof, and made it impossible to speak normally. That was just as well, because this conversation was headed into dangerous waters. At least I could actually get on her case about being here late. "Back to the barn!" I shouted over the din.

Kennedy looked ready to argue, but she must have realized there was no way to sound rational when one had to shout over a raging storm. She picked up her reins and turned Sailor back to the barn, and I followed, face grim. By the time I finished night-check, she had put Sailor and her tack away, and was gone.

Seven

It was the evening before the fall dressage show, and here I was in the arena past closing time again, schooling my youngster sales horse, Hope, on flying lead changes. He seemed to have conveniently forgotten how to do them earlier in the week. There were still boarders in the barn as well, polishing tack and gossiping anxiously, trying to settle horse show nerves. Their anxiety seemed to grow worse with age and the decades-long horse gaps most of them had taken. While they'd been pursuing degrees and careers, though, I'd been showing and showing and showing, and now I slept as soundly on show nights as any other night — if I ever made it to my bed...

Hope flubbed another lead change and I gave him a fairly heavy gouge with the blunt tip of a Prince of Wales spur. I wasn't trying to be mean, but I was sick of his nonsense. He *knew* this stuff. The horse swished his tail in response and swapped leads at last, but such a move in a judged test would get us a two or a three on the movement, torpedoing any chance of a good score. I wanted him to score in the low seventies. I was asking a pretty penny for this horse — it would be nice if he would *act* like he was worth it. I wouldn't get anything like his asking price with this nonsense. Why did I ride horses for a living again? Nothing but disappointment in this game.

"I don't know why I even bother with this," I grumbled, dropping Hope to a walk and slipping the reins through my fingers. He dropped his nose to the ground instantly. We both needed a moment to stretch and regroup.

"Because you love riding," a chipper voice called.

I blinked and looked around. Kennedy was slipping into Sailor's worn old saddle with effortless grace, as if her joints didn't ache with every move, as if the years in the saddle hadn't worn her body to the breaking point. Must be nice. "I didn't realize I'd said that so loud," I admitted. "Bad habit of talking to myself. I guess this life can make you crazy."

Kennedy shrugged. "Depends on how you live it. Maybe you're working too hard. When's the last time you got on a horse for fun?"

"I was probably twelve," I said, and Kennedy laughed, but I wasn't joking.

My idea of fun time wasn't horse-time, not anymore. Fun time was laying on my couch with a romance novel, glass of wine on the coffee table, something soothing on the radio. Horses were *work*. Maybe nothing was as much fun now as it had been when I was a teenager, but it seemed like all work and no play was just part of adulthood.

Maybe I just needed a daily nap to put everything into

perspective. Kennedy seemed like a person who wouldn't say no to a good nap once in a while.

She let Sailor stroll around the covered arena while I picked up the reins and asked Hope to collect himself again. Soon we were pacing around opposite sides of the arena, a study in opposites — Sailor's reins loose on his neck, his ears flopping at half-mast; Hope stepping carefully in an expressive medium walk, foam dripping from his mouth as he held the bit lightly, his ears tilted back on me, weighing my every movement as he waited for the next command.

This was the proper way to walk a horse, I thought, feeling his hindquarters engaged and under his body, feeling the potential pent-up propulsion with every step. I immersed myself in his movements, forgetting all that foolishness about riding being for suckers, because I really did enjoy the hard work and discipline of it all. Unfortunately, merely dropping the subject wasn't enough for Kennedy, because after a few minutes she turned Sailor with a lazy flip of the wrist and brought him over to walk next to us.

"Can I ask you a question?"

I grunted an assent, too busy with Hope to look her way.

"Why do you ride?"

"What?" Her question startled me, and I inadvertently tighter the reins. Hope sucked back from the pressure and pranced a little, in imitation of the *piaffe* we had been playing around with a few days before (before he forgot how to do lead changes). I settled him with loose fingers and a little leg, pushing him back into the bridle. "What kind of question is that?"

"Well, you don't ride for fun," Kennedy reasoned. "And I *only* ride for fun. So what's your reason, if it isn't fun?"

"I love horses," I replied automatically, and turned my attention to Hope's motion once more. Of course I loved riding — I did! Even if I had set barn hours and a mandatory closing day every week in an effort to get away from it. You couldn't live anything twenty-four hours a day, seven days a week, no matter how much you loved it, without getting worn out. I had put mechanisms in place to give me a break from horses so that I could *keep* loving them. That didn't mean I had lost my passion. Had Kennedy even suggested that? Was I being paranoid for a reason?

I settled myself deep into the saddle and concentrated on the measured rhythm of Hope's footfalls, the gentle swing of his hindquarters, the peace of a balanced horse. Yes, yes, that was the good stuff. Oh, I still loved riding. That synergy, that oneness with a horse, was still there, and I still loved finding it and holding onto it for as long as possible, just as I had when I was a kid. So I had to stop and remind myself of that from time to time, so what? Maybe that happened a little more often, these days, running up to the show season, running out of money, running out of time...

Maybe I needed a vacation, in addition to a daily nap.

Well, it was too late for time off now. The show season was here. Tomorrow was just the beginning of a long, busy winter. Maybe in six months I could go on a cheap three-night cruise or something. I ought to be able to get away for three nights, right? Just because a vacation had never happened before didn't make the whole concept impossible.

"I *know* you love horses," Kennedy went on reasonably,

dropping her reins and stretching her arms over her head with an odd artistic motion. I was reminded of some barn gossip — someone had said she'd once performed as the princess at the old horse-themed dinner show down in Orlando. I hadn't believed it before, but something in the way she moved... "But it looks like you could have a better relationship with horses, all the same." She reached way, way up, stretching her back so that she seemed to grow six inches in the saddle, then picked up her stirrups and nudged Sailor into a trot. She left the reins on his neck, and her hands high in the air. For the first time in years, I watched another rider and felt awe.

Unimpressive Sailor became a new horse, his hooves skimming the earth gently as he jogged in long, low frame, guided only by the rail and some sense of inner peace none of my horses possessed. In the saddle, Kennedy posted carelessly, her arms above her head, her fingers pointed towards the roof, her face uplifted and her eyes closed in apparent bliss.

She had impressive balance, I had to give her that much. I let Hope slip the reins and stroll quietly while I watched Kennedy. They made a looping serpentine through the arena, Kennedy turning Sailor in changes of rein with just a twist of her body. Although I had to wonder if you could call it a change of rein if the rider wasn't in fact using reins.

After a few circuits of the arena she stopped posting and stilled her body in the saddle. Sailor immediately dropped to a walk, and Kennedy laughed with pure delight. "I love doing that," she called, turning the horse back towards Hope and me. "We feel so in sync. I try to do it at least once a week, just to remind me of what riding should feel like. Free. Balanced. A little risky."

"I've never done anything like that off of a lunge line," I admitted. "You're very accomplished."

"Oh you must try it!" Kennedy ignored the compliment deftly. For a moment, I thought she'd offer to let me try it on Sailor, who had obviously been trained for such a stunt. If I dropped Hope's reins and asked him to trot around without contact, he'd probably jump out of the arena and take me down the road, even if he *was* schooling upper-level dressage movements. "You just have to work on your bond with your horse," she went on. "If you can't trust him, you won't maintain your balance for long — you'll be second-guessing him and he'll feel that, and second-guess *you*, and you'll both lose your rhythm."

She kept carrying on about bonds and relationships, but after a while, I stopped listening and went back to work on Hope, picking him up in the bridle and asking for a canter. She was very cute and very earnest, but I wasn't trying to build a sacred life-long bond with my horse. I was trying to sell a solid show jumper for a lot of money. Emotional connections were nice, but they paid no bills.

Anyway, I had Ivor. How many horses could one woman love? True wisdom meant protecting your heart. That was a lesson you learned the hard way, but once learned, it was hard to forget.

Eight

Horse show mornings were always too early and always too hurried, no matter how much planning was done the night before. By the time the sun was peeking through the pines, we had the trailer packed, the horses bandaged and loaded, and, with a final check of the trailer hitch and lights, we were off to the local dressage club for the day. *If* you could consider an hour's drive "local," and these days, I certainly did.

I drove north on the county highway with both hands on the wheel, avoiding minivans and SUVs turning out of the subdivisions, their backseats full of kids on their way to soccer practice or whatever it was kids did these days instead of begging to muck stalls in exchange for extra riding time. The decals of smiling stick figure families never failed to depress me on a horse show morning — all those soccer balls and karate belts and tennis rackets. I hated thinking about all of those girls who weren't riding. Why weren't they growing up with horses anymore?

What if that was *my* fault?

I'd let Rodney handle the kids in the neighborhood for all these years, concentrating on the adult amateur market. Kids were a hassle and I didn't really understand them — that was my excuse, anyway. Still, there were probably plenty of moms who were turned off by Rodney's muddy riding ring and ramshackle barn. Maybe their daughters (and the occasional son) would have gotten into riding if I'd welcomed them and their families to my bigger, cleaner, more impressive barn?

It wouldn't have been fair to Rodney at the time, but he was selling — and he'd asked me to take his trail horses, his lesson horses and his students. I hadn't been seriously considering it, but... money *was* tight...

"What are you worrying about?" Anna asked from the passenger seat. As working student, she got to ride shotgun.

"What makes you think I was worrying?" I grinned at her and slid my eyes back to the road just as quickly as they'd left it. We went past the local prep school. The playing fields were packed with children and the parking lot was packed with expensive cars. I had to admit, I would love to have those cars in *my* parking lot on a weekend morning. I slowed to avoid turning cars ahead of me; the highway was always gridlocked here any time anybody did one single thing at that school. These neighborhood kids were active, there was no doubt about that.

"You're chewing on your lip," Anna said. "You kind of stick out your jaw to the right a little and then run your lower teeth over your top lip. It's like a horse with a tic."

"I'm like a weaver, maybe? Or a cribber?"

"You crib on your own lip," Anna chortled. "I'm putting a collar on you when we get home."

"I'm a little worried about business," I admitted, lowering my voice so the gossiping ladies in the backseat couldn't overhear. They were cackling over something silly Colleen's husband had done. "We have a few extra empty stalls. Just looking for a good strategy to fill them."

"Less of that?" Anna tilted her head slightly towards the backseat. She'd always been fascinated that I had built a business solely out of adult amateurs. She didn't know it was non-sustainable, but then again, neither had I.

"I guess there aren't enough of *that* anymore."

"You're thinking kids then? Ponies?"

"Maybe. And maybe..." I paused, considered whether I should tell anyone. It was possible the boarders would riot. It sounded so common. "Trails?"

"Like, rentals?" Anna's eyes were big. Exactly the reaction I was concerned about. This might not work.

"Guided," I clarified. "Not rentals."

Anna nodded slowly, thinking about it. "How often?"

"Charters, I was thinking. From hotels. Not an open barn, just privately organized groups. To keep the integrity of the barn, so there aren't strangers coming in and out. Rodney suggested it..."

"What are you ladies talking about up there?" Colleen asked sharply, and I realized I'd been a bit too explicit with my wording. "Group what? Group tours?"

"Oh, just thinking aloud about hotel groups," I said lightly. "You know, a few people here, a few people there, from conferences, that kind of thing."

"Oh, to do riding lessons," Colleen said comfortably, and I didn't bother to disabuse her. "That's not a bad idea at all. People could do riding lessons while they're on business trips. I would do that. If I had time."

Anna gazed at me steadily, but I kept my eyes on the road. The highway passed under a new expressway overpass and then narrowed to two lanes. We passed a mobile home surrounded by chain-link and banana palms, we passed a nursery with a duck pond out front, we passed a sign for a private airport runway. We were back out in rural Florida at last, it had just taken forty-five minutes longer to get there then it used to.

None of my students were particularly thrilled to spend the day on the flat, but they approached a dressage show with the same intensity that they did the more beloved show jumping classes, because I told them they had to. Dressage kept jumping horses supple and obedient, as I reminded them when I added a dressage show to the calendar and was rewarded with a collective groan of disappointment. Dressage made their horses more athletic and sure of themselves, better able to get out of sticky situations and manage slick footing in the jumping arena, I lectured. Did they really want to deny themselves the show-ring edge they'd have from having horses with solid dressage training? Of course they didn't. So they grimly tightened the girths on their dusty dressage saddles, lengthened their stirrups, and schooled their tests until show day. One by one, the Seabreeze ladies entered the arena at A, halted at X, and saw the dirty deed through, usually bringing home a few ribbons at the end of the day.

That tended to sweeten the deal. If there was one thing my ladies loved, it was hanging ribbons on their horses' stalls.

Personally, I loved dressage more than anything, and it rankled that my students practically had to be bribed into doing one measly test per year. If I thought I could have run Seabreeze as a dressage training center, I would have done it in a heartbeat. But the money, at least in my neck of the woods, was firmly in favor of show jumping.

The students had gone back to gossiping in the backseat, my momentary slip over the group trail ride idea forgotten. Gayle was giggling over some story Colleen was telling, which was a shame, because Gayle was notoriously bad at memorizing dressage tests and hadn't managed to get her First Level test straight all week long.

"Gayle?" I asked her reflection in the rear-view mirror. "Do you know your test?"

The smile dropped from her cheeks. "I *think* so," she said haltingly. "Yes?"

"I'm asking *you.*"

"Yes," she decided in a more resolute tone. "I know my test."

"Can you go over it with Colleen really quick? Just to be sure?" The truck jounced over a bump in the road. Ivor kicked the trailer wall in response. I *knew* it was him — it always was. Picky brat, I thought, even though I liked his bad attitude. It made life more difficult than it really needed to be, but it was part of what made him special. Except for the trailer-kicking; that didn't help anyone. "I won't have time to call the movements for you. I have to be schooling Hope for his test while you're in the ring."

Gayle nodded and pulled her phone out of her pocketbook, opening the app she'd bought which laid out all the dressage tests, step by step, on the screen. Colleen leaned over it as well — she was doing the same test with

Bailey, and she stood a much better chance of bringing home a ribbon, if only because she had actually memorized the movements. Like Gayle, she was a fair-to-middling dressage rider, really no more advanced than anyone riding a Training Level test, but she had the sort of horse who could get her through the movements if she just stayed out of the way.

It was the same with the show-jumping — which was why the horses had cost a small fortune, and why I worried about them constantly, and why I didn't want them leaving the arena, no matter how enticing another rider might make it seem.

The group trail rides would make things even more complicated, if I decided to go down that route. Unless I sat everyone down and explained that they could go on a trail ride if they used one of my trail-broke horses and myself or whoever I hired as a guide to go out with them…

I worried it over, chewing on my lip, aware that Anna was giving me the side-eyed look again. Well, she was just going to have to get over it.

After all, worrying was I did best. I was better at worrying than riding. I thought that was actually the way things *should* be, when you were a barn owner and a manager and a riding instructor and a trainer all in one. I'd seen what horses could do when you gave them half a second of split attention. It was better to keep them in your sights at all times. Worrying over them, clucking over them, shaking your head over them. Anna would learn that over the years.

Ahead, the road began to curve around ancient trees, and undulate with rolling hills. We were nearly there, climbing up onto the ridge where the farms still ruled supreme. Now there were other horse trailers on the two-lane highway, all heading for the same isolated show barn in the middle of a rifle-shaped county in Nowhere Special, Florida. We'd shaken our heads when Kelly O'Brian announced she was leaving behind her small show barn near Orlando and building a magnificent new show-place equestrian center in such a desolate location. But five years later, Kelly was right and we were wrong, and now I was the one they were shaking their heads at as I refused to follow the herd.

Boy, the other trainers would just *love* the trail rides idea. I'd get laughed out of the warm-up arena if *that* news got around. There was a pretty firm line of demarcation between those who produced nationally-ranked show horses, and those who hoisted beginners onto quiet nags for an hour-long walk in the woods. If I went through with it, I'd have to step across that line alone.

Everyone perked up when the scrub oaks and dry grass along the road suddenly parted and gave way to the prancing bronze horse statue that heralded the entrance to Oak Ridge Equestrian Center. A fountain's sparkling waters played against the horse's raised hooves, causing a chorus of *oooes* and *aaahs* from the backseat. I slowed the truck and trailer to a crawl and made the turn slowly and gently enough for even Ivor, while the ladies swooned over the elegant surroundings.

I hated coming here.

"I love coming here," Colleen sighed. "*This* is what a stable should look like."

I glanced in the rear-view mirror, hoping to catch her eye so that I could intimate to her how insulting I found such a statement, but she was still gazing out the window, admiring the white PVC fencing that marched around spacious pastures, dotted with grazing horses. I hoped she realized Oak Ridge was a very different kind of place from the stable I ran — this was a real farm, with hundreds of acres of pasture, with a cross-country course, with warm-up rings and show-rings and boarders and lesson horses of every age and description. Kelly even took in broodmares and foals, something I never would have considered at Seabreeze. This place was an entire horse city. Seabreeze was just a horse apartment complex.

"It would be a hell of commute," I commented, squinting at the temporary signs flapping in the breeze, looking for the field set aside for parking trailers.

"Oh, I know. I'd have to be able to telecommute and move if I ever wanted to board someplace like this." Colleen chuckled. "But you can see why people who really want to ride all the time move out to the middle of nowhere. This is heavenly."

I decided she didn't mean any harm and concentrated on parking my rig at the end of a row of gleaming horse trailers.

We unloaded the eight horses in the close-cropped grass, brassy with the summer sun — six boarders, plus Ivor and Hope. Add their two tests each to all the coaching and hand-holding I had to do today and I was looking at one exhausting Saturday.

Trail rides, I thought, sounded positively heavenly right about now.

"Let's get going," I told Anna. "You support the left side and I'll support the right side. Help them tack up, comb out tails… you know the drill."

Anna grinned. "We'll get them out there just fine," she

said with a wink. "All our kids will do great today."

Nine

Anna was right; all our kids did great.

Tired and happy, we were gathered in the barn to hang up the day's ribbons. It was a cool evening, a hint of fall in the breeze at last, refreshing after the heat of the day and the worry and the frazzled nerves of a horse show day.

I called it a success, despite the summer-like day. No one had gotten hurt and no one had run away and no one had cried (very much) and no one had gotten food poisoning from the roach coach parked by the show secretary's tent, so I was willing to overlook a hot day in October as our show season opener. It would get cooler as the days went by, and we'd started the year on a good note. A successful beginning to the show season was all a trainer could ask.

The hanging of the ribbons was the last thing we did together, a barn tradition, after the horses had been fed and turned out for the night, after the trailer had been cleaned and put away, after the tack had been wiped and the saddle pads put in the laundry and the grooming kits returned to their shelves and the food wrappers and soda cans and napkins had been pulled from the truck cab and tossed in the trash. It was always late and we were always tired beyond the point of caring by the time we got to the ribbons, but the simple act of smoothing the cheap satin and hanging the shimmering prizes along a length of baling twine hung between two stall bars was a calming, refreshing exercise. It gave meaning to the day; it reminded us of our triumphs, whether it was the first time at a new level or the first time winning a championship.

This first show was especially important — these ribbons were a sign of the season to come.

Usually, I felt a jolt of excitement at this point in the day. In show seasons past, I'd been revved up, ready to go, anxious for the big festivals to kick into gear. This year, I just felt a quiet resignation, coupled with an underlying suspicion that I was thoroughly exhausted, mentally and physically. I didn't have to look at the big calendar hanging in the tack room, show dates picked out in red pen, to feel a very real longing for my bed. I wasn't going to see much of it in the next few months. Somehow, my lack of quality sleep felt like a more tiring prospect than it had in years past.

Oh, I supposed that was a normal response. I was getting old, that was all. Every year the show season got longer and harder, with more students, with bigger jumps, with more grueling days in the sun, but I just kept getting older and creakier. Grouchier, too. Just ask my students.

Gayle fingered the blue ribbon I'd gotten for Ivor's

fourth level test, the long tails streaming over her smudged white breeches. "I'd love a blue," she sighed wistfully.

I nodded sympathetically. The fact was, Gayle's Hanoverian mare, Maxine, was fully capable of getting a blue ribbon, especially in the First Level test that Gayle had shown her in today. A few half-circles, a few lengthenings of stride—Maxine could do that sort of stuff in her sleep.

It was Gayle who wasn't quite there yet, and might never be, if you looked at how little progress Gayle had made with her bouncing hands and broken-angled wrists. Maxine was a good girl, and carted her rider around without any apparent resentment about the beating her mouth took. I kept Maxine's bridle fitted with a gentle eggbutt bit, to minimize any damage.

"It'll come," I said reassuringly. It wasn't a lie — nothing was impossible, and First Level wasn't exactly rocket science. You just had to work at it. "You put in a really nice ride today. You're definitely getting there." And you'll get there much faster once you actually memorize the test *and* stop turning your horse by shifting her entire head and neck with your upper body, I thought, but didn't say aloud.

"It's just so stressful," Gayle said. She rubbed at her eyes with dirty palms, leaving black streaks on her sweaty cheeks. "I couldn't sleep last night. I couldn't eat breakfast. I haven't eaten all day! My husband is fed up with it. He wants to know what the point of spending all this money is, if it doesn't make me happy. I don't know what to tell him, you know? I tell him riding *does* make me happy and he says 'this isn't what happy looks like.' And I'm just at a loss."

I looked from Gayle to the nodding heads around her, looking sympathetic and understanding and agreeing with her, and felt a tremor of genuine panic. Elizabeth put down her yellow ribbon, our best student showing of the day, with a gusty sigh of her own.

"It's so *hard,*" she lamented. "My son always says 'I thought this was supposed to be fun' when I'm stressing before a show. And he's only thirteen!"

"What we *need* is to *relax,*" Colleen announced, her tone defiant, as if I had forbidden relaxation. (Of course I hadn't... not in so many words.) "We need to have some fun. I took Bailey on a trail ride last week, and it was great."

"Bailey wasn't spooky?" I countered, because I knew better, and she blushed.

"A little," she admitted. "But he went anywhere Sailor went, and Kennedy said he was bouncing around so much because he was having fun."

Having fun trying to dump you in the dirt so he could run home as fast as his little legs could take him, I thought.

"I love that horse Sailor," Elizabeth sighed, voice dreamy. She was in full throes of a horse-crush. On a trail horse, when she had a thirty-thousand dollar European import parked two stalls down! "And Kennedy is just so chill and relaxed, just like him. They're really fun."

"She invited me on a trail ride," Gayle admitted. "But I was too afraid to skip a training session." Gayle shook her head, looking back at the ribbon-less facade of Maxine's stall. "Should've gone."

I was facing a full-fledged revolt here. It was time to act. Something fun... "Let's play riding games on Tuesday," I suggested. "Or... gymnastics. I'll set up a big gymnastics course—bounces, one-strides, five or six or seven jumps in a row. It'll freshen everyone up."

"I hate gymnastics," Colleen said dismissively. That

bold thing. I added her to my mental shit list, right next to Kennedy. "I'm going on another trail ride Tuesday, anyway. I already made plans. Kennedy found a tree with a bald eagle nest, out by the lake."

I sputtered my protestations, but it was too late — I had already lost control. Heads together, ribbons forgotten, the students plotted right through my reminders of upcoming shows, of fees paid, of points series and potential championships. They agreed to cancel lessons and previously scheduled training rides with cavalier wantonness, as if they had decided in some silent vote to remind their imperious trainer they were the boarders and students, yes, but they were also the *owners* — at the end of the day, those were *their* horses in my stalls and they would do whatever the hell they wanted with them.

No matter what lofty plans and goals I had already set for them.

I hung up my blue ribbons on my own horses' stalls and stalked away to do night-check. Let them go out goofing around on the trails, I thought furiously, glancing through the stall bars at one water bucket after another, turning the faucets on each wall to top off the buckets. I'd be here waiting when they had realized riding in the woods was about as rewarding as getting the oil changed in their car, and nothing felt as good as plain old hard work. I'd be here drawing up a new business plan that would insure I wasn't so dependent on their silly whims. I'd be here when they were ready to get back to their previously scheduled hopes and dreams.

Or when someone got hurt, whichever came first.

Of course, I didn't want anyone to get hurt. I didn't even

really want to tell any of my students "told you so" anyway. It wasn't good for business. The prospect of growing my business was giving me enough worry, without alienating the clients I already had.

Still, I had my chance to say those mocking words almost sooner than I could have predicted — on Tuesday after the show, in fact, when Bailey came back to the barn without a rider, wild-eyed and foamed with sweat. I was out in the covered arena on Hope, practicing gymnastics — well, at least *I* was enjoying the gymnastics course, even if my rebellious students were not. I had to pull Hope up abruptly, though, when I saw Bailey come crashing out of the woods. Hope nearly leapt out of his skin at the sight, and I dug my heels down deep, in case he was the next horse to go wild.

Bailey went clattering across the parking lot, steel shoes skidding dangerously on the asphalt, and raced into the barn. I heard "whoa, whoa, *whoa!*" in Margaret's deepest, most authoritative tones, and the racket came to a clattering stop, so I knew things were fine inside. I worked to steady Hope, who was having a minor heart attack over the proceedings, and watched the trail-head for any signs of Bailey's trail-riding companions, human or horse. A moment or two passed, during which time I was starting to get the awful feeling I was going to have to ride this little dunderhead out there in search of them myself, when a plain nose appeared from the brush, followed by the head, neck, and body of Sailor the Perfect Quarter Horse, *two* riders wedged onto his short back.

I kicked Hope, who really couldn't seem to get his head down from giraffe level, through the grass between the arena and the barn, meeting Sailor and his riders as they came up to the barn. I reined back and allowed Hope to dance an excited jig beneath me, while Sailor came to a placid halt and watched Hope with mild disinterest. I wondered what had happened to that horse's personality. If he'd ever had one, it had been buried beneath years and months and weeks of plodding along sandy trails looking at the same damn palmettos over and over again. Ideal for taking beginners on horseback, but not as interesting as I liked them.

Colleen, meanwhile, was finding her horse was more interesting than she might have liked. She was clutching her wrist and blinking back tears as she slid cautiously from Sailor. Kennedy, following her to the ground, looked rather more shell-shocked — her expression was blank and her movements around her horse were oddly mechanical. I supposed she hadn't expected her little Life Is Good revolution to end in carnage so quickly. She looked at me questioningly — for instructions, for a dressing-down, I didn't know. I went for the former. "Go hose down your horse," I said, and turned to Colleen for the story. Kennedy, I figured, could think about what she had done and apologize to me later.

But Colleen wasn't ready to recount her tale. She was too busy sniffling and looking down at her wrist. "I think it's broken," she gasped when I moved to touch her arm. "I landed on it first."

I winced. It was tough to ride with a broken wrist, not to mention how much more difficult it would make her "real" life, outside the barn — Colleen was a marketing manager at a fairly large firm, and I had a feeling she did a lot of typing and writing and signing of directives in that sort of position. I felt another surge of anger towards

Kennedy — she was putting these naive ladies in danger in more ways than one, threatening their horses, their show careers, and their *jobs*.

Colleen, however, was more than ready to blame herself. "I'm just so embarrassed," Colleen whimpered. The words caught in her throat as she choked back a sob. "I shouldn't have taken him out there. He didn't like it — he kept telling me he didn't feel safe, and I ignored him. And you told me too, and I thought I knew better than you…" her words trailed off as her eyes overflowed again.

I put my hand on her shoulder — I knew exactly how she felt — and with my other hand pulled out my phone and called for an ambulance. This was intense, type-A, powerbroker Colleen, after all. If she was apologizing to me, she was probably going into shock.

The ambulance pulled into the parking lot some time later, the EMTs within looking around rather curiously. I stepped into the lot and waved them towards the barn entrance. Just within, I had Colleen tucked into an Irish knit cooler and drinking water.

"I had no idea there was still a horse farm out here," the driver yelled, hopping out of the cab. "I did a double-take when I saw the call."

"I'm still here," I replied drily. "Rumors of my demise exaggerated, that sort of thing."

The other EMT grinned and opened the back doors of the ambulance, rooting around for equipment.

"You must get offered millions for this place," the driver said companionably, as if he'd just swung by for the conversation.

"Not millions." I smiled tolerantly. "But I do get offers. People are always in a big hurry to build more houses." I gave him a nod and went back into the barn, already sick of the topic. That was all anyone wanted to talk about anymore — developers, construction, selling the property. It wasn't happening, but I was tired of having to repeat it.

Colleen looked up. In her usually perfect skin, a crease was etched between her worried eyes. "Are they going to take me to the hospital? My husband isn't here yet."

"I'll call him and tell him where they take you," I promised. "Gotta get you patched up and show-ready."

She smiled weakly. "I should have been practicing for the show today."

"I won't hold it against you." I grinned to show her I was joking and stood back to let the EMTs do their job.

When the ambulance had gone, the husband phoned, and the horses cooled out, I expected everything to go back to business as usual. Margaret, Tom, and Anna finished up evening chores a little late and went their separate ways. By eight thirty, the boarders had dispersed. There was only one car left in the parking lot — Kennedy's. I gazed at the car for a long moment, feeling a surge of resentment. That girl was giving me nothing but trouble, and now all I wanted to do was flip out the lights and head home for the night... but *first* I had to find her and send her on her way.

I did a loop of the barn aisles and didn't see her. I glanced in the tack rooms — nothing. I looked in Sailor's stall, and he blinked at me from the corner, where he was working his way through a pile of hay. No Kennedy. I ended up back at the barn entrance, gazed up the aisle, and saw that my office light was on, shining brightly from the second floor.

What the hell was she doing in my office?

I charged up the narrow stairs, too angry to bother a stealth attack, and by the time I'd burst into the office she would have been well aware I was coming — those stairs groaned and creaked like a ship in a storm. There wasn't any need for a surprise appearance, anyway. Kennedy hadn't been going through my papers or doing anything shifty. She was just sitting in the chair meant for visitors, turned a little so that she could see the door, her face drawn and anxious.

"What the *hell*, Kennedy?" I snapped, but my temper was already waning. She was afraid of me, but she hadn't been able to sneak away without seeing what her punishment was going to be. I respected that, even if a braver person would have sought me out instead of hiding in the office and waiting to be found.

"I'm sorry," she burst out, sounding half-choked, as if she'd been trying not to cry. "Don't kick me out. I have nowhere else to take Sailor."

"I'm not going to kick you out," I said, although I had been considering it. "Relax."

She looked up then, eyes round. "I thought for sure you would. Margaret said you would."

"Margaret's a groom." I shook my head dismissively. "You want to know something, come to me. Don't ask my employees."

"Okay," she said. And then: "Okay," again, as if she was reassuring herself.

"Go home, Kennedy. I'm tired. I want to be done with this day."

Kennedy got up and went past me onto the narrow landing, careful not to brush against me. She leaned against the railing, and after a minute, I joined her. Something was on this girl's mind. I waited for her to share it.

We looked out for a minute at the moon, setting in orange splendor over the distant trees beyond the county highway. If we stayed here long enough, and looked at the right spot to the south, we'd see a fireworks show. Another world, just minutes away, would be celebrating the night away while I poured a glass of wine and heated up a bag of frozen Chinese food. Kennedy looked in just that direction, as if she'd been here late enough to know what to look for.

"The theme parks are down there," she said after a minute.

"Yup." I pulled the office door closed.

"It's hard to believe they've built hotels all the way up here, isn't it? I mean, when I was a kid, we'd come to Florida on trips and there was nothing out here... it was just farms. I remember seeing watermelons growing for the first time and I couldn't believe it... I'd only ever seen them in a grocery store."

"It's hard to believe, alright," I said grimly.

"Are you going to sell?" she asked suddenly.

"This again? Who is telling everyone I'm selling?"

"No one... it's that big sign next door. I just wondered."

I started down the stairs. I had no need to stay up here all night, discussing real estate and waiting for fireworks not meant for me. "Go home, Kennedy."

She followed me down, the stairs protesting noisily. A few horses stopped chewing their hay and looked up, ears pricked at the late-night racket. "If I can do anything to help keep this place open, I'll do it. You don't know how much having Sailor here means to me."

I glanced back at her, my fingers on the light switch.

"Yeah?"

She stopped and watched me hopefully. "Yes."

"First off, stop taking my students on trail rides."

She swallowed and nodded tightly. "And what's second? I mean it. I'll do it."

An idea was forming in my mind, but it was too soon to tell if it was worth discussing with anyone. I'd have to sit down with a notebook and a calculator tonight, do the numbers, see if it was going to be the future or just a silly idea. Rodney was waiting for my answer. He was antsy to empty his barn and head to his new haven in north Florida. Where there were no fireworks, and no hotels, and no faux Tuscan hills, either.

"I'll let you know," I promised. "Now go home."

I turned out the lights.

Ten

There was a crackle of electricity in the air. A late fall storm was slipping past the farm, with gusty winds causing the trees to thrash and flail. Distant rumbles of thunder shook the windows in their panes. It stayed too far away for rain, though. The cool drafts rushing down from the thunderhead's icy upper reaches, high in the atmosphere, made riding more pleasant, though not more simple, than it had been as the hot summer sun refused to give up its holds. The horses got the wind up their tails and silliness ensued. They pranced through their slow gaits and crow-hopped through their fast ones.

I was on Ivor, jumping combinations in-between helping Anna, who was getting a sort of mini-lesson on her gelding. Mason was a nice jumper, but his limit in scope was really showing today. I was dreading the conversation to come, when I finally told Anna that she was going to need a new horse if she expected to move up the levels. The way he was rattling the poles in their cups today, it looked as if she might not need me to clue her in on the fact.

Finally, after pulling three consecutive rails in the triple combination, Anna called it a day. "We'll watch you," she said resignedly, slipping from the saddle so that she could hoist the poles back into place. Mason followed her like a dog, scarcely needing the security of the rein she'd looped around her arm. They were close, those two. Close like Kennedy and Sailor. A closeness I hadn't shared with a horse since I was a child, with my own Sailor.

I gathered up Ivor to send him towards the combination again, redirecting all my concentration towards getting him down to the fence at just the right spot. There was no time to worry about magical pony-girl relationships, or what might have been. The jumps loomed up before us, one two three, a vertical, a landing, a vertical, a stride, an oxer — big and wide and brightly colored. Anna stepped back from the second element and Mason backed with her, his legs in tandem with hers.

I saw their motions from the corner of my eye, but my true focus was on the fences — and so was Ivor's. He sprang over the first fence, me with him, the perfect spot. His fore-hooves touched the ground, and he was already gathering for the second fence, and Anna said "What the hell?" and I thought "What's wrong? We're perfect," as Ivor bounced over the next two fences like a rubber ball.

I gave him a stroke on the neck as he cantered away from the fence, head nodding with pleasure, and we rounded the end of the arena and looped back at an easy lope, so I didn't see Gayle crossing the parking lot, hard hat unbuckled and mud on her breeches, until she was already climbing under the rail of the arena. Anna was running to meet her, Mason jogging obediently behind her. "What happened?" I shouted, spurring Ivor towards the girls, and Gayle turned a tear-streaked face towards me.

"I fell," she admitted brokenly. "And Maxine took off, and Kennedy said she'd ride after her once she got me back safe."

"Where's Kennedy now?" A red mist of anger danced in front of my eyes. She'd said she'd do anything to keep the barn open. Couldn't she see that she was destroying everything?

Ivor was feeding off my tension and began to prance in place, snorting and throwing splatter of foam from his bit.

Gayle had to jump back to avoid getting stepped upon by my dancing steed. Ivor was not a horse you wanted to crowd when he was feeling nervous. He had feet like serving platters.

"She turned around after she got me to the trail head. She went to find Maxine." Gayle shook her head and put her face in her hands. "This is all my fault. I shouldn't have gone out there... I should have listened to you... my husband is going to kill me if anything happens to that horse..."

That was probably true, all of it, I thought. She *should* have listened to me, and her husband *was* going to kill her. I knew how hard Gayle worked, like a lot of the others worked, to find the money to keep their horses going and their families happy at the same time. No one wanted to give up a vacation or summer camp or a new car because Mom wanted to play with ponies. Families were selfish that way, they couldn't help themselves. It was one reason I didn't have a family myself.

I gathered up my reins. "Anna, take care of Gayle. Tell Tom to cool out Mason for you. I'm going to go find Kennedy and Maxine." To the south, the dark clouds beyond the barn growled, a long low rumble like a shuddering earthquake rippling through the sandy soil. Luckily, my way was east. I wheeled Ivor and trotted away.

Ivor hadn't been on the trails in years, and neither had I. There were still stark white blazes on the trees where Kennedy had first come through with her machete, slashing off overgrown branches and unwanted brush, but the footing underneath was trampled down, hardened by the passing hooves over the past few weeks.

The land around us was scruffy Florida scrub: tall, gaunt slash and longleaf pines, vast and impenetrable thickets of palmetto, clumps of turkey oak, the occasional cabbage palm. The sand was chalk-white on top, charcoal black beneath. Here and there, the ground was scattered with actual charcoal, remnants of the natural cycles of wildfires. The blazes scorched the palmettos to their thick roots and blackened the bark of the pines, clearing the way for new growth. When I was a little kid, I'd dig out the charcoal chunks from the empty lots in our neighborhood and write on the driveway with them, drawing pictures of ponies with rippling manes and flowing tails, like my Sailor.

Ivor pricked his ears at the sounds, tilting his head this way and that to take in his surroundings. The underbrush was alive with peeping frogs in still puddles, clicking ticking insects burrowed into palmetto roots, tiny darting lizards racing about everywhere. We were already deep into wild Florida, though just steps outside my barn, only a few miles from the white concrete and stucco apartment houses of urban sprawl. I couldn't help but look around the countryside with pleasure as we trotted across the flat land, and Ivor seemed pretty pleased with life as well. His strides grew longer, his neck arched, and he drew his hindquarters well beneath him, feeling as powerful as Pegasus before that fabled steed launched into the endless skies. Horses grew bigger outside of the arena. They understood distance and space as freedom more fully than a human, who built fences and houses and walls and rooms almost without thinking about it. Humans were drawn to partitioning and containing as a moths were drawn to a flame, or as a horse to a hay-pile, if you came right down to it.

And there was no better way to see the landscape, especially in the high palmettos of the scrub, than from the back of a horse. Ahead, I could see the approaching dome of the cypress trees encircling the gator pond, and just before it, the oak-crowned hump of the old shell midden standing out like a mountain on the flat land. Above it all, the dark southern sky was ghostly with white egrets flying to their evening roosts. They glowed electric-white against the threatening clouds and the black trees.

Ivor picked his head up a bit higher as we rounded the curve in the trail and entered the hammock of live oaks and whiskery sabal palms overgrowing the midden. Within its shadows, the air was damp and cool. We trotted up the rise and came to a clearing at the very top, where we nearly collided with Kennedy and Sailor. Ivor slammed on the breaks, his ears nearly in my face as he reared up in astonishment, and Sailor jumped backwards, eyes white-rimmed and expression as awake as I'd ever seen on the quiet little horse's indifferent face.

Kennedy didn't look so much surprised as miserable. "I

don't see Maxine anywhere," she said grimly, without any preamble. "Do you think she'll just find her own way home?"

A gust of wind blew dry leaves around us in a little twister, and Ivor sidestepped nervously. Without the exhilaration of forward motion, he remembered he didn't belong out here, and he didn't know what was expected of him. He twisted his neck, looking first one way and then the other, taking little nervous prancing steps. I sighed. This was one of the experienced horses, one of the few who had been ridden out here before, and he was being silly about everything. Imagine how awful Bailey and Maxine must have behaved, without any idea what was going on around them, where they were going, what they were supposed to expect. That was why first Colleen, and now Gayle, had hit the ground. Inexperience, ill-prepared, inappropriate.

I glared at Kennedy meaningfully. "She's never been out here before, so I doubt she'd find her way home."

Kennedy shook her head and looked back out over the scrub. She couldn't have chosen a better vantage point — we were thirty feet above the surrounding plain and there were so few leafy trees to block our way, it was easy to gaze out through the palmettos to search for a large, out-of-place horse. "We were doing pretty well and then a branch fell — that one over there." She pointed at the great grasping arm of a live oak, at least twelve feet long, lying in a tangle of kudzu vine and bracken near the path. "She wheeled and took off, just left Gayle in the dirt. I mean, it was scary — even Sailor jumped. But she went the wrong way — she went back out into the scrub, not towards the barn. I thought that was weird."

"She's never *been* out here," I repeated, shaking my head. "She's disoriented. She's probably never even been in the woods in her life. Maxine's a show horse, always has been. How many times do I have to tell you, Kennedy — these horses are too valuable to just play around with? Their owners have spent fortunes on them. They aren't pleasure horses."

I heard it a split second after I said it.

My words came out completely wrong.

If Kennedy noticed, she let it go. She was in too deep a mess to argue semantics with the barn owner, I figured.

"Where did you ride to?" I asked.

"The lake," Kennedy said. "To see the bald eagles."

"I didn't know we had bald eagles out here." I turned Ivor in the direction of the lake. The old sand road led straight there, due east. "There weren't any when I was a girl. Guess we're heading that way anyway. Let's go see. Maybe Maxine wanted to watch the eagles, too."

Ivor cut out his nonsense once he was allowed to go out adventuring on the trail again. He might have spent most of his time in the show-ring, but he had the heart of an explorer, that much was obvious. Maybe his adventurousness was why he enjoyed jumping big scary jumps so much, I mused. At any rate, he clearly remembered the work we'd done on the trails years ago, before I'd decided I couldn't risk taking him out here any longer. I'd been right to stop bringing him here, of course. Everyone had to draw their own line, and I'd never gotten over Sailor. I knew *that* as much without needing any soul-searching or therapy or self-help books. I'd never gotten over losing Sailor. Ever since, I'd kept my horses in arenas, where I could manage conditions and keep them safe.

Still, there was no doubt that Ivor was having fun now, even without the security of groomed footing and guiding walls. He snorted and blew at alarming shrubs and worrisome bunnies, but his trot was confident and energetic, and our sojourn across the scrub was actually pleasant, despite the cause.

As we jogged east I turned my head to the right and watched the thunderstorm blowing itself to pieces, to the left to see the clearing evening sky, and couldn't contain a sigh of pleasure when the evening sun suddenly emerged from the clouds behind us and lit the palmettos and pines all around in a golden glittering glow.

Beside me, trotting along on a lop-eared Sailor, Kennedy smiled.

I frowned and resolved to get back to business. We were looking for a horse, not taking a joy-ride.

Still, it was overly-observant Ivor who was first to spot the horseshoe, twisted and glinting in the white sand. "She went this-a-way," I observed, straightening out my shying horse. "At least we're on the right path."

We slowed as the live oaks surrounding the lake loomed before us, and the horses walked carefully between their twisting branches, dodging Spanish moss and spiderwebs. It was nearly dark in the hammock, but to our right we could see the dark water lapping around cypress knees. There were alligators in there, and water moccasins, just as I had warned the boarders, but if we didn't bother them, they wouldn't bother us. Probably.

We emerged onto a little swath of green grass on the shores of the lake, just a sink-hole pond, really, a round depression of dark water, and there Maxine was grazing, her flanks sweaty. She lifted her head to see us and the broken reins dangled from her bridle. She nickered with pleasure at the sight of friends, and I sighed. It could have been so much worse.

It could have been Sailor all over again.

"I'll get her," Kennedy said, and started to walk Sailor towards the mare.

Then she stopped. "Look," she said, pointing up.

There they were — four bald eagles, soaring through the golden-lit sky on broad wings. One by one they landed in the highest reaches of a towering bald cypress, heads turning this way and that, zeroing in quickly on us. I felt goosebumps rising on my arm. The eagles were unimaginably majestic and otherworldly, avian kings in a land already populated by dozens of massive, beautiful birds. Ospreys and kites and herons were nothing next to these eagles, which seemed as large as ponies.

Maxine, fed up and ready to go home to her dinner, broke into a trot to meet us, and one by one the eagles erupted from the tree and soared away, shrieking their displeasure with high-pitched, wild cries.

Kennedy took Maxine's broken reins as the mare shoved against Sailor, nuzzling at him with the devotion all horses seemed to show the little Quarter Horse. He was like a horse guru, meditating cross-legged in his mountain-top hut, calming the panicked herd one by one. Well, he couldn't *always* get the job done in time, I reflected, or we wouldn't be out here. There was more to teaching a horse self-confidence than sticking them alongside a confident horse.

"Can you believe that?" Kennedy was gushing. "A whole family of eagles!"

I shook my head. "I've never seen anything like that

before," I admitted. Back when I'd ridden out here as a child, bald eagles were still a rarity. I'd never seen one in the wild before. I never would have today, if I hadn't left the arena. That was something to think about, I supposed, but it didn't change the facts I had laid down for the boarders. It didn't change the risks. I watched Maxine carefully all the way out of the little field, making sure she didn't put a single hoof wrong.

Eleven

We rode back towards the barn, straight into the golden glare of the setting sun, the chill of autumn creeping through the palmettos and raising goosebumps on bare skin. Whip-poor-wills sang in the lengthening shadows, and a flock of white ibis, the curves of their long red beaks glinting in the last rays of light, solemnly watched us from the stark branches of a longleaf pine high above our heads. As we crossed over the shell mound, bats began to flutter drunkenly through the dusk, snapping at mosquitoes, and we urged the horses to a canter, hoping to reach home before full dark. Ahead, winking in the western sky, Venus glinted in a sky fading from yellow to jewel-blue. Everything — every inch of land and sky — was beautiful, and seeing it from atop a good horse made it a thousand times more so.

I hadn't felt so free and alive in years.

I suspected, judging by his pricked ears and out-flung hooves, Ivor felt the same way.

I glanced over at Maxine, jogging along next to Sailor. She alone didn't look like she was having fun — she looked frightened and miserable, drenched in sweat, looking all around with white-ringed eyes. Watching for gremlins, I thought. Her hide shivered as branches scraped against her on narrow sections of trail, and she swished her tail constantly, as if scraping away unseen insects and worries.

"Poor city horse," I said after a few minutes of watching Maxine's nervous tics.

Kennedy glanced back. Her face was flushed with all the trotting and the effort of dragging Maxine along. "What's that?"

"I said *poor city horse*," I repeated. "She doesn't like it out here one bit."

Kennedy looked over at the laboring Maxine. "You really think she's never been ridden outside an arena in her entire life?"

It was the first time Kennedy had admitted any of the horses might be over-faced by adventures in the wild realm beyond the arena. "I seriously doubt it. She came from Germany when she was five and she was already an accomplished jumper. She's been with me for three years and she's never been on the trails in that time. So this was probably her first experience out in the woods."

"With you? I thought she was Gayle's horse. Gayle said —"

"She's been in *training* with me," I amended. "I bought her from the agency that imported her, and sold her to Gayle, but I showed her for the first year, and I still do from time to time."

"Why do *you* show her?" We were trotting three-abreast now, the old white road wide enough for all of us. "If she's Gayle's horse?"

I rolled my eyes. Kennedy was messing with me, right? The reason was obvious. "Because the horse has the potential to go Grand Prix," I said. "Of course Gayle doesn't want to waste that potential, just because she isn't that advanced a rider."

"So why would Gayle buy a horse that's more advanced than she is?"

Oh-ho, Kennedy didn't think my sales were ethical, did she? And what business was it of hers? I took a steadying breath so I wouldn't sound sharp and gave Kennedy some schooling. "Why *wouldn't* she? Maxine was an excellent investment. If we win money in big classes, Gayle gets a portion. The wins increase her sales value as a broodmare later in life *or* if Gayle wants to do embryo transfer and get a foal to keep or sell while Maxine is still competing. And Gayle gets a quality horse to learn on — Maxine was less expensive and younger than what she'd get with a schoolmaster. She's a much better investment than a sixteen or seventeen-year-old gelding that knows the ropes but won't have any future value. A schoolmaster is depreciating every day. A young horse like Maxine, with good temper and huge athletic ability, is just a win-win for all of us. And I'm not sure why you're trying to imply otherwise."

Kennedy smiled at me, attempting, I suppose, to assure me she wasn't suggesting anything... *improper*... about the way I ran my business or advised my students. That girl should really be trying harder to make an ally out of me, I thought.

"I just thought maybe Maxine had turned out to be

more horse than Gayle needs," Kennedy said innocently.

Of course Maxine was more horse than Gayle *needed*, but that wasn't the point. "She's a good investment," I repeated. "If you're going to put all this money into a horse, you might as well get one that stands a chance to pay you back at least some of it."

Kennedy just smiled again, and nodded, and looked straight ahead with a bemused kind of look on her face, as if she wasn't convinced by my arguments but she was too nice to say so. Consequently, as we rounded the last curve and slowed the horses to a walk to leave the woods and step back onto the asphalt of the parking lot, the sun finally sinking below the barn and arena ahead of us, I was in a decidedly less than triumphant mood.

I was definitely feeling less forgiving.

Kennedy was going to have to go. Things had gone too far.

Unfortunately, it was too late tonight to tell Kennedy she was getting an eviction notice. Not to mention, there were too many spectators. Gayle, face still strewn with dirty tears, was running up to catch the wide-eyed Maxine, who was spooking her way across the parking lot as if she hadn't just spent the past half-hour cantering and trotting through the palmetto scrub and pine plantations and was still fresh as a spring filly. Anna was right behind her, snatching one of the broken reins just as Maxine managed to pull loose from Kennedy, and brought the crazed mare down to a trembling halt.

I looked past Anna and Maxine and saw we had an audience. The peanut gallery in the barn aisle were silhouetted against the bright interior lights. I could swear every boarder I had was watching, arms wrapped around themselves to ward off the autumn chill, unwilling to go home for the night without seeing an end to the drama.

I decided not to give them any. A good barn owner didn't air her dirty laundry in front of all her boarders, she kept it behind closed doors. "Kennedy," I said, turning to her as she dismounted Sailor. "Thanks for helping bring Maxine home. Nice job catching her."

I hopped down from Ivor and walked him into the barn, as the boarders parted ranks to let us pass.

After it all shook out, everything and everyone appeared to be fine.

Gayle was shaky but fine, Maxine was tired but fine, Kennedy was apologetic, Ivor was bright-eyed and hungry for his dinner, Sailor was his usual quiet self. The barn was chattering, and from the sound of things, the boarders were ready to swear off trail-riding once and for all and go back to concentrating on showing. Everything was as I could have wished it, if only it wasn't so far past closing time.

I was ready for my bottle of wine and my bed. Maybe a romance novel, maybe even a hot bath, I reflected, feeling a bit of chill in the night air. I pulled a hoodie from the tack room over my polo shirt. The white logo on the back was bright and cheerful against the navy blue: *Seabreeze Equestrian Center: Hunters, Jumpers, Dressage* with a jumping horse soaring over an ocean wave. I rubbed my fingers over the logo before I put the hoodie on, a little ritual of mine. Sometimes I couldn't believe this was all real, even on nights like tonight when the barn was more a pain in the ass than anything, and I was out late settling down the clients and horses after a completely avoidable upset.

But for once, I thought, walking through the barn after everyone had quieted down, after our horses were cooled out and fed, after I had managed to get the boarders to go home to their families and sent the grooms home with my apologies and promises of overtime, for once I didn't mind being out so late. The evening had been so wild and beautiful, and I had seen all of it. Instead of riding in a covered arena, the sky blacked out by the steel roof, or working in the barn, surrounded by walls and stalls and their barred windows and doors, I had been out with only the heavens as a roof, only the palmettos as walls. The charm of it was hard to escape.

So was Sailor. I leaned against the new Sailor's stall door for a moment. The stocky little horse looked at me with his quiet, impassive eyes, and stopped pulling at his dinner hay long enough to come over to give me a *whuff* of hot breath, his nose tickling my palm when I placed my hand against the stall bars. Hay-scented, sweet pony breath, like my own Sailor. My pony, whom I shouldn't have taken out alone. I hadn't thought anything bad would happen — it was before I understood mortality, and chance, and bad things happening to good people and better ponies. I hadn't understood that to a horse, one rabbit was not always like another rabbit. I hadn't expected the spook, I hadn't expected to fall off, I hadn't expected him to run away and leave me there. I hadn't expected to feel so abandoned.

I hadn't realized that sometimes leather reins broke when a leg was caught up in them, and sometimes they did not.

I learned a lot that day. I'd learned lessons I was too young for, and now I could never stop teaching, for fear other people would learn them the hard way as well.

Sailor went back to his hay, giving his tail a little swish as he went, as if telling me to be on my way, to turn off the lights, to move on with my night, to let old sorrows lie. Maybe I exaggerated that last bit. He probably didn't worry too much about my emotions, or the deep knowledge of the game of chance and danger we played with our horses that I had come into that day. He just wanted me to leave him alone to be a horse for the rest of the night. He was right. Horses were often right about these things.

I hung around a few minutes more, somehow not quite ready to go back to the house. There had been something special in the day, and going home would spell its end. I went upstairs instead, to sit and think, surrounded by my memories.

Twelve

I leaned back in my chair and counted my ribbons.

The office walls were festooned with decades' worth of horse show ribbons. Ribbons and so much more: trophies with mock-brass horse statuettes atop them; giant rosettes with sashes, meant to hang around a horse's neck; glass plaques, etched with the date and the championship won; silver picture-frames, with the horse's name under a photo of a perfect jump or the winning presentation. The prizes hung from the wood-paneled walls, leaned against books, teetered on top of shelves, a glorious display of red and gold and blue, the rainbow hues of victory. Blue for first, red for second, yellow for third, and all of them combined into one starburst for the championships. Satin with gold letters stamped into its shimmering cloth — such was the reward for winning a class with an entry fee of one hundred dollars or more, the prize for giving your life over to training and riding.

The oldest, smallest, most dog-eared ribbons, fly-specked and faded, hung in the shadow of the bookcase next to the door. In this corner, the colors were mostly green, or white, with one spectacularly pretty purple ribbon, awarded for ninth place in a particularly large class. Those were my childhood ribbons, at least the ones still suitable for display. After so many years of hanging on stalls, on my bedroom walls, of being crushed in tack trunks and suitcases and cardboard boxes in storage units throughout the country, some had simply dissolved into a colorful pile of dust.

I'd hung everything up here when the barn was still half-finished, the stalls not yet installed in the cavernous space below, the arenas still grass marked with spray-paint while I dreamed it all up. The walls hadn't been filled yet, but that was good — it meant there was plenty of room to add in my victories as a trainer, as a barn owner at last. It had been the first time I'd felt safe, like there wasn't another midnight move in my future, and so it was the first time I'd unpacked all those boxes and seen my life's work in a wall of silver and gold and blue and red. Horse training for hire was perilous work — you seemed to find the craziest people in the country one by one, barn by barn, one tiny spider-infested barn apartment or mobile home or travel trailer at a time. I'd worked at million-dollar barns training million-dollar horses, only to have to leave after three months because the million-dollar owner "couldn't" pay my promised salary. (More like *wouldn't.*) I'd bolted doors against male bosses and coworkers who thought that my training contract included certain extras I wasn't willing to give; I'd left under the cover of darkness to avoid run-ins with bosses who weren't willing to uphold their ends of contracts.

It wasn't a business for the faint of heart.

It had been a rough road, but it had all led to this office with my name on the door and my ribbons on the walls. Just behind me, through the window, I could see the stalls of my boarders, the horses left in my care, the students who trusted me to put their training goals and their safety first.

I spun the chair and looked down at the quiet barn floor below. The horses munching at their hay, or sprawled out asleep on their thick beds of shavings. I'd turned out half the lights, so that it was dim but not yet dark. The massive lamps hung high above the barn from distant, shadowy rafters, illuminating the horses and the aisles and the empty wash-stalls with a pale whiteness. It was the sort of light that showcased every flaw, every missed wisp of hay or horseshoe-shaped clod of clay tracked in the from the arena. I loved it, because I could see the barn was kept perfect, as I wanted it, all the time.

Perfection was why people loved to come here — for the peace of mind that came with perfection. This was a haven for horse owners, just as I had always dreamed it would be. Even on days like today, full of drama, the barn ended up in its natural state again. Quiet, dreaming, peaceful.

My farm was everything I'd ever wanted.

I smiled down at the dozing horses. Everything felt right. The farm would endure. Business was tight, sure, so I'd diversify a little. The boarders were taken in by a fad; they'd get over it. Kennedy Phillips thought she had the magic key to horsemanship, and it didn't look like mine. All I had to offer was a Grand Prix jumping arena with perfectly blended footing, and a covered arena to keep the sun at bay. *She* had a lot of scrubland and the constant possibility of a hospital stay. Boarders who paid the money my barn commanded weren't going to use their priceless horses for trail rides. It was just a phase, and Maxine's misadventures tonight would help its end come that much more quickly.

There was a tap at my door and my smile froze. Everyone was long gone. I fingered my cell phone in my pocket, ready to dial 911, reflecting that I really needed a large dog with a deep bark. A hybrid wolf, maybe.

"Yes?" I called. *Don't be a murderer.*

The door swung open gently. "Grace?"

I relaxed. It was just Anna. Of course it was only Anna. "Hey honey, come in," I said, my voice a little breathless with relief.

Anna came in, pushing honey-colored hair behind her ears, looking fragile as a fawn. She was a little pixie of a thing, with a perfect seat and gentle hands, and big dreams I recognized from my youth. Anna reminded me of myself twenty-five years ago, give or take — earnest, trusting, and willing to do anything her trainers told her in order to follow her dreams. I was just thankful she'd come to *me*. That sort of naivety could get a sweet girl into trouble.

"What's up, honey?" I asked as she slid into the spare chair. "It's late, you ought to be in bed." Her hair was damp and her clothes were clean; there was a fresh smell of soap. She'd already gone up to her apartment over the tack room and showered for the night, washing away the sweat for a few sweet hours of cleanliness before she started all over again in the morning.

"I wanted to talk to you," Anna said hesitantly, her eyes

fluttering from ribbon to ribbon, landing anywhere but my face. "About a couple of things. And I couldn't find the right time in the barn."

"It was a hell of an evening," I agreed. "What's up?" Maybe she'd finally realized that Mason wasn't going to cut it as a Grand Prix horse. Somehow, I hoped not. I wasn't ready for that particular conversation tonight. Selling the girlhood teen dream horse when you realized loving your horse and working towards your career goals weren't necessarily compatible... it wasn't pleasant.

"Do we do enough *fun* stuff with our horses?"

I opened my mouth and closed it again. What. Was. Happening.

"I mean —," Anna cast her eyes about the room again, as if looking for words. "Like, every day is a training session. We never do anything to let the horses relax, or chill out. They're in the arena every day. And Kennedy says, you know, they should be able to go out and have fun, go on trail rides, look around at nature..."

"Anna, what do horses do for fun?"

"Um..." Anna giggled nervously. "Eat?"

"That's it." I have you now, Kennedy. Simple horse sense. "Horses eat for fun. Horses sleep for fun. Horses groom one another for fun. Have you ever seen a horse, without a rider, go on a long walk through the woods, looking around at nature?"

"No," Anna said, catching on. "I haven't."

"If you take a horse out to the arena and let him go, what will he do? Will he jump the fences in the arena, will he leave and go on a long relaxing trail ride, or will he run back to his stall and start eating as quickly as possible?"

"He'll go to his stall."

"Obviously, right?"

Anna nodded.

"If a horse is out in unknown territory, surrounded by potential predators, is he having a good time?"

"Oh my gosh, no."

"So would your horse rather be in the arena for an hour and know exactly where he is, what his job is, and how to get safely home, or would he rather go on a long ride into the woods, where he has to watch out for predators and doesn't know what's coming next?"

"Definitely the arena." Anna was nodding away. She was a good student, I thought. I really liked this girl.

"And if he's a trail horse and he's out with his buddies, he knows *that's* his job, and he's okay with it. He knows how to do it, he knows what to expect, he knows how it starts and ends and begins. A horse is like a person, he can be really really good at one thing, or just okay at a bunch of things. Our show horses are really, really good at their one job. There's no reason to pile on extra things and worry them — then they'll just be mediocre show horses, mediocre trail horses, and confused all the time."

Anna went on nodding. "I see, I see."

"Feel better now?"

Anna leaned back in her chair. "I never thought about it that way. It's almost *mean* to take a show horse out there and act like they're having a good time when they're really just confused and nervous."

"It is," I said resolutely. "It's mean. And if we get those trail horses, I wouldn't ask them to jump a grand prix course, either."

"Are you going to get them?"

"I don't know." I looked at the legal pad on my desk,

criss-crossed with numbers, names, question marks. Rodney had promised me his connections at the nearby resorts, swore it was instant money in my pocket. Taking on trail horses would be a big step in a completely different direction, though, and it would mean I couldn't take on any new boarders, should those mythical creatures appear wanting stalls. I had six... no, *seven* stalls open at the minute. There were six trail horses.

Then there were the school horses. Did I take them on, bite the bullet, start teaching kids? If I took the trail horses, I had room for one school horse. I'd have to stick the others in a paddock. Lord knew Rodney's horses all got along, since they lived together in one unsegregated field. That was something.

Trail horses and junior riding lessons together might make up for the loss of potential boarders. It might even cover losing a few current boarders. It might pay the bills.

Might.

Just looking at all the numbers and squiggled lines and crossed out notes made my head ache.

"I don't know," I said again.

"I could take out trail rides," Anna offered. "I think it's a fun idea."

"What about kids?"

"Kids on trail rides? Sure."

"Kids in riding lessons."

Anna looked doubtful. *"Me* teach kids?"

"I know... sounds awful." We shared a chuckle. "But seriously... what if we looked into getting a nice show pony or two and pushing some of Rodney's 4-H'rs into the show circuit? I'm sure a couple of them must be talented enough. I was hoping you might like the idea."

"I don't have any experience. I guess I could learn. Probably should, right?"

"That's for sure." I sighed. "Niches aren't doing it anymore. I have to try to appeal to *everyone* now."

"I'm sure it will be fine," Anna said reassuringly. She smiled and cocked her head a little, like a mother with a frustrated child. "You run the perfect barn."

I nodded slowly. I did run the perfect barn... for my preferred group of well-heeled adult amateurs. Could I keep it perfect for *everyone?* Might as well give it a try. "Anything else you want to talk about?"

"Oh, nothing." She stood up. "I should get to bed, like you said. It's getting late."

I watched her pull her damp hair back into a pony-tail. "Are you sure? You said you had a few things. I'm here to listen."

"It's just..." she paused. "It was about the trail thing, with the boarder's horses, not the trail horses. I was wondering *why* you were so against trail-riding, if something had happened. But I see now, it's just logic."

"It's mostly logic." I pointed to the bookshelf beside the door. "But how I got the knowledge to make that call, well... you see that little picture there?"

Anna picked up a little brass frame from the shelf, where it leaned against several veterinary manuals. She studied the faded picture behind the glass. "Is this you?" she asked finally.

"That's me," I said. "And my pony."

"He's cute. You are, too." She put the photo down. "What happened to him?"

I shook my head. "I took him out of his comfort zone."

Anna bit her lip, eyes still on the pony in the photo, the

girl in pigtails on his back. I was wearing buff jodhpurs, a navy-blue jacket, a thin velvet hunt cap that would have broken right along with my head if I'd gotten dumped. "He got hurt?"

"He was put down," I said woodenly, as if the words didn't still hurt, decades later. "So yes, something did happen. And that's where the logic came from. That's how it usually happens, with horses."

Anna nodded. "I'm really sorry. I lost my first pony, too... colic. It was a long time ago, but... you know... I loved him. I know where you're coming from."

"It was a long time ago." I got up from my chair, pushing it back. "Like the alarm clock this morning. Let's go to bed."

We walked through the barn for one final night-check together, quiet, thinking of all the horses we'd ever known. "Goodnight, kids," I called as I flipped out the light, as I did every night, as I had since I was a little girl, and I let darkness fall on the quiet, content barn.

Thirteen

No one minds their own business in a boarding stable.

Colleen was the first to ask. "Are you going to tell Kennedy to leave?" she asked one afternoon a few days after the Maxine incident, slamming into my office without warning.

I'd been filling out show entries, and forms were scattered across the desk. I dropped the ballpoint pen and massaged my aching right hand. Arthritis made every equestrian's life so much harder. *"Hello,* Colleen," I said pointedly.

"Hi," she replied breezily, unrepentant. "So are you?"

I hadn't decided yet, but whether or not I kicked out a boarder was certainly none of Colleen's business. "There's nothing in the boarding contract saying the trails are off-limits, or that boarders have to take lessons and join the show team," I said carefully. *Yet.* "She's caused some ruckus, but technically, she hasn't broken any rules." The truth was, I couldn't decide if I was going to kick out Kennedy or not. Between needing her money, a lack of legal high ground, and my half-hatched group trail riding idea, I might have to let her transgressions slide. I wasn't about to tell Colleen all that, though.

Colleen flung herself into the extra chair and heaved a huffy, privileged-girl sigh. I reflected for the tenth time or so how Colleen looked much better in Pikeur breeches than a woman with three children in private school had any right to look. She wasn't the sort to worry about having more than her fair share of anything, though, looks included. Colleen was entitled, to put it nicely, and more outspoken than my other clients. She was definitely of the opinion that where her money went, her mouth was free to sound off. "So she's just getting away with this? She nearly got Gayle and Maxine killed. Gayle's husband is furious, did you know that? I was out with them last night for drinks, and he was all for suing Kennedy for Maxine's vet bills."

"What vet bills? The fifty-dollar trip fee and the twenty-dollar exam? I don't think that requires small claims court." Maxine had come back from her adventure in the Florida wilderness without a scratch. The vet exam had taken ten minutes, including flexions. "Let's not blow this out of proportion, Colleen —"

"Look, I went out riding with her, I admit it." Colleen flipped her hair, eighteen-year-old model style. "And look what happened!" She held out her wrist, which was still bound up with an ace bandage. "This could have been *much* worse. Same thing goes for Bailey. And yes, I should have listened to you in the first place — but don't you think the problem is *her?* She lied to us, after all. She told us it was *perfectly safe* to go trail riding."

"Well," I hedged, trying to think how to reply. I wasn't going to deny I liked Colleen's train of thought. I just wasn't sure it was fair, or *true*, for that matter. "Nothing in riding is perfectly safe, to be absolutely correct."

"Obviously, but —"

"And like I said, there's nothing in the contract that prevents any of you from riding anywhere you choose."

"So you're saying you're letting this go?"

"I'm saying I don't have any legal grounds to kick her out," I admitted. "And even if I didn't like her taking horses out on the trails, she's stopped doing it." No one had gone out on trails in the past three days, Kennedy included. She had shown up within the barn's official hours, not arriving early or staying late. She was behaving herself, and had once again offered to do anything she could to help me around the farm.

With Kennedy behaving herself, and the little matter of keeping my stalls filled with paying boarders, what choice did I have but to let her stay? Yesterday, Angelica Martin had announced, through tears, her job transfer to Chicago next month. Now I'd have one more empty stall. "She has every right to contest if I say she has to go," I told Colleen, thinking of the eighth stall that wasn't going to bring in a dime next month.

Colleen shook her head vehemently. "I think you should do it anyway. What's she going to do, sue you for making her find a new barn? You'd be saving her money. This is the most expensive barn in the county."

I grinned. "Are you complaining?"

Colleen smiled back. "Not a chance. We *like* it exclusive, Grace. Don't forget that — we don't want just anyone here. Keep it classy, okay?"

I nodded. Quarter Horses probably didn't fall under Colleen's definition of classy. "I understand."

She pushed off from the chair, sending it sliding back towards the bookshelf. It bumped the fixture gently and I watched the picture of Sailor wobble. "Easy there," I said gently. "Don't knock my pony down."

Colleen picked up the framed photo and studied it. "He was adorable," she said approvingly. "You know, I'm thinking of getting a pony for Maddy."

"Oh?" *Oh?*

"We don't really have any kids around here, though."

"We really don't. Is that a problem?"

"I'm on the PTA now," Colleen said, making the words oh-so-seductive. "A few of the other moms are pretty interested in a riding stable so close to the school. All the other ones are way out in the countryside. No one has time for that kind of commute. Like, Oak Ridge? It's gorgeous but it's in the middle of nowhere. This place on the other hand... if you don't have anything *against* kids, well then..."

"How many are we talking here?" My mind was racing ahead, building empires, buying horses, selling them to doting children who needed riding lessons and coaching and... Would Rodney's lesson horses work for this? Or would I need classy Welsh ponies? How big? Maddy was in what... first grade? Second? All I knew was, she was short. I wasn't very knowledgable about children, but that could change. I was willing to learn, if it meant some cash flow.

"Maybe five or six? I don't know... some parents are all talk. But at least three of them are definitely interested. Can you help them out?" Colleen put the photo back down.

"And maybe give me a break on a second stall when we find a pony?"

I nodded. In exchange for three potential students from Citrus Prep? I saw the answers dancing before my eyes. Eight empty stalls — it was suddenly a boon. I could make this work in my favor. I'd accept the six trail horses; some would surely be talented enough to pull double-duty as school horses. I'd find two ponies to get started. This was it. This was the sign I'd been waiting for, telling me to move forward. It was time to pull the trigger and tell Rodney to send me his horses. "I think we could arrange that. You have a pony in mind?"

Colleen smiled broadly. "You can handle that side of things, can't you? Nothing over fifteen thousand, though, okay?"

My heart skipped a beat. "Fifteen thousand?" For a pony, for a kid who had never taken riding lessons? This wasn't one of the cute mutts from Rodney's barn, then. This was the real deal.

"My husband got a promotion and a bonus." Colleen smiled contentedly, showing off her perfectly bleached white teeth. "He's getting a new convertible. The boys are getting flying lessons. I've decided that Maddy's getting a pony."

"What are *you* getting?"

"New Dehners." Colleen frowned at her perfectly acceptable riding boots, gleaming in the sunlight from the open door. "These are getting so beat up."

"Very nice," I said approvingly. "You can't go wrong with custom boots." Not quite so expensive as a car or a pony, but probably the same thing I would have gone for, if a benevolent husband had granted me a wish or two.

"So a pony, a break on board, and..." Colleen paused in the doorway. "Three strikes and *she's* out. I don't want Kennedy getting any kids into trouble. The PTA isn't something I take lightly."

I nodded. From what I had heard, no one should ever take the PTA of an exclusive private school lightly. "I'll talk to her."

In the few days since the incident with Gayle and Maxine, Kennedy had taken it upon herself to end the trail guide shtick she'd been using on the boarders. She had been showing up late, after the last riding lessons were wrapping up, but not so late as to hit my strict curfew. She rode alone, occasionally dropping her reins and tilting her face skyward as Sailor cantered gently around the arena.

My six o'clock lesson canceled shortly after Colleen's impromptu meeting, and I decided to take Hope out for a little hack with the sudden free time. He had sorted out his flying lead changes again, thank goodness, and I was hoping for big things from him at the next jumper show in two weeks. I wanted to get him used to the on-again, off-again nature of a horse show, where he could find himself pulled from the comforts of his stall two or three or four times in a single day, so even though I had already given him a very thorough workout early in the morning, I had Anna pull him out and get him tacked up again.

I noticed his pissed-off expression while I was leading him out to the mounting block. Ah, I thought, this was evidently going to be a much-needed lesson in tractability and lowered expectations. I mounted up with my fingers tight on the reins, and was ready for him when he tried to put his head down and buck. "Little punk," I muttered, giving him a solid boot in the ribs. He snorted and leapt forward when the twin pricks of my Prince of Wales spurs caught him in the belly, but his head was up and any thought of bucking was out the window.

"That's what I thought," I told him, and he snorted again and settled down to a prancing walk, looking around at the darkness outside the arena. Fall had settled upon central Florida in earnest, and the sun was gone before dinner-time. I found it rather depressing, but one couldn't complain about the cooler temperatures accompanying the shorter days. It was only in the sixties tonight, and I had my trusty hoodie on, zipped up to my chin.

I leaned forward and gave Hope a pat, to let him know there were no hard feelings, and so I nearly tumbled right over his shoulder when he stopped dead, snorting at the horse who had emerged from the shadows at the end of the outdoor arena.

"For God's sake..." I righted myself and kicked him forward again. The young horse took a few stiff-legged steps forward, his head high and his ears pricked, staring at the apparition in the little-used arena. "Who's out there?" I called when we reached the white railing of the ring, but I thought I knew. There was really only one person it *could* be.

"It's me, Kennedy."

"Of *course* it is," I snapped without thinking. I softened my tone. "Sorry. But hardly anyone ever goes over there, and certainly not at night. Why don't you turn on the lights?"

"They use so much energy, and I don't need them." Kennedy brought Sailor over to the wooden fencing of the outdoor arena. She was only about twenty feet away, separated from us by two rails and a sweep of groomed St. Augustine sod, but Hope acted as if she was riding the Loch Ness Monster. I sighed.

"Hang on, I'm going to ride this ninny over to you so that he can see what a fool he is."

I maneuvered the snorting, spooking warmblood over to the gate near the barn and walked him through the grass to the outdoor arena. A few nudges with the spurs had him rethinking any decisions to nap back towards the barn door. "You're a big fat baby," I told him. "Shame on you." I heard Kennedy giggle in the shadows.

"It's not quite as dark as I thought," I said as we rode up to her. The bright lights of the covered arena created a black-and-white pattern of shadows on the sand footing, illuminating half the jumps and leaving the others in pools of darkness. "It's nice of you to think of my electric bill, though."

Kennedy walked Sailor up to meet us, and Hope danced in a nervous circle before he suddenly realized it was just another horse, and one he already knew, at that. Then he ducked his head against the bit and chewed, pretending nothing had ever upset him and he wasn't actually the silliest horse who had ever been born. "That's your young horse, right?"

"He's six," I said, giving the nitwit a rub on the neck. "Sometimes he thinks he's two."

"Warmbloods take longer," Kennedy said. "I've always found that."

"It's true. But they sure hold up. At least, they do when you're careful with them, and spend a fortune on joint supplements. I've had better luck with warmbloods than Thoroughbreds, in that regard."

"I've always liked Quarter Horses," Kennedy replied. We started walking off together, Hope blowing at the long shadows of the fence line, Sailor watching him with something akin to disgust. "My dad said you couldn't go wrong with a Quarter Horse. His dad bred them, for cows. My granddad."

"You come from a ranching family?" Now I could understand her predilection for wandering in the woods instead of working on jumping courses.

"Way back," Kennedy said. "But it skips generations. My dad left the farm before I was born, got a job in a factory, did the blue-collar thing workingman thing, became the plant manager, went white-collar I guess. He wore a tie, anyway, stopped drinking with the guys after work, joined the country club. So I grew up in the suburbs, but he drove me out to Gramp's place for the summers. My uncle had stayed on the ranch, so I rode with his daughters. My cousins. They all barrel raced and did 4-H and all that. I was so jealous. My dad said I was crazy, but when he made enough money, he said I could have riding lessons. When I picked English over Western, my whole family thought I was crazy." Kennedy laughed. "You woulda thought I'd joined a cult, the way they carried on. Made fun of me in my boots and breeches. My mom thought it was nice, though. My mom always wanted to be a little more fancy than she was."

"So did you show?" I gave Hope another pat for being brave about a shadow he had been regarding suspiciously. I realized that for all the weeks I'd been thinking about Kennedy Phillips, I'd never once asked her anything about her past.

"Oh yes, all the time. 4-H and state fair and all that. I

wanted to do Pony Club, like the kids in the books I read, but they didn't have any nearby. My trainer said it was for rich kids." She laughed. "There weren't any real fancy barns near us. Nothing like this, for sure."

"And then what happened? Between showing and trail riding? You quit riding?"

"Oh, by accident, I guess. I was riding for a trainer out in Indiana and she broke her ankle, so I took over a bunch of her horses and before I knew it I had rented my own place and had a whole string of hunters and jumpers. Not like this place, now." Kennedy shook her head. "Just a little twelve-stall barn and a ring and two pastures, one for geldings and one for mares. We were showing all over the Midwest. I knew all the Quarter Horse people still, through my Gramp, and I bought Sailor as a yearling from a dispersal sale. And we worked and we worked and we worked until one day we looked at each other and said 'why are we working so hard?' And we stopped."

"You just closed up shop?"

"Slowly." Kennedy sighed. "One by one. I kept training long enough to finish grad school — oh yeah, I was doing college too, did I mention that?" She laughed. "God. I was so tired. I moved down here and paid for college with a dinner show job. And then I got a real job. I guess. It has a desk. That's what makes it real, right?"

I nodded slowly. *Kennedy, Kennedy, there is more to you than I realized.* "And now *you're* the white collar renegade who left the farm."

Kennedy pulled up Sailor and Hope stopped of his own accord. We were in a corner of the arena close to the county highway that ran past the farm. "Do you ever sit out here and watch the fireworks down at the parks?"

"No, and neither have you, because it's past closing time."

She grinned. "It's worth it, sister. Stay out late some night and watch some fireworks from horseback. You'll be glad you did."

"Well, not tonight." I dropped my boots from the stirrups and stretched my stiff ankles. "I'm knackered. And cold, besides."

Kennedy leaned forward and wrapped her arms around Sailor's neck. The horse stood quietly, his ears flopped back to listen to her. "I try not to think I'm like my father," she said after a moment. "Picking the easy life over the worthwhile life. But I just got so damn tired. Is it okay to just say you're too tired to go on, when you're not even thirty?"

Nope. I didn't say that, though. It wasn't my life, and everyone's battles were different. "If you're tired, you're tired," I said instead. "It's not for everybody, this life."

"It's for *you* though."

I nodded. "It's for me." The only thing for me. Tired be damned. "But you know how I keep it from getting too tiring, how I keep going day after day?"

Kennedy sat up. "How?" She seemed to hope I had some secret that could bring her back into the fold, back into the world of horses day in and day out, the world that must have seemed so magical to her once, before she burned herself out.

"You won't like it," I warned her, picking up my stirrups and my reins. Hope walked forward and this time, Sailor started walking right alongside him. They had settled into companionship, creatures at ease with each other, with the night and the shadows. A horse could get used to just about anything, with someone to trust and a minimum of boogeymen jumping out of the bushes to startle them.

"Tell me."

"Rules," I said simply. "Rules, and one clear-cut goal. You can't do everything. You have to pick something, and do it very very well. Take me — I decided to concentrate on A-circuit adult amateurs. I have students, and they do A-circuit shows. That's it. I don't have some eventing students, and some dressage students, and some students who are just dabbling. I train everyone the same — for big horse shows. Jumpers. Now — can you keep a secret?"

Kennedy nodded eagerly.

"Now I'm thinking of breaking my rule, but only with my business. It's getting expensive here. I'm thinking of adding kids to the mix, but again, only A-circuit stuff. And I'm thinking of adding guided trail rides, but only from the higher-end hotels. But someone *else* has to teach the kids, and someone *else* has to guide the trail rides. Because I'm sticking to my rules. I take Monday off. I turn out the lights no later than eight. I teach adult amateurs. Rules give you time off, Kennedy, and rules give you boundaries. If you're trying to please everyone all the time, and if you never stop working, then you'll burn out. Every single time."

By the time I'd finished my lecture, we were back at the head of the arena, the barn entrance beckoning to the horses. Hope pulled at the bit, and I reined back and jumped out of the saddle. "It's past seven," I said, glancing at the stable clock above the door. I loved that clock — it was an antique I thought added a special stately something to the barn. "Let's head in for the night, okay?"

Kennedy nodded and jumped down from Sailor, following us into the barn. When both horses were in the cross-ties, she turned to me again, face serious. "Do you think I could have done things differently?"

I shrugged. "I don't know, Kennedy. I wasn't there."

Kennedy took off her helmet, pushed mahogany curls behind her ears. She looked young, not yet thirty — probably because she'd quit riding, got out of the sun, and settled down to life under office lights. "I did everything you said was wrong. I worked all hours. I had hunter students, I had Western Pleasure students, I had pleasure students who just wanted to learn to ride. I was always teaching or riding or mucking or trying to get more business, and I swear I did all those things at once. Maybe if I'd done things like you, I'd still be a trainer."

"You're happy with Sailor as you are," I said gently. "Why would you want to change that?"

Kennedy bit her lip. "I don't know."

"Then don't," I advised her. "Now let's put these horses up and say good-night."

"Do you want to come out and get a beer?" Kennedy asked suddenly, almost desperately. "I'd love to talk more."

I shook my head apologetically. "Not tonight. But thank you."

She nodded her head and smiled. "Another time."

I promised.

Fourteen

Ah, glorious Sunday night! I had total freedom for thirty-six hours. I could put horses and developers out of my mind completely, relax, sleep late, and generally act like a normal person who hadn't devoted her life to needy four-legged animals and their just-as-needy two-legged owners. I could pop the cork from a cheap but not-too-cheap bottle of wine, open a historical romance novel which involved lords and ladies who never had to clean their own stalls when one of the grooms called in sick, and slip into a hot bath, letting all the worries of the stable waft away in the steam.

I really did plan to do all of those things, which was why I sent Kennedy on her way into the night alone. It would have been nice of me to go and have a drink with her, sure. We could have gone to the Applebee's down the road, which was about as upscale a place as we could manage in our riding clothes, and had a few glasses of overpriced white wine while she detailed her regrets about giving up the horse business and I listed all the reasons I could figure for why she had done the right thing.

As a trainer, soothing the concerns and swaying the opinions of my clients was something that I did quite frequently. Would-be buyers had to be finessed into buying the horse I had chosen for them; nervous riders had to be coached into agreeing to go to their first horse show or step up in the divisions. Occasionally, over-eager students had to be gently put down, lest their dreams of greatness take them further than their skills could safely see them through.

I did those things because I *had* to do them, not because I wanted to do them. After all, if I'd wanted to be a therapist, I could've gone to school for psychology, and gone on to make a lot more money than I made now. No, I listened to people's fears, and assuaged them, because that was part of making my living as a trainer and coach. If they didn't buy the horse I'd chosen for them, if they didn't make the jump up in levels and continue to show and progress as a rider, if they pushed too far too fast and got hurt or had their confidence shaken, I was losing money just as surely as they were. Keeping my riders happy and confident was a cornerstone of my business plan.

Kennedy wasn't one of my riders, and fixing Kennedy's life wasn't my responsibility. She'd been a pain since day one. I wasn't going to reward her for all the turmoil she'd brought to the barn by listening to her worries and telling her everything was going to be all right. I certainly wouldn't get anything out of it.

Whereas, I thought with satisfaction, pulling down my bottle of cheap-but-not-too-cheap wine, I was getting plenty out of a night alone in my own little house.

Kennedy *was* interesting, though. I rummaged around in the silverware drawer, finding my corkscrew where it had been buried since last Sunday night. She was more interesting than I had thought. A rancher grandfather who bred Quarter Horses, the black sheep of the family for riding English, who'd have expected that! Then there was the little matter of how she'd stolen her old trainer's students — she'd glossed over that, hadn't she? The trainer had a broken ankle, Kennedy rolled in to help out, and boom, she suddenly had a barn of her own, full of clients! "Little minx," I muttered, twisting the corkscrew into the soft wood of the wine-cork. *"There's* something to watch out for."

Still, I had to admit, in all my dealings with Kennedy I had never thought she seemed shifty or shady. She really seemed without guile — another reason she probably should stay away from the training business.

I threw a bag of frozen pasta into a saucepan, looked at the empty spot on the floor next to me, and thought again about getting a dog. I could have talked to a dog about this whole Kennedy thing. About why her story was bothering me. Then the dog could yawn and lick himself in an inappropriate place, letting me know just how pointless the whole thing was. *Thanks, imaginary dog.*

Usually, I wasn't much interested in anybody's problems. I had problems of my own. I didn't need to borrow anyone's worries. And of course Kennedy was better off with her white-collar job and her big paychecks and her freedom to do nothing but have fun with her horse. Hadn't she said, time and time again, that was all she wanted? Hadn't she been trying to convince everyone in the barn that all they ought to be doing was playing with their horses, not showing them?

I frowned into my wine-glass. Did our dear Kennedy protest too much?

"And what about the rumor that she was a princess at the dinner show?" I asked the imaginary dog, which I had decided was a Jack Russell, for old time's sake — I'd had a Jack Russell terrier when I'd first moved here, ages ago. "Has she been moonlighting as a professional rider even after she claimed to give it up?"

That was the problem, I thought, pushing up from the couch to stir the sizzling pasta on the stove. Now I was interested. "She's reeled me in," I told the imaginary Jack Russell, who had followed me into the kitchen and was watching me, adoringly, little stump tail wagging against the linoleum, pushing hairballs into wispy dust bunnies that would hide under the kitchen cabinets until I got overwhelmed with dirt one day and did a mad cleaning rampage. Maybe I'd get a puppy who hadn't had its tail cut yet, I thought. I liked those whippy tails, whacking against your calf with enough force to leave bruises. *That* was true puppy love. "She's got me hooked."

The pasta was plumping up and the shrimp was nearly done, curling into tight pink balls, the steam rising up to the ancient hood above the old stove. Another person might have replaced the peeling linoleum floor, put in a nice stainless steel appliances, or at least some modern conveniences that didn't look like dangerously aging antiques, but another person didn't have an entire equestrian center just a few steps away, taking up every penny and moment of thought.

"Kennedy has clearly forgotten what it's like to run a barn," I told the Jack Russell. "Maybe she needs a reminder.

Maybe if I give her a few little things to do around here, she'll remember why she quit, and she won't be fixated on it anymore. Or maybe she'll fall in love all over again, and I'll have a new trainer and trail guide." And I ate a piece of shrimp, scalding hot out of the pan, and thought that at least I didn't have to sacrifice one of these scarce little delicacies for the dog. Not yet, anyway.

Fifteen

Colleen brought out her daughter on Tuesday evening. Maddy, fresh-faced and pig-tailed and already kitted out in jodhpurs, garters, and carefully laced paddock boots, went racing from stall to stall, patting noses that were shoved through the stall bars, standing on tip-toe to see into stalls where less-eager horses were lurking within, watching her with wary eyes. "Why doesn't this one want to talk to me?" she shouted, and I whipped my head around to see her leaping up and down in front of Ivor's stall door.

"Don't touch that one!" I shouted, and went sprinting down the aisle to drag the kid away from Ivor's box. Ivor glared at me from the depths of his stall, where he had retreated to avoid the offensively loud small thing that had shoved a hand through his stall bars. "Thanks," I told him, deeply appreciative he hadn't played the stallion and removed a finger or two.

The girl writhed in my grasp. I took hold of her polo shirt collar and spun her around. "You listen to me," I said sternly. "There's no running, there's no shouting, there's no jumping, and there's no touching horses that don't belong to you."

Maddy's thick brows crashed together as she regarded me with an alarmingly adult frown. "You can't tell me what to do."

"Around here I can," I informed her, fixing her with a frown of my own. "This is my barn, miss."

"Maddy, honey, you need to listen to Miss Grace," Colleen said, coming up behind us. To me, she said gently, "I'm sure you can let her go now."

I released my death grip on the girl's polo shirt and she took a step back, watching me rebelliously. *Oh*, I thought. Oh, this is just going to be *way* more fun than I had bargained for.

Maybe having children at the barn wasn't such a great idea.

I remembered empty stalls and a waning supply of students and show fees and fixed a smile on my face. We all have to evolve with the times, after all, or we'd be still be cavemen hunting *eohippus*. "Are you ready to learn to ride, Maddy?" I asked in a voice I equated with kindergarten teachers. "We have a special horse all saddled up for you."

Maddy's face was dark with suspicion. "Is it a *pony?*" She pronounced pony as one might pronounce *worm*.

"It's not actually. I don't have any ponies yet. It's a horse, but he's a nice quiet horse. Very nice for new riders." Douglas was the most bomb-proof of all horses, possibly because he was twenty-six years old. He belonged to one of the boarders, who kept him on out of sentiment after she had bought a racy young Oldenburg a few years ago. Douglas was of uncertain lineage, uncertain soundness, and uncertain history. The only thing we knew for sure about him was he was quiet as a sheep. "Do you want to go and meet him?"

She nodded and put out her hand. I glanced at Colleen, who nodded.

I took the little girl's hand, which was unnervingly soft and delicate, in my own calloused one, and we went to the cross-ties to visit with Douglas.

I went right up to him, waking him from a nap — Douglas spent most of his time napping — and gave him a rub on the face, between his eyes, where you could only touch a horse if he trusted you. "This is Douglas, but you can call him Dougie if you like," I told Maddy, who was suddenly hanging back. "Come on, come and tell him hello."

Maddy shook her head.

I looked at Colleen, who brushed glamorous hair behind her ears and looked right back at me with a challenging tilt of her chin. I wasn't going to get any help from her, I could see.

I scratched Douglas between the ears and considered my situation. I didn't have much experience teaching children — nothing recent, anyway. Back in my younger, hungrier days I had done it, of course. I'd mostly bossed them around, I remembered, but I'd also been a lot younger, closer to them in age. When a young instructor bossed a kid around, it was like having an impatient older sister. When an older instructor bossed a kid around, it was more like they were just mean old people, and kids hated mean old people. That much I knew for sure.

"Maddy," I cooed. "Wouldn't you like to come and pet Dougie? He's the nicest horse in the whole wide world."

Maddy let dark hair hang over her face and shook her head very hard. Not so brave without stall bars between her and the horse, apparently.

A new voice piped up. "Oh, Maddy, you'll make Dougie so sad."

I looked down the aisle. Kennedy was heading our way, a camp-counselor smile on her face and a coaxing tone in her voice. "Poor Dougie," she went on. "He's so old and he's afraid no one likes him anymore. All these flashy young horses and no one to love Dougie. It's *so* sad." She sidled up next to me and gave me a bob of the head. I took the hint and ducked away to watch from the sidelines. Kennedy gave Dougie a rub under his throat, and the old horse stretched out his head to enjoy it. His upper lip twitched with pleasure, and Maddy giggled. "Oh, he *loves* this, Maddy. It's his favorite thing. Want to come and make sure Dougie knows we still love him?"

Maddy nodded and came forward cautiously. When she was a few steps away, Kennedy caught up her hand and guided it to the itchy spot beneath the ridges of Douglas's jaw-bones. She moved it back and forth energetically, and Douglas practically swooned with contentment, his eyes closing and his upper lip stretching to elephantine proportions.

"There you go," Kennedy said approvingly. "Look how happy you're making Dougie."

He looked like the happiest horse on earth. Maddy was smiling from ear to ear, as if she could do this all day long, or at least until her arm got tired.

Kennedy turned to look at me. "Grace," she whispered.

"Can I have this one?"

I held up a finger and ducked under the cross-ties. "Hey Colleen," I whispered, and Maddy's mother turned.

"This is nice," she said, nodding back at the Douglas Appreciation Society. "Kennedy seems to have a way with kids."

Unlike me. "What do you think of having Kennedy teach this one?" I asked quickly. "She has a lot of experience teaching children." *So she says.* "And they'll only be on the lunge line in the covered ring, so you can watch and see what you think of her teaching."

I didn't think she'd go for it, not after she'd practically blackmailed me into promising to kick Kennedy out at the next opportunity. But if there's one thing that will always surprise me, it's people. People aren't like horses. You can never really predict what they'll do next. It's one more reason I prefer horses.

"Sure," Colleen said, and smiled. "We'll keep an eye on her. You thinking of hiring her to teach the kids?"

"Well, she has a job already."

We watched her show Maddy the parts of the horse, the bits to touch and the bits to avoid. Shoulders good, flanks bad. Maddy followed her lead with frowning concentration.

"Looks like she might want a new one," Colleen observed.

"She say anything to you?" Maybe there'd been a tack room confidential.

Colleen shrugged. "The same things we all say to one another. That we wish we'd never quit riding. That we could have been pros if we'd stuck with it instead of going to college, or getting married, or whatever. But she's not married, she doesn't have kids, she doesn't have anything tying her down or keeping her on course or reminding her that she's happy with all those choices. Maybe she really means it."

I nodded. "Maybe she does." Kennedy was pulling down the stirrups, measuring the lengths of the leathers against Maddy's height, making a guess and adjusting them by a few holes on each side. Maddy watched raptly, her face fascinated where a few minutes before it had been stony and closed-off. "Might work out for everyone if she does. She sure looks like a born instructor."

Colleen nodded. "I'll still be watching her like a hawk, though," she said after a moment, and she gave her a wrist an absent little rub.

Sixteen

"Did you see? Did you *see* that riding lesson? I had her trotting by the end of the half hour! She's a natural! What a perfect little hunter she's going to make. I can see her doing small ponies for at least a year before she outgrows it. Maybe two. Her mother's short. That *is* her mother, right? Is she going to buy her a pony? How serious is she?"

I sighed and dropped Ivor's reins, letting the stallion stretch his neck. I'd been hoping for some nice flatwork tonight, getting him in touch with his dressage side so he'd be a little more tractable when we were jumping. He'd been practically running away with me in our last few jump schools, pulling hard and running into the bit on the curves between fences. Show jumping was supposed to be fast, sure, but not out of control. I liked a pretty, rigidly controlled ride. The Germans were my heroes.

There was no concentration to be had while Kennedy

was in the ring, draped over Sailor's bare back like a kid at summer camp, chattering excitedly about the riding lesson I'd let her teach.

Let her teach — hah! She'd saved my ass back there. I'd had zero connection with Maddy, and that girl had been ready to let loose on me with all the terror of the spoiled child. I'd had no idea Colleen let her youngest run so wild. It must be because she was the only girl, and so much younger than her sons, I supposed. Or maybe it was just because Colleen wasn't good at controlling personalities as strong as hers — Bailey had certainly made his preferences very clear to her from time to time, and she'd just sat back and let him misbehave. It was one of the reasons I had looked forward to giving him a very thorough tune-up while her wrist was still bound up.

"You did very well," I told Kennedy now. "You're definitely a natural at teaching children."

"I haven't been around kids in ages," Kennedy gushed rapturously. "I love their little brains. They're such sponges, they just soak up the knowledge. They don't argue, either, they accept everything you tell them as the gospel truth. It's so much easier to mold a child rider than an adult rider."

"Is that so." I ran my fingers through the steel-gray strands of Ivor's mane. It needed pulling again; I swore that horse's mane grew unnaturally fast. I'd put it on Margaret's list — her no-nonsense attitude worked best with Ivor's changeable, demanding personality. He usually came back from a Margaret grooming with his tail between his legs and his nose in the dirt, begging me to forgive him for whatever wrong he'd committed to deserve such a fate. Maybe she'd cure him of this rushing problem he'd suddenly developed.

Kennedy was still talking. "I took five girls to the Pony Finals at the state horse show and we brought home champion, reserve champion, third, sixth, and eighth. Not bad, huh? I mean granted it's no Winter Equestrian Festival, but the competition was pretty stiff! Grace, I don't know, I think this is maybe what I'm supposed to be doing." She paused and looked my way. "Grace?"

I hastily wiped away the skeptical expression I'd been wearing. "Pretty impressive results, Kennedy!" Was she thinking about giving up her office job and going back to teaching kids to ride? I had been daydreaming of having her teach and lead riding lessons for me, but there was no way I could pay her anything like what she was accustomed to making in the real world. Still, I didn't want to discourage her. Maybe there was something I could scrape from the corners of my beleaguered bank account. "Must have been fun," I went on cautiously. "I can see why you would miss it."

"Come on, Grace," she said, which meant she knew exactly what I'd been thinking. "You know it's true. Maybe I burned myself out before, but maybe that's because I wasn't doing it your way! With boundaries, and rules, like you said. Maybe I could do it again, get it right this time. Maybe you could help me out."

"How can I help you out?" Her words made me wary. I wasn't prepared to be the answer to her problems. I wasn't here to be anyone's salvation but my own. Casting about for extra time before I answered her, I asked Ivor for a few wobbly lateral moves without picking up the reins. He crossed his forelegs crookedly, and tripped. The grace of a ballerina, I thought with a wry shake of the head. "Kennedy," I said. "Let's slow down. You already have a good job, and up until a few days ago you were very happy with your trail riding. You want to give up a steady paycheck and go back to teaching, where your salary depends on the weather and who decides to show up for lessons that week? You want to give up your fun rides and go back to competing? That's a pretty big change of heart and lifestyle to happen overnight."

Kennedy rode up beside us, her face serious, and I reined back to let her have her say. Ivor dug his face down against the bit. *Rude.* I was going to beat this horse to death if he kept up this nonsense. Not really, I loved him. But still. "Kennedy," I said wearily. "You are literally having a quarter-life crisis. You are turning thirty and realizing that when you were a kid, you didn't plan on having an office job and a pleasure horse. You're thinking that there's no glory in that. But let me tell you, you're happy with what you have. You really are."

Kennedy shook her head, and her eyes were aglow with conviction. "Oh, Grace, I wish you were right. But you have to understand..." she paused, looked down at the horseshoe tracks studding the clay of the arena, as if she didn't want to meet my gaze anymore. "I've tried to do this before. I keep trying to come back to the horse business, and I keep failing. Although the last time, really, it wasn't my fault."

A-ha! I looked up at her, smiling mischievously. I remembered the suspicion I'd had the first time I watched her ride without reins, and a scrap of gossip floating around the boarders' tack room. "You *were* the princess at the dinner show!"

She nodded, and then looked up with a sudden smile on her face. I could see it then, just as I had the day she'd dropped her reins and started trotting around the arena with her arms above her head — the showmanship, the sudden glamour, the gleaming smile. "It was so fun. I cried and cried when the place closed down."

A failed princess, exiled from a bankrupt kingdom. That was actually kind of sad. "At least you owned your horse. Didn't the other ones go to auction?"

"It was a private auction," she said quickly. "No one went to slaughter. No one sold for less than two grand, actually."

"That's good." It had been in the newspapers, but I hadn't paid the sale much mind. I didn't need a circus-trained Arabian in my barn. Did anyone? Apparently so, if they'd all sold for good money. Everyone was looking for something different in the horse business. Takes all kinds, and all that. "So it turned out all right. And you went back to your job that pays you actual money, instead of princess money, which I assume was not gold coins?"

"Not even close," Kennedy sighed. "But it's just not fulfilling, being away from horses all day. I miss them all the time. Why do you think I was coming so early or so late when my job was keeping me too busy to come during regular hours? I can't stay away."

I looked up at the ceiling and heaved a sigh of my own. "What is your job, anyway?"

"Oh, I'm in finances. Financial blah-blah-blah manager."

That did sound boring. In fact, it sounded kind of terrible. "I'm so sorry," I said, grinning to take away the sting.

"Me too. So help me out," Kennedy said seriously. She was sitting sideways on Sailor now, both legs hanging over his right side. Sailor ducked his head and ran his nose through the clay, looking for bits of grass or hay that might have blown into the arena. He ignored his rider's childish antics better than any school pony I'd ever seen, better even than Douglas, who was just plain too old to care. I considered them for a moment. With Kennedy's natural affinity for children, and her obvious ability to train a completely bombproof horse, I might be looking at a whole new line of business for Seabreeze. A very lucrative business.

The show pony business.

"How's your savings account?" I asked her. "You're going to need to live on it for a while."

Kennedy's face lit up like a child's on a particularly bountiful Christmas morning.

Seventeen

With her notice given and Rodney alerted that we would take five trail horses, two ponies, and his entire client list, Kennedy had already gone online and ordered business cards. *Children's Riding Programs Manager, Seabreeze Equestrian Center*, the stiff little cards announced in regal Roman font. I admired them with her, holding them up to the sun and pronouncing them suitably professional.

"I knew someone who used Comic Sans because he said kids reacted well to that font," I told her, looking at her sidelong from the raised ivory card, and Kennedy pretended to gag and die from horror. I smiled. She was actually funny, and nice to have around, now that she wasn't spending all of her time putting my clients in harm's way and ignoring the barn's posted hours. I found I liked her.

It was a good thing I liked her, because Kennedy took to spending every waking hour in my company. Her constant presence bothered Anna, who was still having trouble accepting Mason wasn't going to be her big show horse after all, and who wanted to be my special little barn buddy since she was my working student. I gave Anna extra riding lessons to make up for it, all of which Kennedy watched, chin in hands, taking it all in, and then reviewed with me in the office afterwards, asking copious questions about lesson plans, student progress, benchmarks.

Now and then, the hero-worship got annoying.

"You know, you told me you were a successful instructor before, and I believed you, but now that you're constantly asking me how to teach I'm starting to wonder if I should've checked your references first." To be fair, I had checked her references in a Google-search manner of speaking, finding newspaper confirmation she had been the starring princess at Horse Country Dinner Theater, and seven years ago her students had taken the top three spots at the Indiana State Fair Pony Finals. There was even a picture of her standing with the three girls and their gleaming white ponies, smiling their faces off. I'd figured that was all the confirmation I needed that her stories were true. But she was acting as if she'd never taught a day in her life.

"No! It's not about that!" Kennedy looked alarmed. She dropped the pen she'd been using to take notes. "I just want to be sure I'm teaching your way. This is your riding program, after all."

I shook my head. "Listen, Kennedy — you're going to have your own teaching style, and you've already proven that's a good thing by the way you connected with Maddy. Just do your thing, be safe, and if we have to discuss anything in the future… we'll worry about that."

Kennedy nodded. She folded up the notes she had been taking and slipped them into her jacket pocket.

"You going to look at ponies later?" None of the ponies we'd be getting from Rodney would be of the show caliber we'd need. The trail horses would do double duty as school horses until I started up the trail rides in spring, but of course, they were hardly A-circuit material either. We would need some classy ponies before these kids were ready to hit the horse shows. I'd put Kennedy on the job of tracking down a show prospect we could put some mileage on and then sell to Colleen once Maddy was ready for her own pony. It would be better than sharing the commission with another trainer on an older, expensive pony with show experience, especially in a few years when Maddy outgrew it and we could sell it on instead of retiring it. If Colleen delivered on her promise of PTA moms with pigtailed daughters, I'd just rinse and repeat. Ponies for everyone!

"Around five." She pulled out her phone and consulted the notes she'd made on it. "At Dennis Lowery's place."

"That's about an hour away. You'd better get going."

"Aren't you coming?"

"I have riding lessons. So don't make any final decisions, and don't let Dennis tell you that he has six other buyers lined up. He doesn't. That's just Dennis." I'd known Dennis Lowery for twenty years. Back before the hotels and houses moved into the neighborhood, he'd been boarding and training just up the road with fifty stalls — a small empire. They used to go on trail rides, I remembered — sometimes riders would just pop up in the parking lot, Dennis laughing at the head of the line, playing trail-boss. That was back before I rebuilt the farm, before there I'd added the covered arena, before my stalls and my parking

lot were filled with European imports. Dennis was old
Florida, a cowboy with a good brain for business, and when
the new neighbors moved in, he'd bought a Welsh stallion
and a few mares and started breeding show ponies. Now his
old place was a golf course and his business was up in Lake
County, where he continued to sell ponies for more than
they were worth.

"I'm serious now," I warned. "Dennis is going to try to
fool you into making an offer for twice what that pony is
worth."

"It's a *Swansdown* pony," Kennedy said doubtfully.
"Gray, already jumping courses, auto lead changes. It's
worth a fortune anyway."

"Swansdown, Farnley, whoever its daddy was, trust me
— he'll ask for more than it's worth. The problem is,
everyone else in town already knows his game. He's going
to see you as fresh blood. We don't *need* this pony. It's
practically finished. There's no point buying a made pony
for Maddy before she's even had her second riding lesson.
We have the time to do that work ourselves. So if it's worth
it, great. If not... just leave it alone." I got up from my
desk. "I'm going to ride Bailey for twenty minutes before
Colleen comes for her ride. He's still being kind of an
asshole. You hop on the computer and see if any other
prospects are in the neighborhood. Look for some more
youngsters, too, if you feel comfortable starting them over
fences." I figured we could always find room for ponies. I
could stick them out in a paddock or something.

"Of course I do!" Kennedy's face lit up. "I'd love to start
some babies!"

"Well, good, because they're cheaper." I had been
examining my bank account, trying to figure out how to

finance this new business segment. The best option, to attain the best ponies, would be to sell Hope as soon as possible, but I'd already paid for several shows with him. If he pinned well at those, he'd be worth that much more. We could float along with one almost-finished pony for Maddy and a few greenies which would be ready when other students were ready to buy, and maybe we could pick up one or two more youngsters come next summer, when breeders were starting to take stock and put some horses on sale.

That would give us plenty of young ponies for Kennedy to train up into show ponies, and when students were ready to buy, we'd have the stock ready for them. No reason to send them elsewhere and split a commission.

Kennedy's taking charge of the children and ponies would leave me free to worry about the current show season until the end of March, and then start the trail rides when everything settled down in the spring. I'd have three businesses then, I thought. Adults, children, trails. It was exciting to think about. I was beginning to realize I had been waiting for something new and interesting in my life for a long time. After a while, even the show circuit had grown rather stale. We all got the show barn blues.

I left Kennedy to her computer horse-hunting, humming happily as she clicked through pages of fine print, typos, and awkward horse photos, and went thumping down the stairs to the barn. November had rolled in with plenty of chilly days and gray skies, not unlike a more northern clime, and the horses were starting to grow wooly coats. I could hear the whine of clippers from a wash-stall, where Margaret was giving someone an early haircut. Ivor whinnied to me from his stall, poking his nose through the stall bars, and I gave him an absent-minded stroke as I passed. He lifted his lip and snapped his teeth with an audible clack. I stopped and *looked* at him, and the stallion retreated into the back of his stall. He knew *that* look.

"You've been a real bastard lately, you know that?" I told the gray horse, and he put his head down and rubbed it against one boney knee, to let me know he didn't care what my opinion was, as long as he was out of my reach. I shook my head. I had Ivor in some pretty big classes in the next few weeks, and with his attitude lately, we were heading for an equally big crash.

I made my way further down the aisle, and was greeted by Bailey, kicking his stall door. The sliding door shook on its runners. I smacked the bars with my bare hand and he jumped backwards. "What is *with* you animals lately?" I snapped. Between Bailey and Ivor, I was looking at nonstop insurrection. Naturally he was being an idiot today, of all days, when Colleen was planning on her first jumping lesson since her spill on the trails. "I'm going to have to give you more than a 'light warm-up,' " I told him, and he snorted hard, blowing snot all over the stall door.

I shook my head and went in search of Anna or Tom to get him tacked up. Behind me, Bailey resumed his bashing of my expensive stall door.

I looked into the row of wash-stalls and Margaret switched off her clippers. To my surprise, I saw the horse cross-tied there, half-shaved like a show poodle, was Douglas. We didn't usually pay much attention to Douglas, as long as he was healthy and had his hooves picked every day. "You're clipping him?"

"Well, look at him," Margaret said defensively, waving the massive clippers for illustration. "He looks like a

Highland cow."

"A Highland cow?" I blinked.

"The shaggy ones they have in Scotland."

"Oh." There *was* an awful lot of hair on the floor. I wondered if he was developing Cushing's disease. Old horses seemed to get metabolic disorders much easier these days.

"I think he needs testin' for that Cushin's," Margaret went on, echoing my thoughts. "Either way, he sure does think it's gonna be a cold winter."

"Let's hope not. Cushing's or winter, either one. Where's Tom?"

"Rotating the hay bales, throwing out the moldy ones."

"Have you seen Anna?"

"She's out riding," Margaret said dismissively, and switched the clippers back on. Their roar drowned out any further conversation we might have had — she was done with me. I waved, was ignored, and went out to the covered arena.

Anna was cantering up to a big vertical — bigger than she really had any business jumping. I stopped in the entry and waited for her to realize her mistake and turn away, but about six strides out, Mason zeroed in on the jump and there was no turning back. He picked his big head up, his strides grew tight and bouncy, and Anna, to her credit, rode him beautifully right up to the base of the jump. He took off, in what would have been a beautiful bascule — if the fence was a foot lower. I winced, waiting for the rattle of the pole in its cups. Mason just didn't have enough jump. Plenty of heart, plenty of love for Anna, but not enough jump.

His tight knees, tucked up to his chin, rapped the top

pole hard, and when he landed and cantered away, he was obviously off, head-bobbing lame.

Anna pulled up as quickly as she could and hopped off. I ran across the arena to her, but I could hear her sniffling by the time I reached them. She had her hands on Mason's right foreleg, feeling for the injury.

"It'll be a sore knee," I told her. "Probably nothing more."

Anna looked up at me, a single tear tracking down her tanned face. She looked very, very young. Well, she *was* only eighteen, I reminded myself. She ought to be in college, not mucking stalls and grooming boarders' horses for me. "I thought he could do it," she said bleakly. "I always thought he could do anything."

"Well," I paused, to stop myself from being callous and saying *Well, guess he can't.* My first impulses were rarely good ones, especially when I was dealing with emotional people. I started again with a more gentle tone of voice. "Well, Mason is a very talented horse, Anna. And you have a great partnership. But he can't go as far as you can. I think you've found his limit."

I gave Mason a pat on the neck, thinking, *thanks for breaking the news to her for me, old boy.* I owed him one. Hopefully he hadn't cracked his knee too badly on that jump pole.

Anna stood up on wobbly legs. "What should I do now?"

She knew exactly what to do, but she was second-guessing herself after making such a mistake with Mason's jumping. I took pity on her. "Take him in slowly and cold-hose that knee for half an hour. Then we'll take a look at how he moves on it, see if we think the vet oughta take a look."

Anna nodded slowly, eyes slightly panicked. She didn't have the money for a vet call. "I'll take care of it," I said reassuringly, thinking sadly of my soon-to-be-depleted bank account. Anna worked for me for room and board, and for her horse's room and board. I couldn't expect her to pay a vet bill when she earned exactly nothing, even if I was throwing everything I had at ponies and trail horses.

"Thanks," Anna said, her voice still gravelly with tears. She pulled the reins over Mason's head and started leading the little horse away. He limped after her with his usual puppy-dog devotion. I watched them from the center of the arena, until the sway of his hindquarters disappeared into the barn, newly amazed and a little envious at their close relationship. I wondered if Anna would be half the rider she was now if she was riding "just" a horse, instead of one who was clearly a heart-horse.

Well, I had learned to do it. If she wanted to be a trainer, she'd have to learn it, too. "There are only so many soulmates out there," I muttered, kicking at a hoof print in the clay, and then I adjusted the jumps to a more appropriate height. I'd have to tack up Bailey myself, I supposed. Anna would be obsessing over Mason for the rest of the afternoon.

I knocked the fences down to about three foot six, wiggled some standards to make some difficult distances, and stepped back to survey the results. I'd made two tight little combinations that could be jumped in a figure-eight pattern. It would be nice for reminding Bailey to start paying more attention to where his feet were and less attention to the big scary world outside the arena, where he had been focused a lot lately. I had a suspicion he was still worried about the trails. Every time he looked towards the woods, he was remembering his bad experiences.

Ivor had been a pain ever since we'd been out in the woods, too. The trail riding episode was a gift that kept on giving, it seemed.

But I wasn't sure why.

"Odd," I muttered to myself. "Very odd. Bailey's scared, because he's only had a bad time out there. But Ivor -- he had fun. What if that brat is ring-sour now?"

What if *I* was ring-sour? The feeling of exhaustion at the thought of upcoming shows, the boredom of endless teaching, the never-ending circles under the roof of the arena... when I thought of what I'd *really* like to be doing on a cool fall afternoon, I couldn't help but conjure up an image of the vast Florida sky stretching out over the lonesome pines, the sound of the wind rattling in the palmettos, the ghostly white apparitions as a flock of ibis high in a cypress tree.

I had the bug, dammit.

Across, the parking lot, a bale of hay came flying out of the hay-shed and joined a small pile of its brethren. I saw Tom up in the heights of the stack, pulling the bales from the back towards the front. The moldy ones would go in the Gator and get dumped in the compost pile. He was too busy to tack up Bailey for me, too. Looked like I was going to groom for myself today.

Just as well, I thought, trudging back into the barn. I needed to keep myself busy, or I'd spend all my time daydreaming about wandering in the woods, both myself and my horse footloose and fancy-free.

Slacking off and ignoring work... that was no way to bring home the bacon.

Eighteen

"I don't understand." Colleen crossed her arms across her chest. "You had me on the schedule, didn't you?"

It was all I could do to avoid shrugging like a sheepish teenager. Beneath me, Bailey panted and heaved. He was dripping with sweat, which was an accomplishment considering the temperature was only in the mid-sixties, with a chilly wind sweeping through the arena from time to time. Still, it had been a really rough hour for Bailey *and* for me, although I doubted Colleen would have any sympathy for me. Standing there in her Pikeur full-seats and the "old" Ariat semi-custom boots she was so eager to shed for a pair of hand-made, custom Dehners, her face like a thundercloud, I was forced to appreciate once again how many of my boarders were made of formidable stuff after several decades in the corporate world. It couldn't be denied, I bullied all of them from time to time, but the ladies with true confidence, used to standing up in front of men in black suits and telling them what to do, sometimes managed to shake my composure.

Still, this wasn't my fault. Things with horses do not always go as previously scheduled. "Of course I had you on the schedule, Colleen," I said in a measured tone. "But I also had a half-hour training ride on Bailey on the schedule. And had he been a halfway tractable horse today, that would have been a nice warm-up for you. Unfortunately…"

Unfortunately, I did not say, we'd had some issues. Some rearing/bucking/bolting/refusing fences issues, to be exact, plus some pretty serious spooking issues. Bailey noticed Tom's amazing flying hay bales, even though the crime was taking place at least three hundred feet away, almost as soon as we'd gotten into the arena. Whether it was because the hay bales were flying out near the trail-head, or just because he didn't want to be in the vicinity of flying hay bales, no matter where they were, was a moot point at the moment. What mattered was the end result: a horse that came unglued, and began spooking at everything, constantly, using every excuse in the book to shy sideways, bolt forwards, stop dead, run backwards, and fling himself up in the air either head or ass-first, whichever seemed more appropriate in the moment. It had been one of the worst hours in the saddle I'd spent in years.

I didn't say all that, though. "Unfortunately, Bailey is just having a really hard time settling down today. Maybe he was just having a bad day. Whatever it was, I wouldn't be comfortable putting you up on him with this sort of behavior."

Usually, that was enough. Usually, I was The Trainer, and my word was law.

But Colleen was definitely feeling her oats today. This PTA thing was obviously going to her head. "That's just not acceptable," she snapped. "This is *my* horse, and I have the right to ride him anytime I want. I will *not* be told I *can't* ride him. What kind of racket is this? Do you think you can just charge me to *train* him, as you put it, and then tell me I have to just keep on paying you because he's having a bad day?"

"That's not what I meant at all," I said urgently. Bailey threw up his head and backed up a few steps. I gave him a dig with my spurs to put him back where I had told him to stand and he kicked out with one hind leg. Jesus, what a bastard. "I just think we have to evaluate his behavior and make a decision about whether or not you should ride him, since this is your first ride in a few weeks. I'd hate for you to strain that wrist again." *Or get dumped and break your neck.*

"I came to ride him today. I don't want this to become some sort of regular thing, where I can't ride my own horse. I'm very busy, and we have shows coming up," she went on, as if I didn't write the show calendar, and fill in the entries, and perhaps had not heard about her busy schedule.

"What's going on?" Gayle came out of the barn, leading Maxine by her reins. Maxine alone seemed more chastened after her trail experience, as if she was thrilled to be home and wanted nothing more than to never leave the confines of the stable again. I wondered what would happen if we tried to take her out to the parking lot, though. There was a show in another week...

"Oh, nothing, just Grace messing around telling me I'm not capable of riding my own horse!" Colleen sniffed.

Gayle's eyes widened and she looked at me for confirmation.

"Bailey is being a tough customer today," I explained. "I just want to make sure we're all erring on the side of safety."

Gayle nodded, as if that sounded reasonable to her. "Colleen, maybe she's just making sure you don't get hurt," she said. Sweet Gayle, the peacemaker. Good girl, Gayle. "I mean, it's not like Grace ever steers us wrong."

Gayle's Christmas present just got very large and extravagant.

Colleen dropped her arms from her chest to her hips, which I considered progress. Bailey tugged at the reins, digging his head against the bit, and I let him walk in a big circle. He swished his tail as he walked, a sure sign of irritation since it was too windy for flies. "Behave yourself, son," I advised him in a coaxing voice, and he actually stomped a fore-hoof as he walked. I considered calling the vet.

He wasn't sick or lame, though. He felt perfectly smooth and even. This problem was all mental.

"This can't become a regular thing," Colleen repeated coldly as we circled past her again. "I refuse to own a horse that I cannot ride."

What Colleen didn't realize was that she'd *always* owned a horse she couldn't ride — without regular schooling sessions from me. "Of course not," I told her reassuringly. "This is a special case. It happens, horses have bad days, something is bothering him. I'm going to cool him out and then we can start again tomorrow to see if it keeps up, or if he feels better."

"What if he doesn't?"

"I'll have the vet out to rule out any lamenesses, anything sore that might be bothering him. He might need the chiropractor — it's been a while. I don't feel anything in his gait to indicate that his legs or feet hurt — you see anything?"

Colleen watched him alertly, as if she was some sort of lameness expert. I sat still in the saddle and let her think so. "I don't see anything," she confirmed after a few minutes. "He looks fine."

"Maybe it's just something in the air tonight," I suggested. "They do get silly the first time it turns cold. It's going to be in the forties tonight."

"I'll get out his Baker blanket," she said. "He'll need that, right?"

I nodded, relieved she had decided to be helpful instead of argumentative. "That would be great. Thanks, Colleen."

Colleen disappeared into the barn, her boot heels ringing on the concrete. Gayle led Maxine to the mounting block and laboriously climbed aboard the mare. Maxine stood still, neck arched, waited patiently and moved off obediently once Gayle had picked up her stirrups and gave her a nudge. What a good mare, I thought. She was worth every penny, and she'd been quite a lot of pennies. Gayle's husband had nearly had a conniption when we doubled down on him at a barn picnic to convince him Maxine was the perfect horse for her. But he'd given in. Gayle had it pretty good, and she seemed to know it. Except for the moments of self-doubt after the dressage show a few weeks ago, and of course the disastrous trail experience afterwards, she was an easy-going, cheerful student to have around the barn.

I needed more people like Gayle, I reflected. I wondered how you could target advertising for that sort of person. *Wanted: low-maintenance, biddable, good-natured student with disposable income and spare time.*

"Looks like you already have a class-A horse show mom on your hands."

I turned around. Kennedy came into the arena, a folder under one arm. I frowned at her. "Shouldn't you be leaving now?"

"I am, I am. But I wanted to run a few prospects by you, and I was lucky enough to see that scene. Welcome to the pony world. She's your first horse show mom, and she's about as bad as they come."

"We haven't even started taking her kid to horse shows yet."

"Then she might be the worst I've ever seen."

I sighed. Pony business. What *was* I thinking? "We should have just gotten a dozen trail horses and gone full-on dude ranch. They come, they do what we say, they leave, they never come back. No coddling required."

"Too late now," Kennedy said cheerfully. "Because look at this dispersal sale happening out in Geneva."

"Switzerland?" I'd gotten a horse or two from a Swiss bloodstock agent. They'd cost a royal fortune. "Bit expensive for ponies, I think."

"Geneva *Florida*," Kennedy corrected me. I pulled up Bailey, who was starting to realize how incredibly tired he was and complied happily, and accepted the folder from her. Print-outs spilled into my hand, of ponies with apple-round hindquarters and beguiling dished noses. Gray, bay, chestnut with plenty of chrome — all the right angles and looks for a show pony.

I looked at the farm name. "Kinsale? Never heard of them." The Welsh ponies preferred for the A-circuit typically came stamped with recognizable and trendy breeder names, like the Swansdown pony at Dennis

Lowery's, or my old Sailor's breeder, Maplewood.

"No, but look at the breeding on them. Basically, they bought a bunch of nice mares, bred them to really nice stallions, and got a ton of nice babies — but don't have the money to stick with the business long enough to get the babies finished." Kennedy pointed to a few of the bloodlines listed — she was right. There were plenty of championship bloodlines on these no-name ponies.

"And it's a dispersal, huh? Is there an auction or is it first-come first-serve?"

"First-come," Kennedy said. "What do you think?"

I shrugged. *What the hell.* "Look at Dennis's pony first," I said. "Tell him you love it but you have to check with me. Then tomorrow get out to Geneva, or wherever, and see what's out there. If there's something we can work with, go for it. Don't tell Dennis or he'll drag-race you there — that man loves a bargain."

Kennedy frowned. "I have to work tomorrow."

"Call in sick," I said. "You're working for me now. Those people are just paying out your sick time now. Use it."

She grinned. "Okay."

I hopped off Bailey and pulled the reins over his ears. He shook his head at me and pawed the earth. I sighed. "This horse needs something. What, I don't know. A stiff drink, maybe."

"He was bad?"

"What gave it away?"

Kennedy surveyed the sweat dripping from his poll, neck, flanks, beneath the saddle pad. "Oh, nothing."

"He was really bad. He's been getting worse and worse. Spooking at everything."

"You know —" Kennedy stopped herself.

"What?"

"Nothing."

"Tell me."

"It's only…"

"Yeah, yeah, Miss Trainer, tell me!" I ran up the stirrups and loosened the girth. Kennedy was still silent. "I'm waiting!"

"He needs a change of scenery," Kennedy said reluctantly. "A little bit of fun."

I shook my head. "You're a broken record, honey." I took Bailey and started walking into the barn, shouting for Anna to come and catch him. Kennedy smiled weakly and waved, heading for her car and her journey out into the hinterlands to look at Dennis Lowery's magical white pony.

Anna appeared and took Bailey's reins, and I watched her walk him into the cross-ties and start stripping my tack. I had a little time to kill, since this was supposed to be Colleen's riding lesson, but I had already lost money since I was going to have to leave this training session off her bill, so I decided to give up the rest of the hour and leaned against the concrete block wall, watching the horse. He eyed everything around him as if it was a potential threat, keeping his eyeball tight on a frog making its leisurely way along the drains in front of the wash-stalls. When it hopped in front of him, he took a quick step back, as if he had never seen a frog before.

We *always* had frogs around the place. They were part of the barn wildlife, along with the feral cats and the occasional raccoon.

Bailey was obviously having some sort of nervous breakdown.

Anna disappeared into the tack room with my saddle and bridle and reappeared with a wash-bucket and a sponge. She filled the bucket with warm water and a big dollop of hard shampoo from the Orvus tub, which was nearly solid now that the temperature had dropped below eighty degrees. When the hose hit the shampoo, the bucket spat back curtains of bubbles. Bailey jumped again. "Settle down, silly," Anna told him affectionately, and started spraying him with the hose instead. Bailey wheeled and shifted, moving as far away from the hose as the cross-ties would let him.

"He's acting like he's never gotten wet before," she said over her shoulder. "Is he okay?"

"He's acting like he's never done a lot of things before," I sighed. "Something's up with him. I wish I knew what."

Anna shrugged. "Maybe he needs a change of scenery."

I cocked my head. "Why would you say that?"

"What? Change of scenery?" She dropped the hose and grabbed the sponge, dunking it into the soapy water. "Oh, it's something my old trainer used to do. Whenever a horse started acting out all the time, she said, it was always one of two things — he was either hurt or bored. First you call the vet, then you take him on a trail ride, that's what she said. Of course," Anna added quickly, "We know Bailey doesn't like trail rides, and he sure doesn't act like he's hurt, so I guess that isn't it."

I nodded slowly. But I was starting to wonder. Maybe a trail ride was exactly what this goofball needed to get his head straight again.

Anna slapped the soap all over Bailey, scrubbing him with her usual efficiency. I watched her and thought about trail rides, and changes of scenery, and feeling like everything good had just gotten very boring.

It was all starting to make sense. Maybe Bailey *wasn't* upset, or hurt, or even scared. Maybe the big brat was bored and looking for trouble.

"You're a wonderful working student," I told Anna suddenly. "The *best.*"

She stopped her brushing and looked back at me, eyes wide with surprise and pleasure. "Thank you!" she said, blushing pink.

"No, thank *you*, Anna." I pushed off from the wall, my mind set on my next course of action. "You have a bright future in this business."

Ready to experiment, I stalked off towards Ivor's stall.

Nineteen

Half an hour later, I was cantering Ivor down the broad white-sand road through the palmettos, watching the uneven ground warily through his pricked ears. The stallion had his head high and his blood up, his canter rolling through the savannah like a cavalry horse charging the enemy. He felt like a million dollars, and so did I.

That itself was a betrayal of all my values. It was dangerous out here, a feeling I mustn't forget for a moment. I kept reminding myself of the hazards of the trail, like the terrible footing. The sand was hard from the unusually dry summer and fall, and there were uneven patches of ground where a horse could take one bad step and put himself out of work for months. There were diamondbacks in the palmetto and coral snakes in the oaks and moccasins in the still, dark water beneath the cypress trees. There might be panthers, if you believed some of the good old boys' stories, and there were definitely bobcats, who were good for a hard spook, a tumble, and a gallop home in the fashion recently demonstrated by Maxine. There were the less-lethal, but certainly unpleasant, banana spiders — yellow and black arachnids as big as your handspan, building thick, entangling webs right across the path in narrow tree-lined sections where it was hard to escape their sticky silken threads and creepy-crawly horror. I ducked alongside Ivor's neck on more than one occasion, praying one of those creatures wouldn't end up crawling down my back after I'd crashed through his web. Talk about an opportunity to tumble right off your horse.

It would be a stop, drop, and roll situation, horse or no horse.

I shivered just thinking about it. Ivor flicked an ear back in my direction, then affixed them back on the horizon. Ahead, the shadowy dome of the shell mound was rising against the fading blue sky. It would be dim and cool in the shell mound, up above the hot sunny sand of the scrub, amidst the boughs of the live oaks and the canopy of vines.

We'd stop up there, I decided, and take a rest and a long look around the countryside we'd been cantering through.

Ivor just carried on, as if he could gallop all day and all night, with no destination in mind but the sheer pleasure he felt in moving forward on a track without fences or boundaries.

His muscles bunched beneath him as we rounded the curve before the shell mound, and then I felt his hindquarters hump up beneath him as he plunged up the steep rise, his neck arching as he rounded his back and dug his hooves into the sand. Ivor was a fit horse, all power from our ceaseless sessions in the arena, jumping which had built up his hind end, dressage which had suppled and smoothed those twitching muscles. I felt his athleticism now in a thrilling rush as he plowed his way upwards, grunting with exertion, focus still forever forward, still lost in the pleasure of the run.

He gave a little buck as we reached the top of the mound, almost as if he couldn't help himself, twisting his back and stretching out his hind legs behind him. I couldn't even make myself discipline him, settling for a sharp "Hey!" that was more instinct than meaningful retort to bad behavior. Such happiness is contagious.

Still, I pulled him up to a prancing walk afterwards. The tree branches hung low up here, and he was tall — too much festivity or airs above the ground from Ivor and I'd find myself hung up in a live oak while he went on towards the eagles' pond without me. Plus, it would be getting dark shortly. I didn't relish a night in a tree with the owls and the snakes and the panthers and lord knew what else while Ivor ate his fill of lush water meadow grass.

I walked him to the clearing on the east side of the mound and pulled him up, letting him duck his head to pull at a few sparse blades of grass pushing through the gray sand. "Watch out for the cactus," I told him, tugging his head away from a small bush of prickles which had found happiness on this sun-drenched hillside, and then let him get back to his scavenging.

The dusk was settling in over the scrub, and as the air cooled cool, a fog from the warm hidden ponds and trickling streams that wound through the savannah. To my left, I could see the dark hump of the cypress dome and the mist trailing out from it like a creeping ghost. It glowed white in the spots where the sinking sun still lit it, a deeper gray against the velvety deep blue of the sky beyond. Florida stretched out beyond the dome, flat and endless and wild clear to the Atlantic Ocean, or so it seemed. The big Florida sky had a way of flattening everything, making the wilderness seem small and empty and ever-lasting, hiding the hotels and towers and houses and truck stops and railroads and power plants I knew were crouching out there. The two of us were standing tall above all the landscape, two deities on four legs.

"It's funny to feel so big when I know for a fact how small we are," I told Ivor, but he went on plucking at the tiny blades of grass, wiggling his lips around in the sand like a starving horse. I supposed it was past his supper time, after all. "We should go home."

But the call of the falling night was a siren song. I looked west, towards home, and saw only the endless reach of palmetto, the tall black sentinels of slash pine against the yellow sunset sky. The stars were coming out all around us. "I should do this more often," I said, and then a mosquito whined in my ear, and I slapped at it, hitting my hard hat, and Ivor jumped like a rabbit, nearly unseating me, and I remembered why sunset rides weren't always the best idea. "Home again, then," I sighed, picking up the reins and pulling Ivor away from his meager snack. "But we'll do it again," I promised him, as we turned back towards the darkness of the shell mound. "This obviously makes you very happy."

It made me happy, too.

The trail riding clients would eat this place up. I had forgotten how wonderful my wild "back forty" really was. I could scarcely wait for spring now. I felt long overdue for a new adventure.

Anna was waiting for me in the Gator, her feet tucked up on the seat, her arms around her knees. She looked cold. "Why haven't you gone inside for the night?" I asked, hopping off Ivor and landing on my toes, the asphalt sending shockwaves through my ankles and knees. I winced; there was a definite upside to mounting and dismounting in the clay arena. "You weren't waiting up for me, were you?"

"I was," she admitted, hopping down from the Gator and taking Ivor's reins. "I wanted to make sure you got back okay."

"Did anyone else know I was gone?" I relinquished my horse and walked into the barn alongside them. The parking lot and barn were empty for the night; the early nightfalls seemed to move up everyone's bed time, even though the arena was lit up like a party every evening. "I tried to sneak away."

"Why?" Anna looked perplexed. "That seems pretty dangerous, to go on a trail without telling anyone."

"I told *you*."

"And that's why I waited for you." She turned Ivor in a tight circle into a wash-stall and tossed the reins back over his head so she could take off his bridle. Ivor took a playful nip in her direction, his teeth clacking together. Anna ignored him with the aloofness of a seasoned horsewoman. She was still focused on my wrongdoings. "I'm pretty sure you'd have a fit if any of the boarders did that."

"Well, that's the boarders, Anna," I said reasonably, taking off my hard hat. The mosquito that had sent us hurrying home was splattered on one side of the leather harness. I made a face and flicked it away. "I don't think we're quite in the same league as some of our boarders, do you?"

Anna slipped the bridle off and the halter on in one smooth motion. Ivor nodded his head and tried to rub his sweaty face against her, nearly knocking her over. "Stop that!" she chided, voice sharp. "I know," she went on in a more normal tone, getting to work on the saddle. "It's just a big change. A few days ago you were on the warpath about anyone using the trails, and now you're sneaking out there, and buying trail horses, and everything." She paused. "Was this about the change in scenery thing?"

I nodded. "Yup. All your fault. How do you like that?"

Anna grinned. "I'm glad to help. But I don't want to be blamed if anything happens to you out there alone! Take me along next time. Mason loves a good trail ride."

"Is that so? You never mention anything but showing."

She nodded, pulling Ivor's saddle off and sliding it onto a nearby stand. She grabbed a brush and started knocking at the damp hair where the saddle and pad had been. "Well, it's like... we've done *everything* together, you know? Even helped move cattle once. He's my buddy. I'm sure he'd love to go on a trail ride. We've been working so hard on the jumping lately, trying to get good enough for WEF... but maybe it's time for a break..."

Anna's voice trailed off, and I knew she was thinking about Mason's bad jumping form. WEF, the Winter Equestrian Festival — it had been her dream since she was a kid. She'd told me as much when she'd interviewed for the job. To go to Palm Beach and ride with the best in the world, that was what it was all about. Not just for Anna, but for me... for all of us, that was why we were here, that was why we were working so hard, eschewing the earthly pleasures of a good trail ride at sunset. I saw her jaw set as she pulled the brush across Ivor's back, and I figured it was time to bring it up. "Anna," I said gently. "If I tell you something right now, something hard, will you promise to just think about it?"

Anna didn't look at me, but she nodded, twice, hard, and bit her lip.

"If we find you a young horse to bring along, you can put Mason in the school program," I promised. After all, Mason would be perfect for any intermediate kids who were too big for pony classes. "He can pay his own way, and your board for one horse can apply to a show horse that you have a future with. Or even a sales horse that you bring up through the levels, like Hope. It would be a big new start for you. And it would ease up the stress on Mason, too. Plus you could use him to guide trails, if you want."

She sniffed, hard, and redoubled her efforts with the dandy brush, pouring all her energy into the strokes of the brush. Ivor grunted and leaned into the rough treatment, loving it. "So you really don't think Mason can go any further? It's not just that he's tired, or that he needs a break?"

"I *know* he can't go any further and I *think* he's tired and needs a break. He'll stay sound and happy much longer if you drop him down a few levels. He's scoped out now, and that's hard work to maintain." I ducked under the cross-ties and put a hand on Anna's shoulder. She stopped swiping the brush across Ivor's back and stood still. "Listen — I know you love him. You don't have to give him up. But you do have to get a new horse."

"If I want to show," Anna said stiffly.

"If you want to show. You can stay on here and take lessons, for as long as you want. But if you want to show... either take him down to something easier, or get a new horse."

She sighed and went back to grooming. I stepped back against the wall and let her take it out on Ivor, who was loving the Swedish massage.

"Part of showing was about Mason," she mumbled after a few minutes of silence. "I wanted to do it with him."

I nodded. I could completely relate to never wanting to give up your baby.

"He's *special*. Would it be as special with another horse?"

I shook my head regretfully. "If you're lucky, you'll get it a few more times. Maybe not the next horse, or the one after that. But every now and then, you'll find one that makes it *that* special again. That extra-special feeling."

Anna put down the dandy brush, all groomed out, and turned to face me. There was a redness around her eyes that hadn't been there before. She was so young. The way we worked and rode together, I often forgot that there were decades between us. She crinkled her brow. "Is that what it's going to be, just horse after horse, Grace? Like grooming in the barn — I groom one, then another, then another, and I don't really care about them on a personal level, they're all nice or not nice or whatever, but I don't love them or hate them, I just do my job... is that what it's like, being a trainer? Being a show rider?"

I nodded, my eyes on hers. This was what made training a job, not a hobby. One of my old bosses had put it best: *Do what you love, and you'll turn what you love into hard work.* "That's what it's like. A succession of horses. Some you love, some you hate, some you like, some you just ride because they're on your schedule."

Anna tossed the brush back into the grooming bin and unsnapped the cross-ties from Ivor's halter. She fixed on a lead-shank and walked him past me, out of the wash-stall, into the main aisle. I followed them slowly, and by the time she had come out of his stall, folding the lead up in her hands, I was there to slide the heavy door closed behind her. "It's not a bad life, Anna," I told her, slamming the latch home so Ivor didn't go on one of his late-night tours of exploration. "It's just that not every single horse is going to be one you have a connection with."

"I know," Anna said dully. "I just have to decide if it's worth that."

She hung up the halter and lead and left me behind, crossing through the center aisle of the barn. I knew she was going to Mason's stall. I hesitated for a moment, then left her to it. She'd know to turn out the lights when she was done. We both had plenty to think over tonight.

Twenty

Three ponies went whirling around the last little paddock in the row of little paddocks across from the barn. Three flashes of silver, streaked with green and brown from other, dirtier playgrounds. Three four-legged devils, manes flying and ears pinned, kicking and squealing and bucking and snorting.

Three ponies I'd dropped quite a bit of cash on, looking for profits in all the wrong places.

Only Kennedy was unconcerned with the hellions she had acquired for Seabreeze Equestrian Center's burgeoning pony business. Which was good, because she was in charge of the little brats.

She leaned over the fence now, one heel hooked on the lowest board, and risked her life by resting her chin on her arms, her face actually inside the paddock, within kicking distance next time the herd of hell-ponies came tearing around in a dust cloud of trouble. "Aren't they something else?" she asked, delightedly.

They most certainly were something else, although her something else was probably different than mine. "I thought they'd be half-broke, at least," I said resignedly. The tallest of the ponies, still not fourteen hands in height, kicked on the brakes in a rather epic sliding stop right before he slammed into the far fence, and the other two skidded sideways and kept running without losing much momentum. The lead pony went flying after them, but not so fast he couldn't throw in a few bucks along the way.

"They'll be a piece of cake," Kennedy said. "Don't worry, I'll have them eating out of your hand before New Year's."

I sighed. That wasn't what I had been hoping for. I would have preferred them jumping fences by New Year's, and courses by spring break, and ready to lease or sell to students by summer. But these three ponies were green as grass. "This just slows down the business plan, a little... but it's fine," I said carefully. I didn't want to upset Kennedy — how times had changed! She was proving herself remarkably useful as a youth instructor. Along with Colleen's spoiled daughter Maddy, there were two more kids already sharing Douglas in weekly lessons, and the first wave of Rodney's students were starting next week, after his horses arrived. It was the start of something big for Seabreeze.

If Kennedy could get these ponies going in time.

She waved her hat at the ponies as they ran by a fifth time (or sixth, or seventh — I'd lost count and the little devils had endless energy) since they'd been turned out, shooing them away from the fence-line. "I know it's slower than what you had hoped for, but look, three nice gray ponies for less than the *one* at Dennis Lowery's place! And he still hasn't found a buyer, by the way. You could probably make him an offer and get that pony anyway. Then you'd have one finished pony in the barn, if anyone is ready buy."

"There's not enough money to make him an offer he'd consider." The pony fund had all gone to the Kinsale ponies. The ones acting like complete sociopaths right now. I shouldn't have agreed to buy them. I should've bought Lowery's pony and just one prospect. But these had been such bargains, and Kennedy had sung their praises so highly... I'd gone insane and flung all the money I'd budgeted for ponies at these little terrors.

"Are they going to do that all afternoon?" I turned at the sharp voice and saw Colleen marching out of the barn, arms folded across her chest, elegant eyebrows drawn together in a frown. Just what I needed. "They're making the horses in the barn jumpy. I want to take out Bailey and I'm a little nervous that he's going to spook and get away from me."

"I'll come help," I said. To Kennedy, I hissed, "Control them or get them back in the barn." I left her to deal with the little monsters on her own. She'd taken the money I'd given her and she'd bought them, she'd taken responsibility for them — I washed my hands of them. As long as they didn't upset my nice, quiet, full-size horses and adult riders in the barn, we'd all get along just fine.

Colleen waited for me with hips jutting and jaw set. "I wasn't looking for help handling my own horse," she said sharply as I entered the barn with her. "Just wanted to know if those ponies were about through acting so crazy. What's with them, anyway? I thought you were going to buy nice ponies for the girls to ride."

"Nice ponies for the girls to *show*, down the road," I corrected her, picking up Bailey's leather halter from its hook. "Show ponies are expensive. I'm saving everyone some money by starting out youngsters and getting them ready here, rather than buying finished ponies."

"More expensive than a horse like Bailey?" She narrowed her eyes.

Colleen, you are too smart for your own good — or mine, I thought. "A different kind of investment," I said lightly, rolling back the stall door. "You'll ride Bailey for ten years or more. A kid outgrows a pony in a fraction of that."

Bailey snorted at me and then looked back out his window, where he was watching the Killer Ponies make their rounds. He whinnied, his mouth wide open and his nostrils dilated, then snorted again when none of them replied.

"They're not worried about you," I told him, slipping the lead rope around his neck and sliding on the halter before he could bounce away, still high on pony crazies. "They're not worried about anyone but themselves."

Bailey quieted under my touch and ducked his head helpfully into the halter, eager to get out of this stall. As well he should be. I'd taken him out for a few late-evening trails the past three nights, followed by a hard dressage session in the covered arena. It had meant staying well past closing time, breaking my own rules, but the results had been pretty impressive — by last night's ride, he was trotting like a tired old mule along the white sand of the trail, our path lit luminescent in the glow of a full moon, and giving me pretty solid lateral work and flying lead changes in the arena afterwards. A change of scenery, indeed, I'd thought as I untacked the weary horse last night. He was a new horse, fresh and eager and moving forward with enough impulsion to wow any dressage judge.

I found the rides were calming for me, as well. Shifting focus, new goals, more relaxed rides... I was sleeping better now than I had in weeks, *months* even. This was especially impressive considering the ever-escalating signs the neighborhood was about to get a lot more crowded. Driving past the property next door was growing more depressing by the day — cars parked along the highway verge, men in suits looking at papers and pointing into the pine trees, surveyors peering through their spyglasses. Yesterday I had passed by on my way to the store, and there had been a trailer unloading a backhoe — a sight that made my heart sink.

This morning I hadn't been able to resist taking the Gator down the driveway to have a look. Sure enough, there was now flattened brush and the white scars of broken tree branches, a narrow path carved into the heart of the pine woods. I was facing the dismaying reality that just as I was learning to appreciate the natural world from horseback once more, a big chunk of it was about to disappear from my life forever.

Still, there was no telling how much of the property next door would be flattened. Maybe they wouldn't want to build homesites up against a smelly farm, full of manure and livestock. Maybe they'd leave me a nice buffer zone of trees and palmetto, so that from here, in the sanctuary of my farm, I wouldn't have to remember hundreds of acres just next door had been converted to golf courses and Italian Revival McMansions.

More importantly, the development next door wouldn't affect the trail business one bit. We would be using my land all the way to the lake, after all, and that was good for an hour or so. I didn't know who owned the land beyond the lake these days, but I didn't think it was accessible to anyone but horsemen. There were no roads, there were no houses, for quite a few miles east.

For now.

The only thing I knew for certain was life was about to change. I just wasn't sure how much of the change would come from the ponies and the new trail business — which no one knew about but Kennedy and the grooms — and how much would come from external forces like nearby construction.

I led Bailey down to the wash-stalls and put him the cross-ties for Colleen, who was still looking annoyed at my assistance. *Wait until you get on him and he's a perfect gentleman,* I thought, leaving her to groom her horse on her own terms. She could tap her toes and cross her arms all she wanted, but when she got out there and felt a nice polite horse beneath her again, she'd be singing my praises in no time.

Anna passed by with Missy's big chestnut, Donner, who was blowing after the tough lesson I'd just given them. Their ride had started like a lion and gone out like a lamb — over the first jump, Missy had come off in a tangle of legs and stirrup leathers and reins and whip, and then she had proceeded to jump the same course of fences six times in a row without letting Donner put a foot wrong.

"Cool him out really well," I called to Anna, although she already knew what she was doing, and watched the horse and rider panting with some satisfaction. Hard, grueling work was exactly what these teams needed to make horse shows seem like a piece of cake.

Which was good, I thought, glancing at the calendar in the tack room, because today was Wednesday, which meant in three days we'd all be packing up for the Maywood Horse Show, and there would be plenty of tough customers there. Maywood was one of the first big shows on the circuit. "WEF, here we come," I muttered, crossing off a few days I'd missed on the calendar. "Watch out for Seabreeze."

They better watch out for Ivor, too. Just as I'd been taking Bailey for evening rides, I'd been taking Ivor out for a few early morning spins. Just an easy gallop out to the shell mound and back, nothing too crazy. But it stretched his legs and freshened his mind, and the gallops seemed to wake me up better than coffee.

Only Anna knew about the extra rides, and Anna was still wrapped up in her private misery, trying to decide if showing horses was her life's work, or just something fun she liked to do with a pal.

Anna walked Donner past the tack room door again and I stepped out to watch her. There was no spring in her step, and she didn't even glance at the horse dragging a few steps behind her. Anna usually conversed with her horses, and gave them a few pats on the neck every so often. None of that now.

Poor girl. It wasn't easy, realizing loving a horse and making a living with horses wasn't the same thing. But the sooner she learned that lesson, the happier she'd be. Horses could make you crazy if you let them all into your heart. For the few chosen ones who *did* worm their way into your affections, you still had to be able to step back and be rational, and know when to cut your losses.

I reached out and touched a pony-sized bridle hanging from a rack near the door. Kennedy must have dug it out, going through my tack trunks in search of gear that would fit the little newcomers. I ran my fingers over the brass nameplate on the crown, my throat tightening a little. Then I slung the bridle over my shoulder and took it with me, heading back towards the house to find some lunch. Kennedy would have to find a different bridle for her little gray demons. *This* one was off-limits.

Twenty-one

"Gayle, what's the matter?"

"N-nothing," Gayle stammered, but the white, pinched look around her mouth said otherwise. Gayle was having show nerves.

I sighed.

"Is it something on the course? Is it the triple? Because you have triples down pat, and so does Maxine. You have nothing to worry about." I put a hand on Gayle's shoulder, and felt her trembling beneath her navy blue show coat. "You have nothing to worry about," I repeated. "Just take Maxine out, take each fence as it comes, and have fun."

"Have fun," Gayle said woodenly. "Have fun."

"You *will* have fun," I said firmly. "Go mount up and you'll feel better. Anna has your horse." Maxine was near the temporary stabling being amused by Anna, who was running her fingers up and down the mare's nose and evading her lips every time the horse tried to catch her. One of these days Anna would get bit and she'd stop playing that game, but for now, it was nice to see her having fun. We all learned these lessons the hard way, and we all had the scars to remind us, too.

Maxine was already dark with sweat. The day was warm for November, one of those hot humid days that seemed to crop up just when you'd thought the fall weather had come to stay, and twenty minutes lunging with side-reins meant some hard work and hard thinking — plenty enough of both to work up a summer sweat. Margaret was out in a field beyond the horse trailers lunging Bailey, and as soon as Gayle was mounted up, Anna was going to head out with Donner. Then Margaret would come back for Hope, and I'd handle Ivor myself. *Everyone* got their giggles out on the end of a long rope before they were mounted on a show day. I made sure my horses understood a show day wasn't an opportunity to revisit old lessons for a refresher course. This was a day to put down your head and behave.

Gayle scuttled over to Maxine, and Anna went into helpful groom mode. She tightened the girth and then first held the mare still while Gayle struggled in an her futile attempt to mount from the ground, then tactfully turned the mare so that Gayle could use the wheel-well of the horse trailer to get into the saddle. I frowned and marched over as Gayle turned Maxine towards the chaos of the warm-up arena. "Where's the mounting block?"

Anna looked around, as if she expected the mounting block to step out from behind a horse and wave helpfully. "I don't know?"

"Did you not pack it?"

"I don't... um..." Anna cast deer-in-headlight round eyes at me.

"Anna! You packed the trailer. You have a checklist. What else did you forget?"

"Grace? Have you seen boot pulls anywhere?"

I wheeled around. Missy was walking towards me in breeches and flip flops, a pair of field boots in one hand. Old-fashioned field boots, without zippers in the back — the kind of boot you needed boot pulls to get on and a bootjack to get off. "Let me just check," I told her, and swung around on Anna once again. She quailed.

"I'm sorry..."

"What *else?*"

"Well, are there boot pulls?"

I turned again. "We can use hoof picks," I told Missy. "Assuming we have hoof picks."

Anna brightened. "We have hoof picks!"

"Thank goodness. Go and find us some."

Anna went off to rummage through the grooming buckets. Missy smiled uncertainly and cast her gaze around, taking in the tumultuous show-grounds. "Is Donner ready yet?" she asked after a minute, looking worried.

"You have half an hour," I said. "Plenty of time."

Anna returned with a pair of hoof picks and handed them over silently. Missy settled down on the wheel-well to pull her boots on. "I should get zippers," she said apologetically as she wiggled the hoof picks into the fabric loops inside the left boot. "But I've had these boots for so long..."

They were ancient Der-daus, custom-made, built to last a lifetime. "How long have you had them?" Anna asked.

"Since I was seventeen," Missy said with a rueful smile. "At least my old boots fit, even if I don't ride like I did then."

"You rode as a kid?" Anna started to knot up a hay-net along the trailer's wall. "Like, you showed?"

"Oh, I did it all." Missy paused and focused all her effort on getting the slim boot on. She might have to give in and get new ones soon, I thought. Nothing lasts forever, especially not pencil-slim calves. "I showed, I hunted... I wasn't afraid of a thing back then."

"And you stopped? What happened?"

"The usual," Missy laughed, but it sounded rueful as well. "College, love, marriage, work, babies. And my horse died, and I never found another one I was so comfortable with. So I stopped riding, and then eventually I realized how much I missed it, and then, years after that, I finally had a little spare time to start taking lessons again. And then Grace helped me find Donner, and here we are. But I'm definitely not the brave teenager anymore."

"You're very brave," I objected. "You *never* tell me no. You do everything I tell you in lessons."

"That's just my nature," Missy said, and she grinned at Anna as if they shared a private joke. "I'm not good at saying no. I'm very easy to bully. That's why Donner tells me what to do so often. He jumps those courses because he likes to, how he likes to. I'm just along for the ride. And that's why he's a good horse for me now," she finished. "When I was a teenager, we would've fought all the time."

Anna was nodding along with Missy's every word. "Your horse when you were younger, he was really different from Donner?"

"He was night and day with Donner," Missy said. She

stood up and stretched up and down on her toes. "God, these are getting tight. I'm getting old. Yeah, he and I were partners — we were equals, all right. And now if I had an equal, we'd never get around the course — we'd just sit inside the barn and look nervously at each other. Things change when you quit riding, you know? There's a spark — you have to keep that alive, or it goes out. You're not less of a person, or anything like that. But you're not willing to do the same things for a ribbon, either."

"I never thought of that," Anna said. She'd given up pretending to work now and was just watching Missy. But that was fine with me — Missy was giving Anna the talk I couldn't. The talk from the other side, the talk from the decision to walk away from it all and live a normal life. I thought I could see the result already.

Just like Kennedy with her inability to give up horses, no matter how burned out and tired she'd thought she was, Anna had a look on her face that told me she wasn't going anywhere, no matter how much it hurt her to give up Mason as her partner.

I owed Missy big-time. I didn't want Anna to leave, after all — training a new working student was no fun.

Anna turned and saw me watching her. "I'll go get Donner lunged," she said hastily, mistaking my silence. "Sorry about that." She went scurrying into the depths of the white tent where the horses were stabled for the weekend, Missy and I watching her go. Then Missy turned to me.

"She was thinking about quitting?"

I nodded. "Pretty sure. She wasn't sure she wanted to keep showing with a different horse, but that's her only option at this point. You just did me a big favor."

Missy shrugged and smiled at the same time, her emotions neither here nor there. "I guess I'm the example of what not to do, in this case."

"Don't think of it like that. Everyone has a different road."

Missy nodded, watching as my working student emerged from the stable tent with her horse and went off to lunge away his excess energy. "I never saw this road coming," she said softly. "Not when I was Anna's age. But I guess you're right." She smiled then. "Thank goodness I found you!"

Another Sunday night, another hanging of the ribbons. Happily, this time everyone had a little something to show for their hard work. Gayle sniffed and wiped away tears as she hung up her blue ribbon — Maxine had pulled out all the stops once again, proving if Gayle just sat tight and remembered the course, Maxine would take care of her. Missy had two thirds and a fifth, which she was pretty happy with; Stacy had a first, a second, and a sixth; even Anna had brought home a first place ribbon with Mason, from an under-saddle class — the only class she'd ridden him in, after withdrawing from all the jumping.

Colleen was the big winner of the weekend, with three firsts, a second, and a fluttering sunburst of a Grand Champion rosette which dwarfed all the other ribbons. She pinned the massive award on Bailey's stall, where it sat like a planetary body above the little moons of the other satin scraps, and we all clapped for her while she curtseyed and waved. Bailey, annoyed by all the action outside of his stall, turned his tail towards us and dragged his hay pile to the back corner.

"Who cares what he thinks?" Colleen crowed. "Look what we won!"

I sent them all home with smiles on their faces, a big difference from the evening after the dressage show. "I might rethink my dressage commitment," I told Kennedy, who was hanging around because she thought as an employee she ought to be at the barn at all hours.

"But the dressage is important, you said," she argued, hanging up bridles she'd carted in from the horse trailer. "You said that's their edge."

"It's the *horses'* edge," I corrected her. "I'm not sure it's doing much for their riders. They like to get on and jump. The dressage is just bumming them out, and I'm the one who teaches it to them, anyway. You should have been here after the last show — everyone was threatening to mutiny. It was like the *Bounty* in here. I'm not aiming to be Captain Cook, and I don't want everyone jumping ship to get away from me. If they don't like dressage and only want to jump, well then, I'll just keep on doing the dressage on their horses and they can jump them. That way everyone's happy."

"But they're not improving as riders."

I glared at her. "Are you going to argue with me about every single decision I make? Kennedy. For the tenth time. They are here to show their horses and bring home ribbons. They are not here to become the next great horse trainers."

Kennedy frowned and picked up the loops of lunge line and side reins that had gotten tangled up on the wheelbarrow ride back to the barn. "I just don't get how you can deny them the opportunity to progress and say that's what they want."

"Look." I sat down on a tack trunk and prepared to

make her understand the business once and for all. She wanted to make a living as a riding instructor and show trainer? Fine, she needed to get this. "Take this in. There is a difference, in this business, between people who just want to show, and people who want to train and maybe show too. And people who just want to show *do not need* to learn how to train. No one in this barn needs to know how to start a young horse under saddle or over fences — no one but you, and me, and Anna. Because we are the only ones who *want* to, and that information is not required in order to show. Does that make sense?"

"I guess, but—"

"No, no buts. That's it. That's all there is to it. Colleen does not need to know how to train a horse to do lead changes. She needs to know how to *tell* her horse to *do* lead changes. These folks have limited time to ride. I help them make the most of it and reach their goals. And if someone wants to learn to train a baby — then we'd teach them very differently. But it hasn't come up yet. So we're okay?"

Kennedy sighed. "Okay."

"The kids are the same," I said warningly. "Until they're older. Don't get technical with a ten-year-old. Teach them to post. Teach them to do a crest release. Got it?"

"I got it, I got it!" Kennedy laughed. "God, you're so serious!"

"It's my business," I said simply. "You want to know how to make a living at this without killing yourself, I'm telling you. Keep it simple, that's all you have to do."

"And what about the older kids who want to know how it works and why it works?"

"Oh, them." Who knew? Teens were different. They could grow up to be like me, or Kennedy, or Anna. Or they could be another Missy, riding like hell until college and boys and careers took them out of the barn for decades. "Sprinkle the technical stuff in and go with your gut," I decided. "But remember that parents are paying the bills, so keep them moving towards the show-ring. Ribbons make repeat customers."

Kennedy nodded. "Ribbons make repeat customers. That's pretty good. You should put it on a cross-stitch pattern and sell it."

"Trade secrets," I sighed, slipping from the tack trunk. "I'm going to bed. Have a nice day off tomorrow."

Kennedy looked up from the reins she had been untangling. "I'm going to ride the ponies tomorrow."

"No you're not. Tomorrow's Monday. On the eighth day, the horse trainer looked and saw that it was good. Yea and she rested. The Horseman's Gospel."

"But they had the whole weekend off!"

"They've had three years off," I said wearily. "Tomorrow won't kill them. It might kill me."

I headed for the house, trusting Kennedy would turn out the lights, ready for thirty-six hours without seeing a single horse.

Twenty-two

Except, I broke my own rule.

I didn't spend all of Monday on non-equestrian things, as I was supposed to do. I didn't even make it to sunrise. By the time the first mockingbirds were lazily wheezing from the branches of the live oaks that sheltered the bungalow, I was wide awake, the covers flung away and squashed down at the foot of the bed, staring at the darkness above me and thinking about that feeling.

That feeling — the one I'd been having on Ivor before the show, when we'd been together out there in the scrub, galloping on a ramrod-straight path, the sound of his hooves rolling across the firm white sand, the hoof-prints left behind us perfect black horseshoes waiting to lead us home again at the end of our frolicking. The sight of the endless reaches of Florida wilderness between his pricked ears, the lift of his head as he sought out the horizon, the fluidity of his muscles and ligaments and bones and tendons as he moved like one perfect, incomparable machine. It haunted me, it woke me in the night, it woke me before the dawn, with the lazy Florida sun still somewhere far east and not even the mourning doves awake to coo from the treetops.

I curled up my toes in the rucked-up covers and resolved to go back to sleep.

I closed my eyes and then I scrunched them up to keep them closed, like a toddler pretending to take a nap. But my mind was racing, and so was my heart.

"Stupid horse," I said aloud, and I meant it. Because I was tired, and today was my day off, and I wanted to sleep until eight o'clock and then drink a pot of coffee and make pancakes and read a romance novel in my pajamas. The way normal people did on weekends, the people who didn't have horses and hadn't devoted their lives to animals who required constant care and surveillance seven days a week. I liked to pretend to be one of those people every week — just once, just enough to keep my sanity. Now, it looked like I had finally cracked. Waking up in the night to daydream about riding a horse in the woods — that was the sort of thing teenagers did, and teenagers were the sort of people who pushed themselves until they burned out completely a few years later.

Exhibit A: Kennedy. Look how crazy horses had made her. She'd given up horses and gotten an office job she hated, and now here she was back at square one, teaching beginners and breaking ponies for someone else, when once she'd had her own farm and her own show team and her own name out there.

Was I going to let myself go right over the edge and

risk the same fate? I shook my head on my feather pillow. After I'd worked my whole life to reach this point? Hell no. I was going to *go back to sleep* like the sane, intelligent, professional woman I was.

After a few moments of weakening resolve I got up anyway. What was the point of laying in bed wide awake, after all? I was awake, I should get out of bed. I *wouldn't* go to the barn. No sir! I was going to make coffee, sit on my pretty front porch that got so little use, and watch the sun rise.

Fifteen minutes later I settled onto my creaking old rocking chair, which wobbled alarmingly atop my creaking old porch floor, and gazed through the swirling fog at precisely nothing. The barn wasn't visible from the porch; it was hidden by a grove of oak trees, draped with picturesque Spanish moss like a scene on a drug-store postcard, and now those oak trees were shrouded with a silvery mist, curving and snaking through the boughs in sinuous shapes. I sipped at my coffee and waited for the sky to grow gray and pink, for the birds to start carrying on as they did every morning. Out on the highway, a semi went rattling by, its sound amplified by the damp air, and I frowned at its intrusion. I remembered when the only trucks on this road had been farmer's trucks, pulling flatbeds of watermelon in summer, citrus in winter. The watermelon beds were gone now, and the last remnants of citrus groves were ghostly ruins, an acre here or an acre there left behind of gray, skeletal trees, their few remaining oranges gleaming bravely in late winter before someone — the old owners? Kids from the subdivisions? Migrant workers? — plucked the fruit from the withering branches and left the trees bare for another year.

Maybe that was where my silly fixation on galloping through the scrub was coming from. Maybe I was so tired of watching the countryside I had known get paved over, my exhaustion with all things man-made was extending to the show-ring. Maybe I was on the verge of a mental breakdown entirely different from the one I had been staving off with all my rules about barn hours and days off. Maybe I was fixing to head out west to some forgotten corner of mountainside or meadow where I could live in a shack, haul water from a spring, and commune only with my horses and the wild creatures that would come visit me, like Snow White's animal friends. Maybe I was one step away from hermit-hood.

I took another long, restorative gulp of black coffee. Fair-trade, Sumatran beans. I would have to take quite a few bags of this blend, I reflected, if I was going to make it somewhere that actually had a winter. I hadn't seen snow in ten years, and only then on a vacation I had regretted (because of said snow). I could live like a hermit, sure, but I was going to need good coffee and a good percolator. Probably I should find somewhere tropical. Maybe Costa Rica? They grew their own coffee there.

I heard the rattle of the front gate as it hummed to life and swung open for the first groom to arrive. That made the time six thirty. The horses would hear the gate too, even though the barn was a quarter mile away. I had been down in my office before their breakfast-time before, seen the way their heads lifted and their eyes brightened a few minutes before the first car pulled into the parking lot. They were like dogs — they could tell the sounds of different motors apart from hundreds of feet away, and knew which car belonged to a groom (which meant food) and which car belonged to a boarder (which meant a confused person walking up and down the aisles wondering what time everything got started around here).

Sure enough, the sound of the motor had barely reached the house when the nickers and whinnies began to filter out of the barn, their melodies rippling through the sea of fog. Happy horses, ready for their breakfasts.

New sounds amplified by the fog followed: the gate wobbling its way shut on hinges in need of good greasing, the car making its way to the parking lot, the engine shutting off, the slam of the door. A few kicks on wooden walls — Ivor's calling card — and a cacophony of high-pitched neighs as whoever-it-was entered the barn. Who was on breakfast duty this morning? Was it Tom? I couldn't remember who did what any more.

I did remember the Monday morning routine, though, and I knew by ten o'clock, the barn would be empty of people, the horses on day turn-out would be in their paddocks, the horses who stayed in all day would be munching extra hay, listening to the barn radio (set to classical music from the local NPR station), all tranquil and completely isolated until four o'clock.

A window of six hours, during which I must fend off this insane urge to go riding.

I could get up right now, get dressed, get into my car, and drive into town. (It wasn't very far). I could have a nice breakfast. I could go shopping. I could go to Ikea and buy flat-pack furniture and re-do my shabby little living room for under five hundred dollars. I could go to the tack shop on the other side of town and indulge in the little things I wanted, like six new pairs of boot socks, or a quilted white saddle pad with argyle trim. I could go to a used bookstore and look for old English riding manuals, pages dusty and yellow with age, and breathe in their musty scent as I flipped through glossy insets of grainy photos, images of model riders jumping six foot rustic poles without ground lines or hard hats or saddle pads or martingales or flash nosebands or gag bits or any clue that in sixty years all of those things would be *de rigueur* for every show-rider from Pony Club to the Olympics.

I could see a movie. Play tennis. Go fishing. Take a knitting class. I could do a million things that wouldn't involve breaking my own rules and going down to the barn on a Monday, on a Monday after a show no less, and falling pell mell down a rabbit hole which would lead to an eventual disillusionment with my entire life, right when I was on the verge of shaking it up from its doldrums.

I went in for more coffee, my imaginary Jack Russell at my side, heels clicking on the scarred old hardwood.

I could go get a *real* dog, and that idea actually had some merit. The thought gained some traction in my brain. Dog-shopping! I picked up my tablet from the kitchen table and took it back outside with me. The birds were carrying on now in truth, tweeting and singing and, in the case of one deranged mockingbird who had obviously spent too much time in a nearby subdivision, caterwauling like a car alarm. The silver fog was thinning, and the sky above was gray and pink, shot with blue. The day was getting underway. A second car went by — the death-rattle of Margaret's old Subaru, telling me Anna was the lucky duck who had a full day off today. She was probably still asleep, her white noise machine on to drown out the happy horse sounds in the stable below. Anna was still young enough to sleep the day away. Lucky duck, indeed.

I sipped at black coffee, cooling now and with an oily rainbow pattern swirling atop its depths, and flicked my finger idly across my tablet, scanning through the local dog rescue's available listings. Pit bull cross, rottweiler cross, Staffordshire Terrier (come on now, I wasn't stupid), chihuahua cross. The former dogs would frighten the boarders, the latter was hardly what I had in mind for a barn dog. I put the tablet down on the floor next to my rocking chair. So no new dog today. It had been an idle thought anyway, easily forgotten, easily pushed to one side. I was happy enough with my imaginary dog right now. He didn't eat any pillows, and no one had peed in my closet in more than six years, which had to be something like a world record in horse trainer terms.

The only thought that wouldn't leave my head was of Ivor's pricked ears, of his forelock blown back by a breeze of his own creation, of the wild rhythm of his shoulders working between my knees.

I'd wait, then, I thought. I'd wait until everyone had left, and then I'd give in to temptation. Who knew, maybe it wouldn't lead to my eventual nervous breakdown. Maybe it would be just what it looked like on the outside: a merry gallop on a favorite horse.

Twenty-three

Anna came downstairs just as I came creeping back into the barn, a sweaty Ivor stepping up eagerly beside me. I heard her door close and my head snapped up to see her, leaning curiously over the railing of her little landing. "What on earth are you doing?" she asked, seeming rather delighted to have caught me sneaking around my own barn.

"Nothing," I said quickly, like a guilty child. "I mean — I took Ivor out for an extra ride. He's had a lot of excess energy lately."

Ivor pawed at the concrete aisle, leaving a white streak behind from his steel shoe. "See what I mean? He's still asking for more."

"More galloping on the trails, you mean." Anna laughed. "I can't believe you're going to this extreme to hide that you've been riding out there! And I'm really shocked to see you out here on a Monday," she added. "I thought your

Mondays were sacred."

"They are," I admitted. "But for some reason I just couldn't help myself. I wanted to get out there. It's such a pretty day."

It had been a perfect day out in the scrub. The temperature no higher than sixty-five degrees, the sun bright in a sky of unrelenting blue, not a single fluffy white cloud to be seen. It was as dry as a desert and as green as a jungle out there today, and Ivor and I had enjoyed every moment of our ride. He pawed again, as if to punctuate my thoughts.

"You know," Anna said rather darkly, coming down the steps. "Ivor worked very hard at the show yesterday."

"I know." My fingers slipped up to his noseband, began to undo the fastenings. I was suddenly as guilty as a child who had snuck out on her pony. "I shouldn't have taken him out."

Anna stopped on the bottom stair and I saw she was barefoot. I'd never seen her feet before — she always wore boots — and I was mildly surprised to see her toenails were painted yellow, bright as the center of a daisy. "I'm sure he would have much preferred to stay in his stall all day, staring at the walls," she agreed, and smiled mockingly at me. "You were so cruel to take him out to have a fun gallop. And he looks just utterly depressed."

Ivor fluttered his nostrils at her, stretching his neck out to see if she had any treats. I tossed her a peppermint under his neck and she caught it neatly. Holding it out, she crackled the plastic temptingly and Ivor nearly took her fingers off before she could get it unwrapped. "Yup, he's abused all right," she sighed, watching him crunch the peppermint. "Someone should call the authorities on you."

I shook my head at her and pulled the saddle off in a heap of leather and metal and sweaty cotton pad, leaning it against the wall to wait until I had Ivor showered and put away. "I know, it's silly. But it *was* bad. I have these rules in place for a reason. I shouldn't be breaking them, anymore than any of the boarders should be. I would come down hard on anybody who rode when and where they shouldn't be, after all. So I have to respect those rules, too."

"You make owning a farm sound so appealing," Anna said dryly. "I can't wait to spend my life working up to this point, where I have sunk my entire savings and career into running a barn with rules that I don't like, but that I have to follow for my own good. Come on, Grace, if that's the future I might as well just board my horse and give someone else the headache of paying for all this and keeping it running."

"I don't have rules like this for *fun,*" I argued, but Anna cut me off in a very un-Anna-like fashion.

"You don't do *anything* for fun! Or if you do, you beat yourself up about it afterwards. I was *proud* of you when I saw you riding out there this morning. Of course I saw you, do you think I sleep all day? I was sitting at the kitchen table and I heard hoofbeats. So I looked out — what if someone had gotten loose? I'd be the only one here to do anything about it. And what do I see, but my boss heading out on her big bad stallion, the one that's too valuable to waste on trails. Except that's all the horses, they're all too valuable to waste on trails. The trails that they like, and that their riders like, of course. I know what you told me before, about the horses having one job and all that, but I don't think you believe it anymore. So why not admit it and start having some fun? And maybe let everyone else join in?"

I struggled for words. *Was* I defending something I didn't believe anymore? I didn't know. I needed time to think. In the meantime, though, Anna was glaring at me and I was on the hot-seat. "But that's not the whole truth. You've seen what's happened. We've had dangerous falls, we've had runaways, we've had the ambulance out here —"

"You're saying that they couldn't learn?"

"I'm saying it's not the right use of their time." I felt like I had said this a hundred times before, and somehow it kept falling on deaf ears.

"I know that's what you *think*," Anna said. "But have you asked *them* about this?"

I picked up Ivor's reins again and started to lead him down the aisle, feeling weary to the core. This had been a mistake. Maybe, in another life, without a barn full of other people at all hours, I could have just made a random decision to take my horse out for a pleasure ride without getting into an argument or getting the third degree from someone who clearly just couldn't mind their own business. No, that wasn't my life. My life was the professional life, training horses and teaching students, and nothing about it was private. Nothing in the barn, anyway. "Anna, I'm not having this discussion," I said simply, without bothering to turn my head and see her reaction.

I heard her steps going back up the creaky stairs to her apartment above the tack room; I heard her door open and close gently. Anna would never slam a door, lest she spook a horse. I led Ivor into the wash-stall, slipped his bridle from his head and gave him a good shower, trying to pretend everything was as it had been when I was a kid, and a trail ride on your horse and a shower afterwards was nothing but another day.

Twenty-four

Instead of taking my own stern counsel, I simply went back to riding late at night, sneaking out under the cover of darkness, because of course that's what all above-board barn owners do. I took out Ivor, I took out Bailey, I even took out Hope a few times, just to let him stretch his legs, although he was a spooky devil and really too silly to be ridden out alone. I considered asking Kennedy to come out with me, but I wasn't sure I wanted anyone else to know about my clandestine trail rides. Anna had kept her mouth shut, and I had rewarded her richly: extra riding lessons and riding time. Time she might previously have spent knocking down cobwebs in the stalls or polishing brass buckles on little-used show bridles, she spent working on jumping grids and dressage. It was all the bribery a horse-crazy girl needed.

Our trail rides weren't really about training anymore —

Ivor had settled down, and so had Bailey, and while they both clearly enjoyed being allowed to move out on the sands without a fence telling them where to turn next, it seemed they'd gotten the worst case of the sillies out of their systems. I supposed the never-ending grind of it all had just gotten to them, the way it got to all of us from time to time, and once they'd had a taste of the freedom out there on the trails, they had wanted more. Now it was no longer a novelty, now it was just another ride. An easier, more fun ride, perhaps, but still — it was no laying sprawled out in the sunshine, fast asleep, or munching on a fresh flake of alfalfa in the tranquility of one's own stall.

Horses were easily lulled back into routines, and easily bored by them.

I was the problem. It was me who couldn't get enough of the total solitude and freedom out in the wilderness. My life was spent surrounded by a peanut gallery, gossiping and begging favors and complaining, from the arenas to the barn. Employees, students, boarders, horse-shoppers — there were always people around, and no one gets into the horse business because of how much they enjoy *people*. Granted, I had better people skills than the average trainer, to which I could attribute much of my success. For example, I never went into screaming fits of rage at horse shows when students didn't follow my explicit instructions — behavior which was much more common than non-equestrians might believe.

Still, I certainly wasn't on par with, say, a society party hostess, or a motivational speaker, when it came to building people up and making them feel special. *I* wanted to feel special, and I got that feeling from riding. Students were just there to pay my bills along the way.

Or rather, they had been, back in the mists of time when I had started this whole crazy game. Somewhere along the way, the training and the teaching and the coaching had come to be the paramount factors in life.

The moonlit gallops reminded me of why I'd started riding in the first place. Or, if not why — there was no real explanation for *why* a young girl thought of nothing but horses, morning, noon, and night — then of *how*. Of sneaking away from the barn when my riding instructor was away at shows. Of riding my bike to the stable on moonlit nights just like these past few we'd had, clear skies and a brilliant moon gleaming down on shimmering white-sand roads, the palmettos casting jagged black shadows I avoided with giggling superstition. Sailor's pricked ears, miniature versions of Ivor's, gleaming in the night. Too expensive to be a toy, worth too much to take out on the trails, never meant for fun — Sailor was the pony equivalent of a collectible car, promising fun and power and excitement without boundaries, if only it wouldn't spoil the resale value to take him out and really feel it.

But tell a headstrong little girl she can't take her pony for a gallop, and you'll find a junior jockey in training, sneaking around the barn with the stealthy skill of a cat burglar.

The moonlight and the white ears — that was what was going to be my undoing, I thought. I was sitting in my office on a windy afternoon, looking through show forms. It was the Thursday after Thanksgiving, another show this weekend, the prospect of moving horses to the Ocala show-grounds for weeks at a time on the horizon. I was aching for a ride with all the twitchiness of an addict, but the moon was waning, and there were clouds on the northwestern horizon, threatening rain.

"And so much the better," I said to the empty office. "We need rain, and I need to stop this crazy habit." I looked at the bookshelf, where the little framed picture of Sailor wobbled gently. The wind was slamming against the barn walls, and the second-floor office was rattling like a ship on rough seas.

I got up and adjusted the picture so it was more secure, leaning against the equitation manuals behind it, and Sailor's bright eyes glittered at me from the faded picture. The way he had jumped... I ran my fingers over the smudged glass, at his perfect knees, tight and close to his chin, which was set in tense concentration. He had loved to jump as much as I had, and he had done it with far more style. I barely glanced at myself, my garters-and-pigtails self, with my hands too high and my back too arched and my toes turned too far out. It had always been Sailor winning those ribbons.

Which was why I'd turned out to be a jumper rider, anyway. I smiled and turned away, leaving him leaping there as he had done ever since I'd moved my things into this office, my little shaman pony, overseeing everything I did.

Right or wrong.

I went back to my show entries, making a schedule for each day, assigning grooms to horses, marking out what ring I needed to be in, and when, for each rider's warm-up and classes. I thought about drumming hooves on packed sand. I sighed.

The door rattled and Kennedy came bursting in, full of all that life and energy I barely knew how to deal with most days. Quitting her office job had been like a tonic — now her face was bright and animated and her limbs seemed to fly around the room in a permanent Muppet flail. I found her equal parts exhilarating and exhausting. "Hi Kennedy." I put down my pen. "What news from the pony front?"

"Only good news, only awesome news," she trilled, flinging herself into the extra chair so hard that it rocked on its back legs.

"Please be careful," I suggested in a motherly tone. "That chair was very, very cheap."

"I rode all three of them," Kennedy continued in the same exuberant tone. She leaned forward, elbows on her knees, as if to try and contain some of her energy, but it was flying around the room anyway, irritating me. Outside, the rushing wind smacked into the wall and the joists creaked in response. "In the round pen? All three, one after another. Bing bang boom. They're super-easy. Magic, the oldest one, he's the toughest obviously. Bucked a couple of times. I gave him a couple whacks and settled him right down. Wonder, she's a piece of cake. I think all Wonder wants is a little girl to kiss her on the nose every night. She's like a unicorn in disguise."

I could barely respond with all the glitter and rainbows in the room. "And Dream? By the way, I hate these ponies' names."

"They're perfect pony names! What little girl wouldn't want a pony named Magic, or Dream, or Wonder? These Kinsale people were geniuses."

"Geniuses who couldn't stay in business long enough to get their ponies broke."

"It happens." Kennedy sat back and slapped her thigh as if she'd just remembered what we were talking about. "I think Dream is broke already. I even free-jumped her and she has knees up to here." A hand, hovering near her nose, to illustrate Dream's jumping prowess. "Pony jumpers much? She turns on a dime, too."

I rolled my neck on my shoulders. Pony jumpers, that was a whole other thing we hadn't even talked about. "Teach her to be a hunter first. It's quicker and it's where our first students will be aiming, anyway."

"Will do." Kennedy nodded sharply, like a private taking orders. "I have a lesson in about an hour and I think it's going to rain later, so I'm going to ride out on Sailor real quick. You wanna come?"

I bit my lip, just for a moment. "On the trails?"

"Yeah." Kennedy grinned. "Come on. Bring that big silly stallion of yours, I bet he'd love it."

I thought about it. I thought about the cool wind roaring through the pine trees, and the exciting rumbles of thunder as the storm slowly approached. I thought about the fresh air in our faces and the excitement in our fresh horses, dancing down the path as the sky above turned black. I thought about the gallop back to the barn, shrieking with laughter as we dodged the raindrops and tried to beat the first bolts of lightning. It all reminded me of being a kid again, of wild days in a wild Florida I thought had disappeared.

Then I thought it probably really had disappeared, and anyway what that would look like? We couldn't go galloping off into the woods as a storm front rolled in. The most irresponsible people at the barn were the ones in charge, that's what the boarders would mutter. Besides... I looked at the mound of papers on my desk. "I don't really have time. Plus, it's definitely going to storm sooner rather than later. I can't go. And I'd rather you didn't go out in the woods with the weather like this."

"Oh, it's nothing. I bet it doesn't rain before midnight."

"Trust me on this one. I've lived here a long, long time."

"You just don't want me on the trails." Kennedy's chin jutted out. I was reminded of the way we'd butted heads just a few weeks ago, when she'd first come to the farm.

"You're right," I said lightly. "I don't want you on the trails, getting hurt, when we have a new business venture and I need you sound, whole, and healthy to make it happen. I especially don't want you on trails with a cold front pushing in. Anything could happen — a tree branch could snap and hit you, or spook your horse—"

"Are you always such a worrier?"

I considered this. On the one hand, I was engaging in insanely dangerous rides several nights a week. On the other... "Most of the time," I answered finally. "About other people and their horses? Yes, definitely."

Kennedy slouched in her chair, excess positive energy gone. "Why don't you just come out with me and see? We could make it quick. You'll get a break from all this paperwork. And if Sailor spooks at a flying tree branch, you can rescue me. See? We both win."

I went over to the door and peeked out. The dark clouds were definitely closer. "No way. No one goes on a trail ride. I'm calling the trails off-limits today."

"Off-limits!" I heard the chair squeak as Kennedy jumped up. Her voice was fierce. "You're *forbidding* me? Come on, Grace. Maybe you don't want to go but you can't tell me I'm not allowed. I'm not a child. I'm not even one of your rich students that you have to baby all the time."

I turned around and fixed her with a disapproving

frown. *Oh no you don't!* "First, how dare you refer to my students that way? Completely inappropriate, coming from an employee of this facility. Second, I absolutely *can* tell you you're not allowed to use the trail. The facilities of this stable are used at my discretion. Because, in case you forgot... they're *mine.*"

Kennedy glared right back at me, but I had her. I rarely put down my foot quite like this, but if she seriously thought she was going to go out there, in front of boarders, and take her horse out into the woods with a storm coming on, she had another think coming. She had to set an example now. She was an instructor, an employee, a person whose lead boarders and students were going to follow. "You have to weigh everything you do by the influence you have on other, less experienced people, Kennedy," I said in a gentler tone. "And going into the woods with the winds howling and dark clouds rolling in is not a message of safety and common sense. It's a message of risk and self-indulgence. That's something you can't do anymore."

Kennedy sat back down, looking deflated. "What else can't I do, now that I'm influencing the little people?"

"Anything that could be remotely dangerous. Leading a horse without a lead-rope. Riding without a hard hat. Walking around the barn in flip flops. The kind of thing you might do without thinking, because you know the risks and know it's pretty unlikely you'll get hurt, but that a boarder could see and think was safe for them to do, despite having less experience." We all had to give this stuff up at some point. The short-cuts, like leading two or three horses out to a paddock at once — when you had impressionable clients, you had to do everything the long, hard, Pony Club-approved way.

Or else do it your way under the cover of darkness, once everyone had gone home for the night.

"So that's it," Kennedy said morosely. "I'm a professional again, and all of a sudden, all the fun is sucked out of life."

I threw her a sarcastic grin. "That's it, I'm afraid. You'll learn to live with it."

"And if I don't?"

"There's always your old cubicle!"

Kennedy grinned suddenly, then hopped up and headed for the door. "You know, a nice quiet ride in the covered arena sounds like just the ticket right now."

"Good girl," I said. "Don't forget your hard hat."

I settled back down to my paperwork, fingers itching to wrap around a pair of reins instead of pen and paper. The wild winds of the storm would have to blow through some other horse's mane. This was professional life, all right.

Twenty-five

December went rushing by in a series of horse shows and cold fronts. There were hot days, heavy storms, and a few icy-cold days, then the cycle started all over again. Each Friday we loaded the trailer, drove to some far-flung corner of the peninsula, and set up shop in our temporary stabling, living out of tack trunks and the trailer dressing room, driving miles and miles each morning and night from Hampton Inns and Best Westerns along the interstates. Once, the horses got actual wooden barns, but mostly they stayed in white tents with collapsible stalls, the bars between each one allowing for plenty of stall-to-stall communication. In these cases I had to rent extra stalls to keep Ivor from getting too close to any mares, or perhaps geldings who had puffed-up ideas about themselves. Having a stallion as a show horse led to all sorts of additional expenses.

I thought the extra precautions would be worth it in the end. He was jumping absolutely brilliantly this fall, and at the last show before the Ocala circuit began, he won a five-thousand-dollar grand prix and made me a very happy woman.

The Winter Equestrian Festival was looking more and more lucrative with every weekend that passed. Lock down a few grand prix placings in international competition, and Ivor would have some semen worth bottling.

"Every woman's dream, of course," Kennedy laughed when I told her my big plans.

"A freezer full of horse semen," I agreed, laughing along, but I was still serious about every word. I sprayed water on Ivor's legs and considered icing them down. He'd just worked hard in the covered arena, and the ground was kind of hard these days. I needed to order a load of clay, an expense I was putting off in hopes of winning another big purse next weekend. "Every straw worth a thousand dollars."

"That's one nice freezer," Kennedy chuckled. "Most people only aspire to having an extra fridge in the garage for their beer keg. You want a million-dollar freezer of sperm."

"Stop making fun!" I aimed the hose at her and she squealed and ducked behind the wall of the next wash-stall. "You could only wish for a freezer full of my horse's sperm."

Anna walked by with a tacked horse. Douglas, the beginner horse. I froze. Kennedy popped her head up from behind the wall and her mouth dropped. Anna stopped Douglas and looked at us. "Yes," she said. "You're absolutely right. You do need to stop shouting about horse sperm. Your three o'clock is going to be here any minute. And she's eight."

Anna walked on, the sane and sober one in the barn for once. I turned to Kennedy and burst out in horrified guffaws. She did the same thing, face red, while Ivor stood and patiently awaited the rest of his bath, apparently unaware we were discussing his value in terms of fences jumped and semen stored away in freezers.

As the horse gods would have it, the next day, Ivor came up lame.

I had tacked him up with the plan to just give him a light ride. It was Wednesday; we left for a show in south Florida the next day, which meant he'd have that day off, but it would be a travel day, and that meant stress on the legs anyway. He'd have a couple of easy classes on Friday, to get used to the footing and the surroundings, then on Saturday and Sunday both we'd have big classes, timed and with money on the line. HITS Ocala was right around the corner, an extravaganza of horse showing that wouldn't leave Florida until late April. Everyone would have a few weekends off after this show, to rest up and prepare mentally and physically for HITS. Because once that got started, it would be really and truly on, with very little downtime, for three amazing months.

"Amazing, well, that's what I *used* to say," I sighed, girthing up Ivor myself. Anna was occupied with Mason, Margaret was tacking up a lesson horse for later, Tom was scrubbing water troughs in the paddocks. Kennedy cast me an inquiring look. "I usually can't wait for HITS," I explained. "This year, I have to admit, I'm a little tired."

"You're getting old," Kennedy announced. She was grooming one of the ponies: Dream, or Wonder, who knew? They looked so alike. "Pretty soon you'll be sitting on a bench to teach, and you'll give up riding altogether. And saying 'whipper-snappers,' probably."

"That sounds really nice, actually." With Ivor's saddle secure, I checked his polo wraps before I went over to a chair and put one foot up to zip on my half-chaps. My ankles felt too tired to deal with tall boots today. "I could do with a bench, instead of standing there on the hard ground for hours while everybody else is comfy on horseback."

"Believe me," Colleen interjected, walking by with a tired post-riding-lesson Bailey. "No one is comfy when you are teaching them. My body feels like I just climbed a mountain."

I grinned at her. "That's what I like to hear from my students," I called. She stuck out her tongue and continued down the aisle, taking Bailey outside so he could graze and dry off from his bath.

"Ringing endorsement," Kennedy agreed. "I'll remember that's what they're looking for in a trainer."

"Not the kids," I said warningly. I worried the half-chap zipper over my calves with more effort than usual (Were they getting fatter? Or bulky with muscle? Probably the former.) and stood up again, stretching. In the cross-ties, Ivor flung his head up and down, his eyes locked on me. "You ready to go, big guy? Kids," I added, for Kennedy's benefit, "do not always understand that pain equals gain."

"Neither do I," Kennedy joked.

I slipped on Ivor's bridle, hooking up buckles and straps mindlessly. It was all second nature now, after so many decades with horses. When I'd been very small, a bridle had seemed like an impossible puzzle I would never master.

"Very funny," I told Kennedy, and led the horse out of the wash-stall. We turned left, to walk into the aisle.

That turn was the moment I saw Ivor's head shoot up suddenly, and his eyes widen. Just for a second, no longer than the moment it took for his left foreleg to bear his weight and then leave the ground again. I pulled him up sharply and peered at the offending leg. Kennedy peered out from the wash-stall. "What happened? What're you looking at?"

"Watch him walk," I commanded. "Come on, Ivor." I walked forward again, careful to leave plenty of give in the reins so I wasn't tugging on his head, and damn if Ivor didn't do it again — the head-bob was much more slight now, since he wasn't turning, but still, now I knew it was there, it couldn't be missed. "See it?"

"No..." Kennedy came out of the wash-stall, brush still in hand. "Turn him on it?"

We took a hard left. Ivor followed me willingly, but his head snapped up again, the white sclera suddenly showing around his eyes, as the left foreleg took all his weight.

"Well, damn," Kennedy said. "He's lame as hell, isn't he?"

I stood very still in the aisle and glared at Ivor's leg, trying to see what I might have missed in grooming. I had brushed off his leg, and polo-wrapped it, and hadn't noticed a thing. No heat or swelling had stood out. I knew Ivor's legs like the back of my hand, from years of running my hands down the popping veins and sleek cannon bones, day after day, trying to stave off an incident just like this. "I didn't see a thing in his lower legs," I admitted finally, and kneeled down to start unwrapping the polos.

"Maybe it's higher up," Kennedy said, running a hand

along the big bold line of Ivor's shoulder. He shook his head and flattened his ears at her, not so unusual behavior, since he was a snotty stallion, but still... we both paused and looked at his expression together.

"I think you're right," I said after a moment. Ivor flung his head up and down, his lips pulled back and his teeth bared in a tiny grimace. Kennedy took away her hand and he shook his head once more before subsiding into good manners. "Hell."

Unwrapped and untacked and settled back in his stall to pull at his hay and make threatening faces at every gelding that walked past his private space, Ivor seemed content enough with his fate. I leaned against the tack room wall, waiting for the vet to pick up her cell phone, and counted the horse shows on the big calendar hanging from the door. How many was I going to miss?

The vet answered at last. I explained my problem. She broke in with, "Can it wait?"

My face twisted in a confused grimace, which concerned Kennedy. She had elected to stand and stare at me while I called the vet instead of riding Dream/Wonder the pony, which I did not find particularly helpful. She mouthed "What?" at me and I mouthed "Go away!" at her and she mouthed "What?" again and I gave up and looked at the floor instead, the linoleum curling from years of heat and humidity. "How long do you need me to wait?" I asked Dr. Bartlet, who was making great sighs and sounds of exasperation on her end of the phone.

"I don't know, until tomorrow? I'm heading to Hawk Landing for a nasty colic and it'll probably have to go into surgery, and I have about ten other calls today that I'm going to have to reschedule if I so much as hit a red light on the way there."

"We're going to Fort Myers tomorrow."

"Can't you leave the info with a groom?"

I rolled my eyes. "This horse is going too."

"Well if he needs me to look at him, maybe he shouldn't go. Look, I'm sorry to be so rude, but I am really having a hellish day and I think this colic is about to make it a thousand times worse. This horse is a repeat offender and of course he belongs to a little girl and —"

Dr. Bartlet launched into a diatribe about the state of the paddocks at Hawk Landing, which were admittedly pretty bad, and how simple it would be if people just fed their horses hay on rubber mats so they didn't eat so much sand. I tuned her out and looked at the ceiling and looked at the toes of my boots and looked out the doorway into the barn aisle, where people were living their lives and riding their horses without a care in the world or a vet shouting in their ear. Finally she stopped and took a breath and sounded halfway-normal again, like the vet I liked very much despite her temper.

"Which horse is it? Is it a boarder or is it yours?"

"My gray stallion," I said, feeling blue just saying the words. "Ivor, the big show jumper."

"Ah, shit." Dr. Bartlet was quiet for a moment, and I imagined her mentally calculating how many minutes of her day were accounted for. "How late will you be up tonight?"

"As late as you need me." I hopped up from the tack trunk I'd perched upon, feeling much more hopeful. She was a very good vet, after all. Who knew, maybe it would be something simple. Maybe she'd get Ivor all sorted out and we'd go on with our weekend as if nothing had happened.

"It might be crazy late, if this horse goes into surgery,"

she warned. "Don't stand me up. If I say I'm coming tonight, I'm coming."

"Are you saying you're coming?"

She sighed. "Yes. I'll come tonight. I'll call ahead. Leave your phone ringer on, sleepy-head. It might be past your bedtime."

"Thank you thank you thank you thank you —"

"Okay." There was a click and Dr. Bartlet was gone.

I looked at Kennedy. "She's coming late. But at least she's coming."

Kennedy lifted an eyebrow. "Is she always so… hard-boiled?"

"She's a character." I slipped the phone into my pocket and started rummaging around the shelving unit where a thousand bottles of medicines, shampoos, potions, and liniments had accumulated over the years. "She gets very tense when she's driving. And I guess this horse she's going to see is a candidate for his last surgery before he's toast."

"That's pretty sad."

"Yup." I lifted an unlabeled bottle of liniment, just the concoction I'd been looking for, and held it up triumphantly. "My grandfather's secret recipe. Rodney still makes it. I'm going to go give the old boy a massage. You go ride that pony of yours."

Kennedy gave me a salute and marched out of the tack room, a pony bridle slung over her shoulder. I went back to Ivor's stall, ready to risk a few bites for the sake of maybe soaking some of his soreness up with this bottle of camphor and menthol and lord only knew what else. "Maybe it's nothing," I told myself over and over. "Nothing at all."

Twenty-six

"Oh, it's something," Dr. Bartlet said ominously, prodding the offending shoulder. "Not sure what, though."

Ivor clacked his teeth together, *snap snap snap snap*, like a cat hunting a mouse. I had a lip-chain on him, there to remind him if he tried any funny business on my vet, it was going to go very badly for him. This was his usual response, to stick his tongue out of the side of his mouth and rattle his front teeth. I knew he only did it to annoy me. That's the thing about stallions. They have big, funny personalities which verge on the obnoxious when you want them to just settle down and be quiet.

At eleven o'clock at night, all I wanted was a little quiet.

I'd been in my slippers, or more accurately, in my flip flops, for the night when the phone had finally rang. I draped my limbs in ungraceful folds across the couch, vacantly staring at the ten o'clock news, which I found very boring because there weren't any horses on it. As always, I waited for the weather report with great anticipation, although I could've flipped to the Weather Channel at any point and just seen the forecast. Still, it was interesting this time of year, and I liked a detailed analysis by a local meteorologist with lots of nerdy details. The weather forecast in summer months was always the same; in the winter you never really knew what was going to happen next.

An enthusiastic young man swung his arms around the map of Florida. He announced blue skies and seventy-degree temperatures for the weekend. Well, that sounded simply heavenly, compared with the massive cold front he predicted for Monday night. We'd have to leave Ft. Myers bright and early Monday to avoid getting caught in that, I thought.

When Dr. Bartlet finally rang up, sounding exhausted, I slipped my feet from flip flops to Wellingtons and pulled a cardigan on over my t-shirt. No bra, no problem, I thought. The benefit of having a lady vet.

Now Ivor gave me a hard nudge in the chest and I thought longingly of underwire. I gave him a little wiggle on the lip chain, just a statement of fact: *I can nudge you right back, buddy.* He went back to clacking his teeth. "Blithering idiot," I told him, and Dr. Bartlet looked back from her perusal of his leg.

"I've never seen you so fond of a horse in my life."

"You haven't known me very long," I said airily. "And anyway, I just gave him a shank with the lip chain and called him an idiot. So you're actually being a little insulting right now."

We'd known each other fifteen years, when she was fresh from vet school and had a much longer fuse, and when I was just starting to poke my head out of the assistant instructor shell and wonder if it was time to go into business for myself. After so many years, speaking to one another without sarcasm was reserved for the most serious of cases. Now she grinned and went back to her poking and prodding. "If you didn't like him, you wouldn't even talk to him. You'd just stand there and look irritated."

I couldn't deny this. "Are you going to talk all night or are you going to figure out what's wrong with my horse?"

"He's just sore," she said, straightening up. "In the shoulder, though, not in his lower leg, so no suspensory or tendon issues. That's good. Sore shoulder's hard to diagnose, though."

"That's bad," I said.

Dr. Bartlet sighed. "Has he been on hard ground, maybe? Or took a jump funny? Damn, Grace, he looks *extremely* fit…" She ran her hands over his slim neck and down his face, and I realized for the first time how tightly his skin was stretched over his bones. He wasn't thin, but he was somehow more elastic and taut than usual. She traced the hard knob of bone above his eye and he playfully tried to snatch at her arm. "Have you been galloping him? Like, a lot?"

I hesitated, and that was all she needed. Dr. Bartlet whipped around, took one look at my face, and had me figured out in an instant. "What have you been up to?"

Old friends are overrated.

"We've just been going out for some gallops," I said cagily. "He's had a lot of excess energy. Getting bored easily. The galloping keeps him fresh."

"Are you taking him to a training track?" she asked suspiciously. "Because the closest one I know of is thirty miles away, and I know you don't have room in that covered arena to get up to a good gallop before you have to slow down and turn."

"No." I sighed and brushed the end of the lead-shank against Ivor's nose. He snapped at it with yellow teeth. "We've been doing it out back, on the trails."

Dr. Bartlet whistled. "That's not like you at all! Where did this wild streak come from?"

"I told you. He was getting bored. I was having trouble with him, a couple of others — they just needed freshening." I paused. "I just really liked galloping him out there, so we kept doing it."

"It's the dry season, though," Dr. Bartlet pointed out. "That ground's getting hard, isn't it? You should have been icing him afterwards."

I didn't bother to explain my rides were done in secret, under the cover of darkness, when the moon was bright enough to light our way along the white-sand trail, and fitting him with ice boots would have aroused suspicion in the grooms. It didn't matter — she was right. I had been treating the gallops like they were nothing but fun, without even taking into consideration that Ivor was working very hard even though he was enjoying himself. I'd thought about the hard ground in the arena, but not on the trail.

That did explain my tight half-chaps, though. At least my calves were bulking up from muscle, not fat. The half-seat I'd been using when we galloped had my calves taking the brunt of my weight. My lower leg had been bulking up all along, without my notice. We were both harder and stronger, but it was only a matter of time before one of us got hurt. It just happened to be Ivor.

"Let the soreness work its way out, rub him with liniment if you want. And put him in ice boots next time if you want to keep those lower legs tight," Dr. Bartlet said, rummaging in the bucket she'd brought along from the truck. I leaned over to see what groundbreaking veterinary tool she was reaching for. She came out with a wet-nap and wiped her hands clean. Very anti-climactic, but good at the same time. It meant nothing very serious (or expensive) was happening. "As long as the ground is hard, ice him. If it's softened up, poultice is fine, but do him up in wraps every time you gallop! His legs already take a hammering from jumping. I'm sure the galloping is good for him — my God, Grace, he's ready to run a race. A Thoroughbred trainer would say he has his game face on." She ran her hand along his bony face once again. "I mean, he really looks fantastic. I don't think the week or two off is going to do him any harm."

"That's it?" I asked, trying to ignore the sinking feeling in my stomach at the loss of this weekend's show. I should be grateful, I told myself. Grateful she didn't think it was anything serious.

"That's all I think it is. A bad step on hard ground, maybe he was feeling sore on one side and worked too hard on the other. Shoulders are funny — you think the shoulder hurts and it turns out it's coming from his hip, or his back, or wherever — anywhere but where you thought. So just give him some time off. But, I mean..." she stepped back and surveyed Ivor from nose to tail once more. "He's not giving you any other trouble. You said he was acting like he needed freshening, which could be a warning sign, but the trail rides brought his attention back. So I'd say it's just soreness from a bad step."

"Oh, thank God." I felt a little dizzy at her speech... if it had been his spine!

"But if he's not feeling one hundred percent better in a week, we do a bone scan."

"Oh." I felt more dizzy.

"Shoulder injuries can be a bitch," she said thoughtfully. "Hard to diagnose, hard to fix…"

I couldn't speak at all. Surely she was just playing with me now.

"But honestly, since he hasn't had any incidents to blame this on, I'd say it's nothing a week off won't fix."

I poked Ivor in the nose again, for lack of anything better to do, for lack of any words to say. He snatched the end of the leather lead-shank in his mouth and yanked at it, nearly pulling me over.

"Yeah," Dr. Bartlet said, watching him play with the lead, watching me recover my balance. "I'd say it's nothing." She picked up her bucket. "Welp, I'm heading home to my bed."

I watched her go, wobbling down the aisle with her big bucket full of bits and pieces of veterinary equipment she hadn't needed. Then I looked back at Ivor, who was wiggling his nose contentedly on the leather shank. He didn't seem to mind that it was nearly midnight and that the barn was lit up bright as day, although quite a few of the other horses were grumbling and pacing, trying to figure out why their night had been disturbed. That was the thing about Ivor — since I'd had him longer than I'd had any other horse in years, he had settled into life with me like a comfortable glove. "And here I am risking you out on the trail," I told him, planting a kiss on his nose and then backing up before he could take off my face with one playful nip. "All the hell I gave the boarders about hurting their horses, and I did it myself."

And wasn't that just typical? I slid back his door and deposited the stallion back in his stall, where he went back to stuffing his face on hay with his usual abandon. How had I thought I could risk such an amazing horse, anyway? It must have been temporary insanity.

Well, that was all over now. He'd have his week off while I took Hope and the gang to Fort Myers, and then in January we'd come out with guns blazing, ready to take on the international show jumping world by storm.

Mama needed a new load of clay in her arena.

Either way, I'd sleep better tonight knowing that Ivor's sore shoulder wasn't the end of the world.

Probably.

Twenty-seven

"Sleep well last night?

That voice could cut through the sweetest dream. My eyelids flew open, and for a moment I wondered where the hell I was. Then I lifted my head from the back of my office chair and smiled apologetically at the hatchet-faced woman glaring down at me. Reality flowed over my shoulders in a chilly stream. *That's* right. *That's* where I was. "Oh, Colleen, I'm so sorry. I really didn't, actually. I was up late with the vet. I meant to go down and help Anna get the trailer packed, and here I am sleeping the day away."

Colleen came into the office stiffly, holding out cherry-red talons. "Just came from the salon," she explained, setting down her expensive handbag gingerly, careful not to expose her freshly lacquered fingertips to the embossed *Ls* and *Vs* all over the leather surface. I'd never understood why rich people wanted someone else's monogram on their things. As a horsewoman, inscribing as many possessions as possible with my own initials was kind of a religion.

"I don't know how you're going to ride in those," I observed school-marmishly.

Colleen regarded her fingernails critically. "They'll have to go before the show, but I missed nice nails," she responded gloomily, eyeing her fingertips. "I don't ride until tomorrow afternoon, so it can wait. Anyway, I have to look fabulous at one of Tom's parties tonight — you know how it is. A fundraiser, lots of wine glasses, lots of powerful men judging each other's wives."

I *didn't* know how it was, thank goodness. "I hope it doesn't keep you out too late tonight," I offered sympathetically. Colleen must feel upstaged by her husband at these events, and Colleen was not good at being upstaged.

"Oh, it will." She brushed the subject off. "I wanted to talk to you about something." She glanced back at the open screen door, the blue winter sky sparkling over her shoulder. There wasn't a cloud in sight. "I'll close the door."

I furrowed my brow as she pushed back her chair and tripped back over to the office entrance in her beaded flip flops — she'd had her toes painted up too, I noticed — and delicately pushed the heavy door closed. When the latch had clicked, she turned around and gave me an insincere smile. "Let's talk."

"Okay." I pushed aside the receipts I'd been sorting through before I gave in to my heavy eyelids. "What's up?"

"It's about the party I'm going to tonight." She looked away nervously, something that Colleen never did, and I shifted uncomfortably in my seat. Was she going to move or something? Sell Bailey, stop Maddy from riding? I could see that fifteen-thousand-dollar pony cantering down the road, gray tail waving in the dust, taking my commission with it. "It's for the Hannity and Roth Group."

I shook my head. The names didn't mean a thing.

"Developers? Built the Venezia Bay Resort, just down the road? Building that golfing community, the Preserve at Sunset Pointe?" I could hear the extra "e" in the word point. "You must know those places."

"Hard to miss." I sat forward, suspicious of where the conversation was going—and damned uneasy. "Sunset Pointe was built on the last ranch in the county." And it wasn't called Sunset Pointe... it was just the Dale Ranch, back when old Willy Dale had been running cattle on two thousand acres of Florida scrub, savanna, and swamp. When he'd started, it had been one ranch in a sea of ranches, cattle marked with brands like it was the Wild West. When Florida had been the Last Frontier, not Alaska.

"Well, they're Tom's clients. His *biggest* clients. And... he asked me to feel you out on this."

"If they want the farm, they can't have it." The audacity of those developers. Paving over the countryside like the gods were making more of it. Didn't they know this was all we got? And Seabreeze was my heart and soul... I'd die before I'd let them tear down my barn and my paddocks and my sweet little cottage and obliterate every trace of my dreams. "I will *never* sell. They can build a hotel here when I die, but first they'll have to spend a million dollars figuring out the trust."

"The trust?" Colleen narrowed her eyes. "What trust?"

The trust I'd never gotten around to making a reality. "Let's just say this land will stay native Florida forever, if I have anything to say about it." I really needed to make some time to sit down with my lawyer. After HITS. After WEF. When I could breathe.

"What about the back forty?"

"The what?" My grandfather had called the hundred acres out back "the back forty." No one else.

"The woods behind the farm. The trails? That scrubland? You own that, too, don't you?"

"Oh yes, but it can't be developed without buying *this* farm," I explained. "There's no road access. It's landlocked." Unless the golf course going in next door included some sort of access I hadn't known about... I felt a little curdle of worry twist in my stomach.

"It can't be developed *yet*," Colleen said comfortably. "And neither can the Wilcox property. Not yet."

"They bought out Hugh Wilcox?" This was sad news. Hugh had hung onto his old ranch long after he'd decamped for a houseboat out near Homossassa. That meant the parcel of land east of the lake would no longer be safe... I bit my lip as Colleen made a *who's that?* face, shook her head, and went on with her story.

"That's why the country club going in next door hasn't broken ground yet. They were trying to get the county to build a new road to connect back to the Wilcox property. Turns out there's only one place they can do it without taking ten years or something crazy like that. Changing zoning, blah blah, legal speak. Because there's *technically* already a road there. You know anything about that?"

I sat upright, my heart hammering. The trail. Stories my grandfather told me came rushing back. They weren't just stories. There was a reason it was so wide and straight and hard-packed.

Colleen liked that. She leaned forward, looking chummy. "Here's the thing — I'm not on anyone's side. If it's a good deal for you, great, you should do it. All I know is, I saw the maps in Tom's office. There's some old road that's been on the maps since they started keeping records... I forget the name now, the Tomahawk Trail, maybe —"

"Timucuan," I interrupted automatically. "It would be Timucuan."

"Timoocoon," Colleen repeated, waving a hand to dismiss a forgotten tribe. "Whatever. The Timmoocoo Trail was a road that ran from nowhere to over yonder, between old Indian villages maybe, which is why it's not much more than a break in the bushes now, but it can be *paved* without all the environmental impact studies. Like, anytime the owner wants to pave it. So the part that runs from alongside the farm, back through your woodland, and into the Wilcox property — that's now worth a fortune to them. If they can build a road back to that piece of land, they can skip years of arguing with the county and the state and the EPA."

"And the water management board."

"What does water have to do with it?"

"Water has everything to do with everything here," I sighed, suddenly feeling I'd had it up my neck with Yankees. "And the Timucuan Indians lived here five hundred years ago, more or less. That's what the road name means. They must have had a game trail or something here." I didn't know if that was true, but my grandfather had claimed it was.

I wanted to go out there right now, and get away from Colleen and her red fingernails of doom and her thinly veiled threats from the developers. I wanted to climb onto Ivor's back and gallop away from all this.

Ivor was lame, I remembered sadly, and anyway, we had to get to the horse show.

A trail ride would have to wait, as would everything else. Including this ridiculous meeting. "Colleen, I appreciate the warning. I have to get going now, though. We need to get the horses on the road." I stood up to let her know I was serious, and barely managed to hold back a yawn. This was going to be a three-Starbucks drive south, at least.

Colleen got up slowly, dramatically, as if determined to draw out the meeting on her own terms. "This is something you need to take very seriously, Grace," she warned. She plucked up her bag with those cherry-red claws. "I want to make sure you get a good deal. I'll be listening in tonight and get you as much info as I can. Values, land prices, that sort of thing."

I smiled politely. "I won't be selling."

Colleen shook her head knowingly. "Let's talk after the weekend. I think you'll be surprised at what I uncover."

"After the weekend," I agreed, and watched Colleen sway down the steep staircase to the barn aisle on her beaded flip flops, her red toenails flashing beneath the bright overhead lights. There was no way I'd ever sell one square foot of my land, but if she wanted to dig up some dirt on the developers, that was certainly her business. I had work to do. I turned back to the desk and started gathering up the show entries and horse registrations into the show binder. Time to get busy.

Twenty-eight

I settled down in the little metal grandstand alongside the warm-up ring and watched my students canter around the ring, feeling the warmth of pride in my belly. There went Gayle, with her thumbs turned up like a dressage rider and her knees turned out like an equitation rider, but her heart was in the right place and she wasn't hanging her weight off of Maxine's mouth for once, so I couldn't complain and really, neither could Maxine. There went Missy, rolling her thighs oddly with every canter stride, a mannerism I couldn't quite figure out to correct, but I kept her out of the eq classes and it wasn't a problem. There went Colleen, stick-thin and smug because she knew it, designer sunglasses tucked under GPA helmet and her perfect coif knotted in a bun and hidden away in its net, her lower legs a tad too forward and her shoulders a tad too back because she was waiting for Bailey to spook at something. Bailey, however, was not complying. He looked as quiet as a Labrador Retriever after a good swim, and I knew why.

I'd fixed his wagon, all right. Mr. High Energy, bolting around like an idiot. Taken care of with those extra rides. He was fitter, but he was saner, too.

I was just lucky the firm ground hadn't done the same number on him that it had on poor Ivor, on bed-rest back at the farm. I resisted casting another wistful gaze towards the grand prix arena, where the colorful jumps had been raised up high for tonight's first big class. Bad enough I wasn't earning any prize money this weekend, I'd also had to forfeit the my entry fees when I canceled, and money classes weren't cheap. I was out a pretty big sum, and with coaching and trailering fees I was still going to come out pretty close to dead even this weekend... not thrilling for an entire weekend away from home, working my tail off in the hot southwest Florida sun.

"Phew!" Gayle pulled up Maxine along the rail in front of me and swiped at her sweaty face with the back of one glove. "Isn't it supposed to be winter? It's hot as hell here!"

"It's always hot here," I agreed. "I don't think Fort Myers gets even the little bit of winter that we get." I couldn't think of a single show down here at Foxes Corners where we hadn't baked in the sun, unless it was raining the whole weekend, and even then it contrived to be hot. "You going to be okay?" Gayle wasn't in the best of shape, and she always seemed to feel the heat more than my other students.

"Oh yeah," she panted. "I'm fine. Just... need a drink..."

I dug in the soft cooler I'd brought along and pulled out a Gatorade. I hopped down from the grandstand and handed it over the rail. "Drink as much of this as you can."

Gayle tipped the bottle back, both reins scrunched up in her spare hand. Maxine sidestepped and Gayle spluttered, spilling purple drink down her front. Luckily, she was still wearing her pale blue Seabreeze Equestrian polo over her white ratcatcher. "Oh shit!" she gasped. "Would you look at that!" She batted at the stain, and Maxine began to jump around, utterly confused by the commotion in the saddle and the tugging on the reins. I slipped through the fence and snatched the bottle in one hand and the mare's reins in the other.

"Take off your hard hat and pull the shirt off as quick as you can," I hissed.

Gayle, flushed with heat and embarrassment, fumbled with her hat's snap, finally pulling off her gloves and stuffing them between her legs and the saddle so she could get hold of the straps, and then got her hat off. She held it helplessly, trying to figure out where to stash it while she pulled the polo off, and I grabbed the hat as well.

"Be quick, before a steward sees you!" No one was allowed on horseback without a hard hat at Foxes Corners. They were very strict... I suspected it had something to do with all the junior classes. There were ponies *everywhere*. Well, I'd have some ponies here myself before too much longer, I supposed. Gayle flung down the wet polo shirt and I handed up her hat. I looked the white shirt over. "Don't think any of it got on you. We'll get you a straw next time."

Gayle's smile was pained as she buckled her hard hat back in place. "I'm so clumsy. I'm always spilling things on myself."

"Well, as long as you're spilling things and not taking a

spill, you're doing just fine," I said reassuringly. I handed off Maxine's reins again and gave her a pat on the knee. "Why not take her over some of the fences at a slow, easy canter and then we'll call her warmed-up, okay? No reason to overheat the two of you."

Gayle nodded and smiled, looking happier again, and she gathered up Maxine and sent the pretty gray mare cantering down the rail, remembering at the last minute before a collision with a very determined junior that she was meant to be on the inside, veered hard to the right, and nearly collided with Colleen, who was cantering up on her inside rein.

I climbed back through the fence so I wouldn't have to see any more, and found Anna sitting by my cooler, a friendly smile on her face. "Hey you, managed to sneak away from the stalls?"

"Everyone's out here or taken care of," she said happily. "Thought I'd catch some showing before someone was shouting my name again."

I settled down next to her and pulled a Diet Coke out of the cooler. "Have a soda and watch my students give me gray hairs," I suggested.

She reached in and dragged out a bottle of water, dripping with melted ice. "I've had about eight sodas today," she admitted. "Bad Anna."

"Shameful," I agreed. "Oh look, there goes Gayle over the vertical." We both winced as Gayle flubbed the distance, hit Maxine in the face over the jump, and sat on the cantle before the mare landed. But the gallant Maxine didn't touch the pole with her hind legs, tucking them up tight and flicking her tail in the air for good measure. "Thank goodness," I said. "I don't want to have to run out there and put the pole back up."

Anna smiled politely. "Can I ask you something?"

"Of course."

"You won't tell anyone."

"Anna, you're my working student. You're here to learn so that you can run your own barn someday. What kind of trainer would I be if you couldn't talk with me honestly?"

"Well, it's kind of about that." She took a drink of water, buying time. "It's like... Gayle. Gayle is not a good rider. We can agree on that, right? Her horse is like, amazing. But Gayle would be lost without a horse like that. She'd fall off every time. So... is Gayle ever going to *be* a good rider? And if not... why not?"

I opened my mouth, thought, and closed it again. Why *wasn't* Gayle ever going to be a good rider? Easy answers crowded my mind, but I couldn't say with any authority whether any of them were true. Because she wasn't a natural athlete? Because she was edging towards fifty and had stopped riding for twenty-some years? Because she was a bit top-heavy and didn't work out, so she had no core strength to keep her balanced?

Because she had skipped riding foundations in order to pose on a perfect packer of a horse who could cart her around the show-ring?

"It's a lot of reasons," I said hesitantly. "Probably a combination of a lot of things."

"But should she even be jumping fences of that size?"

We watched Gayle jump Maxine over the oxer without too much drama, wobble on the landing, and just manage to save her own balance by digging her hands into Maxine's neck. Maxine shook her head a little, ears pinned, but cantered on. "She's only jumping 3'6" right now. That's not huge or anything."

"No, but I wouldn't have been allowed to jump fences like that if my form was so iffy." Anna bit her lip. "Sorry. I'm not saying you're doing anything wrong. I didn't mean —"

"No, it's fine. I know what you're saying." I shifted my focus to Colleen for a moment, who was still cantering around in a perfectly balanced pose atop the mighty Bailey. "Here's the thing — Colleen looks much better than Gayle, right? But they're both about equal riders, believe it or not. Colleen might be slimmer and have more natural balance on a horse, but they're both at about the same skill level. Which is — they can take a well-trained horse around a course of fences and look decent doing it."

"But is that enough?" Anna persisted.

"Not for you, and not for me. But for them... yes. It's what I promised them. It's what they wanted. And they get to show and they bring home ribbons, and everyone's happy." Gayle caught Maxine in the mouth again and the mare threw up her head in protest. "Almost everyone," I amended. "I have to do something about Gayle's hands when we get home."

I turned to Anna. "Listen, you keep bringing this up, and I know it's because you're worried about being a trainer yourself. So here's the thing. It's all about deciding on your customer base and giving them what they want. Hey, if you want to go to the Olympics and then train young Olympians, that's your choice. Just be aware, it might not pay that well. *This* pays my bills, or it almost does. I have a farm and a house and some nice horses. I'm happy with my choices. You have to be happy with yours." I settled my elbows against the seat behind me and reclined. "End of speech."

Anna nodded solemnly. "Got it."

Colleen sidled up to me after the classes were finished and everyone was grouping together, discussing where they wanted to head for dinner. The consensus was Big Pig Barbecue out on 441. Since the restaurant was within totter-home-and-pass-out distance of the hotel, I had absolutely no problem with this. I stepped away from the conversation and walked the shed-row we'd been assigned, making sure everyone was fed, watered, and happy. Anna had done a good job, as usual. I leaned over a stall door and watched Maxine nibble delicately through a flake of timothy and alfalfa, nosing out the sweet green alfalfa leaves so that she could gobble those up first.

"Give any thought to what I said last night?" Colleen murmured in my ear, making me jump.

"Jeez, Colleen, are we playing spy movies?" I laughed to take the scold out of my voice. "You scared me."

"I just don't want everyone alerted," she shrugged. "I know Gayle would have an absolute conniption if she thought the farm was... if anything was going to change." She neatly sidestepped the word "sold."

Gayle's horse snorted, and I couldn't have agreed with her more. "Colleen, I think I was very clear."

"And so was I, wasn't I? They'll stop at nothing. You can name your price with these people. You could even just sell the back forty — the stable and arenas can stay intact."

Just hearing her say the words *back forty* while talking about selling the land made my throat close up. That land had been my grandfather's playground. That land had been where I had spent the most golden hours of my childhood.

That land was where I had made the most wonderful memories, and the greatest mistakes, of my life. "They're not getting it, Colleen. My answer is always going to be no."

She narrowed her eyes at me, her perfectly plucked eyebrows coming together in a thin line of elegant outrage. "You're going to regret that kind of attitude, Grace. You don't know who you're dealing with. The Roths —"

"Are developers," I snapped, my voice rising. "The worst sort of people, the wolves who are tearing up Florida and destroying it, acre by acre. I wouldn't sell to them if they offered me a million dollars."

"Oh, it would be way more than a million dollars!" Colleen retorted. "You idiot, do you have *any* idea —"

"What's going on?" Gayle's childlike voice, lost and afraid, penetrated my enraged brain. I realized that I'd said the magic words — *developer, sell* — much louder than I'd intended. "Is someone buying the farm? Grace, are you selling the farm?" Her voice wavered, and the pink ribbon she'd been holding was suddenly crushed within her fist.

I took her hand and gently opened her fingers. "Of course I'm not, Gayle," I told her gently. "The farm isn't going anywhere. Now, let's hang up this ribbon on Maxine's stall, and go get some dinner. I could eat an entire pig, I think."

Colleen turned on her expensive heel and stalked off down the shed-row, scattering mulch with every angry step. Her horse, who had been hanging out of the stall to see what the commotion was, darted back into the stall as she went storming by. I knew exactly how he felt. That was what I wanted to do every time Colleen came around, too.

I turned and faced the little cluster of wide-eyed ladies.

"Sorry about that," I said, forcing a smile. "The conversation is getting old, and I guess I get a little short-tempered."

Missy cocked her head. "Does Colleen *want* you to sell?"

"It sure sounded that way," Gayle ventured. Her lip trembled a little.

I considered for a moment. Colleen had presented herself as an ally, someone who could get me details on the developers. I had figured it was so that I could beat them and send them packing. It hadn't occurred to me that maybe she'd wanted me to get the best deal possible.

I stifled a groan. Colleen must be in with the developers. She must be counting on a commission, or a piece of the long-term action, once the farm was bought, the barn was razed, and the road was paved.

Missy shook her head. "You can't trust that woman. She's been leading you on, letting her think you're her buddy, that she's going to buy some expensive pony. It's all a load of crap. I bet she can't even afford to adopt a pony for that snotty kid of hers."

"Oh, there's no way. They're in debt to their eyeballs," Stacy confirmed, her voice knowing. "Colleen's a big spender. She keeps David hustling, that's for sure. He was driving an old beater until he got that promotion and managed to buy a new car. And then she was making fun of him for being sensible and getting something used. She wanted him to buy a new BMW with all the bells and whistles. He's used to getting bossed around, but at least he had the sense to defy her on that one."

"Is that true?" I asked, dumbfounded. Colleen had never missed a board bill, never passed a bad check, never batted an eye at vet or farrier bills. She rode when she wanted, paid me to ride the rest of the time, and luxuriated in the finest tack.

Stacy grinned, enjoying my chagrin. I couldn't think of any reason to disbelieve her. If anyone would have the gossip on the barn bitch, it would be Stacy, our own bitch-in-waiting. "Well, shit."

I leaned back against the barn wall and closed my eyes, not even caring that the boarders were watching me. Ordinarily, I'd never have let them see me caught off-guard like this. But it didn't take a genius to see that the farm was in trouble, and losing a promised deal like the one I'd had with Colleen was going to be a massive blow. For once, I figured, the boarders could see that their trainer was a real human, capable of really freaking out.

I bowed out of dinner at the Big Pig and went back to the hotel alone. I'd order a solitary pizza and leave the ladies to their gossip. They'd shake their heads knowingly, go off to dinner together, and talk about where they'd move their horses when Seabreeze closed down over brisket and pulled pork and puddles of barbecue sauce. After all, they had money. I might lord over them at the barn, but at the end of the day, when I was broke and they were not, *they* were the ones in control of the situation.

Twenty-nine

"Hey boss!"

I stopped in the barn entrance. Tom ran up behind me, the Gator rumbling and growling behind him. It was becoming a noisy idler. Probably needed tuning-up, I thought with a mental sigh, then pushed the thought of my head. I wasn't thinking about anything that required dollar signs. "What's up?"

Tom brushed pale hair from pale eyes, which were wide and worried now. "Maybe nothing, but... Saw some guys standing out front when I took down the trash cans. They were wearing suits, looking at the farm sign. Walked back towards the property next door when they saw me."

I narrowed my eyes. *Developers*. I would have their heads if they stepped foot on my land. "You think they're from the realty company?"

"Might be. Maybe they're worried about building next

to a farm?"

"They oughta be. You done with the Gator?"

"Yeah, I'm just going to the tack room for some coffee."

"Good." I went past him and slipped into the driver's seat. If there were developers scoping out my property, I wanted them to hear it straight from the horse trainer's mouth — this place wasn't for sale. If I told them that, maybe they'd spare me the blank check scenario Colleen had sketched out at the show last weekend. I was really afraid of what I'd do if something like that were to happen — especially after seeing this month's hay bill. Best to send them on their way now before I got the feed bill.

Sure enough, there they were — still on the neighboring property's highway verge, but definitely looking my way. Two black Mercedes sedans were parked along the highway shoulder, and when they caught sight of the Gator for the second time, the two men started to beat a retreat to the safety of their cars.

"Oh no you don't," I muttered, and gunned the Gator up the shoulder to the pair of cars. Seeing that I was intent on confronting them, the men both stopped by their car doors and waited for me.

"Gentleman," I said when I had parked in front of them. "Good morning."

"Good morning," said the closest man, taking off his sunglasses. Tan, fifties, gray hair and good clothes — nothing special, just another Florida businessman, cutting down a few more trees and getting rich doing it. I felt a sudden wave of anger that made my vision dance. Why must they destroy everything in sight? Why couldn't they let the farmers have their farmland? Did every inch of Florida have to be converted into golf courses and condos before they'd be content?

So I glared at him with a stare I usually reserved for rank stud colts about to learn what happens when Someone Bites Grace. "You involved with this?" I nodded my head towards the sign announcing resort villas, making sure to convey exactly what I thought of their despicable plans.

"Why yes," the man without sunglasses said, not a trace of trepidation in his oily voice, and he stepped forward to shake my hand. "I'm Rich Hannity, and this is my partner Mike Roth. We're very excited to move into the neighborhood. It's nice to meet you...?"

I pointedly hesitated before I took his hand, then made sure he saw exactly how dirty and calloused my hand was before he was obliged to clasp it in his own soft, clean one. "I'm Grace Carter," I said simply, and waited for him to continue stating his business.

"Oh, *you're* Ms Carter!" Rich smiled. "Just the person we want to talk to."

"Yeah?" I took my hand back and placed it on the steering wheel, ready to leave some dust in his face.

"Well, it's about some land that you own, Ms Carter."

"Not for sale." I smiled sweetly.

Rich opened and closed his mouth, flustered for a moment. "Not the equestrian center, I assure you," he said after a moment regaining his train of thought. "That's an asset to the community! The undeveloped land, though —"

"Also not for sale."

Mike Roth, in the background, shook his head. He was younger than Rich, with a mop of dark hair falling over a white forehead. His skin was pink-tinged with heat. I could see that Mike didn't play outside much. His expression was menacing, though, dark eyes glittering and lips turned down in an angry frown. "Ms Carter, now hear us out before you make any snap decisions —"

"Not for sale!" I sang out, favoring them with a brilliant smile. I gunned the Gator's engine and Rich Hannity stepped back just as I took off, showering him in the dust storm I had been happily imagining. I did a quick u-turn in the highway and went roaring back down to my own driveway without looking back.

But when I pulled the Gator up at the barn again my heart was pounding and my hands were shaking. Colleen hadn't been wrong — they really did want this land. They wanted *everything*.

I'd love to think that I wasn't going to be the one to hand it to them. But I'd betrayed too many old promises as it was.

I heard a car coming up the driveway and whipped around, thinking it might be the developers, intent on a second interview. I ought to meet them with a shotgun.

When it turned out to be Colleen's purring sedan, I wondered which scenario would be worse. I kind of wanted to be mean to Roth and Hannity again. That would certainly be more fun than getting Colleen's hard sell again, especially since she'd probably stopped to chat with her buddies in suits before she pulled into the barn lane.

I turned and headed for the tack room. I needed a ride on Ivor if I was going to make it through the rest of this day. Thank goodness he was off stall-rest. I'd be so wrapped up in riding, Colleen wouldn't be able to catch me for a business chat. Good strategy, Grace. Sure to work.

Thirty

Of course, a ride on Ivor wasn't enough to save me. Colleen was willing to wait. She cheerfully followed me back to the house after I had done everything I could think of to wait her out, including cooling out Ivor myself instead of handing him off to Anna. I finally gave up and went home, sweaty and dirty and with my angry client tailing me, silently fuming that I wouldn't go up to the office and let her tick me off the way that she wanted to.

I thought she might stop at the front door, but she didn't. She followed me right in. I sighed and offered her coffee.

Although caffeine was the last thing this crazy person needed in her veins.

She accepted gratefully, and then went off, eyes blazing. "Don't think I don't know what you've been up to!"

"What's that supposed to mean?" I dropped the

professional businesswoman veneer without a thought. I didn't like accusations and insinuations from anyone, boarders and clients or not.

Colleen sneered. "Act all innocent! You've been giving my horse extra work. The only thing I don't understand is, why haven't you been charging me for it? You're terrible at money, Grace, or you'd be living in a nicer place than this. You could be fleecing us all and it wouldn't even matter — we've got the cash, you know! I gladly pay you for your services and so does every other boarder here! But look around —" She flung her arms around the room, at my tiny dark living room, at the splintering hardwood floors, at the faded racehorse throw on the broken-down sofa, at the home I loved just as it was. "You're living in a shack out here in the middle of paradise. Million-dollar condos and golf courses and resorts and you're squatting here like some kind of gypsy —"

"That's *enough*. Why don't you just get out of here, Colleen? Why don't you go board somewhere else, if you have such a problem with me? Or is the problem that you don't want to be in horses anymore? Maybe you can't afford me, huh?"

"You're a fool," Colleen spat, but her face flushed red, and I knew my arrow had met its mark. Still, she persisted in her argument. "You're turning down a tremendous opportunity for everyone here."

"How is selling off the last bit of land in the county helping anyone?" I shook my head, dazed by her logic. "If a golf course is right up against the farm, there's going to be guys out there drinking all day. There's going to be loud equipment when they're building it, and mowers and all sorts of noise when they're doing maintenance. There's going to be pesticides when they try to keep the grass that unnatural shade of green. And the kids are going to lose any sense of what Florida used to look like, and that's probably what I'm most against. Come on, Colleen — you can't see that only having a hundred lousy acres of scrubland left is some kind of crime against the planet? Against the place where you're raising your children?"

Colleen didn't rush for the door, or for my throat, as I thought she might have. She just stood in the middle of my living room, fists on her hips like a mad Peter Pan, staring at me with a face that was half amused and half outraged. "Those hundred acres that no one ever sees? The hundred acres you scared us off of and that you're out riding on in the dead of night like a criminal? Those are the hundred acres you are preserving for my precious children? They're not even *allowed* on it!"

"Well, not yet..." I back-pedaled, hard. She had me there. "No one is ready to go out of the arena yet. But give them time..."

"And what about *me?* You can ride my horse out there, but *I* can't. When are you going to give me the green-light to ride outside of the arena, instead of treating me like a trained monkey that's only good to sit on my horse and look pretty?"

Whoops. Suddenly I was on the defense. "Colleen, I never meant you weren't a good enough rider," I said cautiously, searching for the right words. "I meant that you and Bailey were in different places training-wise, and I didn't want a green horse and a green rider going out together and getting hurt." I paused, considered, and then forged ahead more confidently. "And Colleen, you *did* get hurt. Everything I have done has been a considered reaction plan to the incidents that we had in October. Between you and Gayle both taking falls out there, I decided it would be best to wait until the show season was over and then work on trail-riding safety. And if you'd have asked, I would have told you so."

Colleen's face fell just a bit, as if she'd been counting on me telling her my entire evil plan to keep her and the others as my horse show puppets forever, like some sort of villain in a comic book, spieling off their entire backstory just before the hero steps in and makes an end of it all. But she couldn't argue with facts: she *had* fallen off out there, and she had been the one and only boarder to get hurt, as well.

Then she shook her head. "It doesn't matter. You had no business training my horse without my knowledge. You had no right to take him out there and risk him like that."

She was right, but, I reminded myself, I'd done it to settle her horse and make him more safe for *her* to ride. I was her trainer and that was my job. I softened my tone. "Colleen, you're talking in circles. First you want to ride on the trail, then I'm risking him by doing it. And we have a training contract that says I give your horse the schooling that I believe he needs. I don't have to run every little training exercise past you before I try it."

"Maybe not, but you do have to schedule the ride and make sure I'm okay with it!"

She might have a point there. The extra rides were on pretty shaky legal ground. "Extra rides that I didn't charge you for are generally considered a bonus," I said, defending myself anyway. What else could I do? "*Most* people just say thank you. Why don't you sit down and play nice? We'll have some coffee and sort this whole thing out."

Colleen sighed and flopped down on the couch. The

sagging springs groaned in reproach. "You should consider a new couch," she said, shifting her weight uncomfortably.

"I don't have many guests over," I replied. "By choice," I added, before she could make a comment about my lack of social skills, and escaped into the little kitchen, leaving her to continue her judging of my shabby little house.

The kitchen would really have set her off, I thought, pulling down the canister of coffee and sliding out the coffeemaker from where it crouched beneath a few hanging mugs. The canister brushed the porcelain rim of the largest mug, a prize from a horse show with a blue jumping horse stenciled on the side, and the mugs tinkled together gently, like a very practical wind-chime. My flip flops stuck to the old brown and white linoleum, perpetually gummy thanks to never-ending humidity and sheer age. The peeling squares could probably be historical landmarks themselves, and the aging refrigerator wasn't much better. It growled away to itself in the corner by the narrow window, rust making crooked trails through its cheeky yellow face.

"Goldenrod," I told the fridge. "You're vintage, not old." It went on murmuring, making fridge noises that I had been nervously translating as death rattles for some years now. Still, it went on keeping things cold, as it had done for decades. It was possibly the most reliable thing I'd ever encountered in my life. The coffeemaker was less so. I glanced at it nervously. I went through one every couple of years, possibly because the outlet I plugged it into was so old and probably gave it constant power surges. This one had been making a few unnerving sounds lately.

I opened the fridge and pulled out the milk, listening to the coffeemaker hiss away. There was just enough room on the counter for the coffeemaker, the milk, and two mugs; I found some stale Oreos in a cabinet and shook them onto a plate, then set it on top of the little stove, which was probably the same one Marjory Kinnan Rawlings had in her rustic cottage where she wrote *Cross Creek*. I felt a kinship with the author now: bad-tempered, hermit tendencies, unwilling to let precious Florida countryside feel the developer's boot, living in a rattle-trap old cottage that had seen better days. All I needed now was to adopt a fawn.

"Because I need more animals," I muttered, and took the Oreos and the milk out to the living room, where Colleen was glowering at the stack of horse magazines on the tack trunk in front of her. I swept them aside and put the snacks down in their place. "Do you like sugar?"

"Do you have Splenda?" she asked.

Predictable, I thought. "Nope. I drink mine black."

"I have some in my purse," she sniffed, and went to rummaging in her Louis Vuitton.

More cookies for me, I thought, and went back into the kitchen to murmur encouraging things to the coffeemaker.

The coffeemaker lived to fight another day, and the caffeinated pool of darkness in my show-jumping prize was all I needed to work through the rest of the negotiations with Colleen. Well, the couple of stale Oreos helped. I preferred them soft and squishy, anyway. I was gross like that.

"So what you're planning on doing," Colleen said after a few minutes of contemplative, sipping silence, "is teaching everyone to ride out on the trails after WEF ends?"

"Everyone who wants it," I amended. "Some people are never going to do it. Trail-riding isn't for everyone. There's always an element of danger — horses spook, and they are excited out there and more likely to do something silly. Sometimes just the way they act when they're having a good time is enough to scare a rider who isn't used to it, or is a little timid." I paused. "I think it will be good for the kids, too," I added, although my stomach churned a little at the thought of white ponies on trails, white ponies running away, white ponies and dangling reins — I swallowed and forced my thoughts back on track. "They'll be more well-rounded horsemen for it. And they'll have fun."

Colleen nodded. "I liked it," she admitted. "Well — I *was* scared. But I liked it."

"So you agree it's worth keeping."

She shifted uncomfortably, as if she wanted to agree but something still stood in the way. "I can see its value. But I'm not convinced it's the best use of the land. I think this is all coming too late. Grace, you have to admit, this farm can't be here forever."

"What?" I put down my coffee mug with a sharp clink on the wooden trunk. "Now you're after the entire property?"

"No, no, it's not me. But it's going to happen. Your taxes are going to keep going up. The neighborhood is going to get more and more built up." Colleen shrugged. "Don't get me wrong — I'm happy you're here, and that I don't have to drive an hour to see my horse. But eventually... *you're* the dinosaur here. This won't last, even if you're diversifying. Ponies and everything... it's a nice idea. It's just not going to win against a new resort."

"You're wrong," I said shortly. "For one thing, every dollar that my taxes go up is a dollar I'm charging new boarders. And the more fancy houses get built around me, the more boarders and students I get. People just like you, who don't want to drive an extra hour."

"And the tourists? There are more hotels than houses being built around here."

"Trail rides," I answered stoutly, and even as I said it I *knew* that it was the answer. I'd throw all of my reservations out the window and make it happen. Diversification, with a vengeance! I'd buy Rodney's nags to do the nose-to-tail thing, and hire a trail guide — or just make Kennedy do it. "Real Florida. Eco-rides. Get out of the theme parks and into the country, just steps from your hotel. The brochures write themselves."

Colleen sipped her coffee. Buying time, I thought with satisfaction. "That might work," she allowed after a moment. "If you really think you can do it."

"Of course I can! It's the simplest thing in the world. A few more horses, an update on my insurance plan, a few calls to concierge desks around the neighborhood... It's done." It really was that simple, I thought. How had I not thought of this before? All of this time laboring over adult amateurs, and now I had little kids who couldn't be convinced *not* to ride... add in a little tourist trade and my accountant was going to give me a kiss on the lips. I considered Derrick's fishy round lips and revised that to a hug. If he tried to kiss me I'd probably punch him before I even realized what I was doing.

Colleen set down her mug. "Of course, the boarders won't like the trail rides." The smugness had returned to her tone, and I had the uneasy feeling that I was being threatened.

"Why would the boarders care? We're talking about a few small groups a week... probably in the middle of the day... no one would even be here but myself and the grooms."

She shrugged eloquently. "I certainly wouldn't want to be a boarder at a trail riding barn. It makes us sound like some sort of tourist attraction. And who knows how far it will go? What about when a minivan full of tourists comes in off the highway because they heard you have trail rides? They'll be running up and down the aisles, feeding the horses candy, spooking horses in the arenas... this place will be like some sort of cheap amusement park —"

"Well, it would hardly be cheap," I chuckled, with an attempt at humor that fell completely flat. "Nothing here could ever be *that*."

Colleen gave me a look that said *nice try, but no.*

I sighed. "Colleen, look, I understand your fears but you have to believe that it's completely unvalidated. There's no chance I would allow my farm to be anything like a... a tourist trap. We are talking about corporate groups coming on group trail rides. Professionals here for conferences and training. Hardly a rowdy group.

She laughed outright. "Oh Grace, I can tell you've never been to a corporate training. You poor, sweet, country girl." She got up, still chuckling, and picked up her bag. "You've misjudged everything very, very seriously. No one is going to stand for this idea, and it's not going to save the barn. You should get out while you can, Grace. I'm telling you this for your own good... it's all going down whether you like it or not.

I cocked my head. "I don't understand why you want me to give in. I'm doing this for all of us — your daughter included."

She shook her head, the blunt fringes of her

immaculate blonde hair brushing her shoulders. It reminded me of a show-jumper's tail, banged perfectly straight. "I see your point, Grace." Then she sighed, and her face turned regretful. "I just hope it isn't too late."

"What's that supposed to mean?" It all sounded very melodramatic... as if she had set something sinister in motion which she had neglected to tell me.

"We're just dealing with very determined people," Colleen said, shrugging. "Hannity is used to getting his own way in this county. No one ever thought the Dale family would sell their ranch, either, but The Preserve at Sunset Pointe is selling out, and they haven't even cleared all the lots yet."

"Willy Dale was eighty-seven years old," I reminded her. If she'd ever even known who he was or how old he was. I'd known Willy, of course. Back in the day all of us farmers had known each other, whether we had Angus cattle or Hanoverian horses. "His kids had no interest in ranching. That was a loss, but it had nothing to do with taxes or a developer who doesn't like to be disappointed. You make it sound like the mob was twisting his arm behind his back or something."

Colleen just shrugged again. "You'd know better than me, I guess. I'll tell Tom. I just wanted you to understand... they're still going to be knocking on your door."

I nodded and got up to see her out. We appeared to be on friendly terms again... it was the least I could do as a hostess. "I appreciate the head's up," I said, and I meant it. "See you for your lesson tomorrow?"

"Yes." Colleen started out, then paused in the doorway. The hot sun glared on the white porch steps, and picked out the highlights in her perfect hair. "I understand you thought you were doing the right thing for Bailey, too. So, thanks. It obviously helped him."

"I do it all for you guys," I blurted, suddenly feeling the springing of a well of affection I had thought was nearly tapped out. "I wouldn't let anything happen to any of you, not for the world. You guys and your horses are my *students*. I care about you. That's why I'm in this business, you know — to make partnerships possible, and help them bloom."

I remembered this with a start, as if the notion had slipped from my mind over the years. That *was* my mission, that *was* why I was a horse trainer. It wasn't to make money, it was because nothing felt better than being a partner with a horse — and I wanted to share that feeling with as many horses and humans as I possibly could.

It was the mission statement I hadn't been able to put into words all these years. It was the mission statement I had forgotten about in the grind of making enough money to pay the bills and keeping people happy enough to spend more and more.

I looked at Colleen, waiting for her to agree, waiting for her to catch on and realize that she was part of something big here, but she just shook her head sadly and walked away. As she went down the path, she pulled out her phone and started texting madly.

Thirty-one

I'd made up my mind for sure this time, and I had the confrontation with Colleen to thank for it. The trail horses arrived on Tuesday afternoon, just as Kennedy was busy getting dumped off Magic in the jumping arena. I glanced out at her from the barn door, waited until she was getting up and dusting the sand from her breeches, and then ran out to meet the trailer in the parking lot.

Rodney's trailer was an ancient stock trailer that had once been painted barn-red but was now hued a more rusty tone. The six trail horses glared out at me through the steel slats, their eyes rolling and their nostrils flaring at the indignity of being trailered away from their life-long home. They were used to another lifestyle, I thought with a pang of guilt. While Rodney's personal horses would continue their idyllic pasture existence with occasional trail rides for excitement, these guys would have to get used to living the show barn life. A twelve-by-twelve stall, limited turn-out, and, unfortunately, no grass.

They'll be fine. Horses were tough, and with proper care, they'd adjust. They were no different from horses all across the country who were having to learn to live with less land.

Rodney slowly swung down from the cab of his ancient Ford, and a blue-eyed Australian shepherd wriggled down after him. I didn't allow dogs on the property, but Jack was an unwritten exception; the dog was the latest in a succession of shepherds who had been Rodney's best friends and constant shadows over the years. My grandfather would have rolled over in his grave if I'd told Rodney he couldn't let his dog out of the truck. "Sit, Jack," he muttered absently, and the dog plopped down on furry haunches and gazed up at him adoringly. "Brought your horses," he said unnecessarily, hooking a thumb towards the trailer.

"Thank you! I have their stalls all ready. Are you going to keep their halters or anything? I have spares."

Rodney shook his head slowly. "No... no... I won't have no need for 'em," he sighed. "Got more old tack and halters than I know what to do with, if you need any."

I could always use tack, but it wouldn't be the ratty old nylon and Indian leather that Rodney used in his barn. That stuff would be about as out of place in my barn as... well... I blinked at the scruffy horses poking their noses through the rusty trailer slats... as these horses were going to be. "That's all right," I said. "Just the Western saddles will be fine, like we talked about."

A horse kicked the trailer wall and whinnied, and that set them all off. We got busy, Anna and Margaret and Tom and myself, hauling the upset horses off the trailer and dragging them into the barn (or being dragged into the barn), and in about ten minutes the future of Seabreeze Equestrian Center had been installed into the barn and was trampling frantically through the bedding, neighing incessantly and sending reverberations through the entire herd.

"They'll settle right down in a little bit," Rodney assured me, shouting above the din. "You know how horses is."

"I know." Sometimes I thought Rodney still saw me as ten-years-old and chasing my pony after my grandfather's big mare. "We'll be fine."

He looked at the horses as they circled their stalls, and ran a finger along the steel bars of the nearest one. Inside, a roan quarter horse crossed with God knew what — maybe a Belgian, with those feathery fetlocks — was carrying on like the end of the world was nigh, whinnying and pacing and throwing occasional kicks at the wall. Rodney's lined face was uncertain. "Maybe they ought to be outside like they're used to."

"They can go out in a little bit," I assured him. "Just as soon as the afternoon set comes in. And they can stay out all night."

He nodded. "They'll like that." He looked back at the roan horse, who paused for a moment and shoved his narrow nose through the bars. Rodney stroked the whiskered nose. "Alright Rainbow," he told the horse. "Miss Grace will take fine care of you... just like her grandpa'd have done."

One by one he stopped in front of the stalls and placed a hand on his horses' noses. Watching the stooped old horseman, in his ragged jeans and dirty old hat, with his dog at his heels, say goodbye to his horses was almost more than I could take. I bit my lip and put my fist at my chin, forcing myself to hold it together. I couldn't deny the prickling in my eyes and the lump in my throat, though. I was watching the end of an era. The last cowboy was leaving town. I was the only one left.

And I was on thin ice.

Unfortunately, I was the only one who saw the arrival of the trail horses in such a light.

The boarders were a little horrified by their shaggy coats, uneven manes, and uncertain lineage. Even sweet little Gayle was taken aback. "But, what *are* they?" she asked, standing in front of the roan's stall. Rainbow, the roan gelding who had stumped me with his breeding, blew his nostrils hard at her and went back to his constant circling of the stall. The horses' displeasure with their new surroundings had not dissipated during the three hours they had been incarcerated in box stalls.

I shrugged, trying to ignore the fact that I was the one who had instilled such a sense of breed prejudice in my students. "They're just nice trail horses," I said lamely. "Rainbow here, he's probably quarter horse and draft, so he'll be really quiet and easy-going and —"

Rainbow the quiet and easy-going trail horse kicked his stall wall and squealed.

Gayle took a step back. "Are you sure they aren't kind of... wild? Like, he might be a mustang. I heard mustangs can stay wild deep down. He might run off with someone."

"I think we know that any horse can run away with anyone for the right reasons," I reminded her. "Which is precisely why we need trail horses who are nice and calm out in the woods... even if they're not big fans of living indoors like our show horses. They want opposite things. These guys are used to living in a pasture."

Gayle nodded.

We watched Rainbow in silence. His strawberry roan coat was dark with sweat, and the white patch between his rolling eyes somehow combined to make him look even more wild-eyed. I could see how Gayle might equate him with a mustang.

Anna came up behind me and whispered in my ear. "Colleen just drove in."

Oh God. "Thanks. I'm hiding — feel free to do the same," I told her, and clapped Gayle on the shoulder as I scuttled past, heading for the office steps. I wished Rodney had delivered the horses at a different time, like, say, the dead of night, or on a Sunday evening after Colleen had already gone home. It would have been nice to present them as clean-shaven civilized members of society, instead of the drab, hobo citizens of a failed farm down the road. Ever since Colleen had started talking up the farm to her PTA cohorts, her standard for barn appearances had surpassed even my own.

I had my hand on the stair railing when Colleen's shriek reached my ears.

"What in God's name are these?"

I turned around. In front of the trail horses' stalls, Colleen was waving her arms around while Anna quailed. She obviously hadn't run off to hide fast enough. I sighed. Now I had to rescue her. I ambled back down the aisle, trying to fix a professional smile on my face. *Jesus give me strength.* Fortunately, I had several decades of idiot-placating on my resume.

"Colleen," I said pleasantly. "How are you today?"

Colleen rounded on me with a face like a particularly well-made-up demon's. "Not great, Grace! I have two friends bringing their children out tonight to see the barn and these *donkeys* are not exactly what I was describing to them!"

Two friends with children! Exactly what my bank account was crying out for. If not my mental health. Two of *Colleen's* friends sounded downright repellant, but with unfortunately attractive bottomless bank accounts — if they weren't as spendthrift as the girls would have me believe Colleen was. "I'm sure they won't mind these guys. And we'll have them cleaned up in a few days. Clipped, manes pulled, bathed... you won't even recognize them!" Although there would be no mistaking these plain plodders for the expensive designer warmbloods that Colleen would prefer to see in these stalls, they'd still look just fine cleaned up.

At least, I hoped so. Rainbow's strawberry speckles did not exactly cry out to my aesthetics, but the bay gelding next to him, plain and pleasant as chocolate milk, would look nice with a haircut, and so would the nondescript brownish gelding at the end of the row. I had a suspicion that *he'd* turn out to be a darkly handsome liver chestnut once the burnt ends of his coat were clipped off and he had some good feed pumped into his system.

Either way, they were quality horses who were going to make me some easy money, and that was what was important. I couldn't have *any* horses in the barn, fashionable or not, if something didn't give really, really soon.

Colleen was glaring at me with that patented steely glare. "When you said you were going to expand the lesson business, you said you would be bringing in well-bred ponies. This is not what we discussed."

"Colleen," I said patiently, imagining her head exploding into a million particles, "these aren't the lesson horses. These are the *trail* horses."

If her head didn't explode on the outside, the blank, shocked expression on her face suggested it had on the inside. I had just blown Colleen's mind, and not in a good way.

There was a sound of slamming car doors in the parking lot, and then some children laughing, sneakers pounding on pavement. "Your guests?" I asked.

Colleen blinked and came back to the world. "Yes, that will be them. But we're *not* through here. You made certain commitments to me. I have made promises based upon those commitments. We need to have a conversation to make sure that we're both on the same page. If the barn is staying in business, it will be because of *my* patronage."

I watched her stride away in her elegant new boots, her childish pony-tail flipping from side to side. For all intents and purposes, I supposed, Colleen *was* a child — a teenager, raised with too much money and too much entitlement, so used to getting her own way she had forgotten there had ever been anyone else's way. If she had ever known it at all. She really seemed to think she owned me, and the barn, since I had welcomed her suggestion to bring out new students from the prep school.

"What commitment did you make?" Anna asked softly.

I'd forgotten she was there. "Just to bring in ponies, really," I said. "Which I've done."

"But not for lessons."

I looked down the aisle, where Tom and Margaret were

leading in Wishes and Dream for the night. Outside, Magic whinnied shrilly, annoyed at being the last horse out. "They'll be good for lessons eventually."

"Kennedy fell off Magic a little while ago."

"Well, they haven't been under saddle that long."

Anna looked skeptical, but she subsided.

"Go bring Magic in," I told her, and she scurried off.

Thank God there was always work to distract us from our problems.

Thirty-two

A Saturday in February, with a packed show barn full of wealthy women and expensive horses, brought the first taste of true winter in the air. I was huddled into an old barn coat and feeling like I should have moved to Miami, but the horses were in ecstasy.

There was an icy blast of wind down the barn aisle, and the boarders shrieked with something halfway between shocked horror and laughter. In the wash-stalls, Anna hastily turned off the water and grabbed a fleece cooler from the stack I'd left nearby, throwing it over Wonder's furry little body. The rug was about four times too big for the pony, and after she was done tucking up the loose ends and knotting them together, all that was visible was his white face and ears, peering curiously from a cherry-red bathrobe.

I happened to be walking by and flipped on the heat

lamps above the wash-stalls. Anna jumped and looked up. "I didn't even know those were there!"

"Your first winter here," I observed. "Hopefully your apartment doesn't get so cold that you come sneaking down here to use the heat lamps to stay warm."

"Hopefully!" She grabbed a towel and all but disappeared under the cooler, rubbing down Wonder's sopping wet legs.

"Where did this weather come from?" Kennedy grumbled, leading Dream in from the arena. He was sweaty and hot as well. I grabbed a sponge and a bucket and turned on the warm water. At least the wash-stalls, situated behind the center aisle of stalls, were fairly well protected from the gusting wind.

"It's already February. You can expect a big cold front right about now," I said simply, helping her strip the tack from the tired little pony. Kennedy sure wore out these little monsters. They didn't tear around the paddock when they were turned out anymore — they went out, had a nice dignified roll, and munched at their hay like model citizens. "It will be thirty tonight, fifty tomorrow, and eighty on Monday."

"That's insane." Kennedy piled the pad, saddle, girth, and bridle over her arm and marched them over to an unused saddle rack. "I'm going to have to find my feather comforter."

I just shook my head and went to work sponging off Dream's sweaty spots. He sighed at the touch of the warm sponge on his tired muscles, hanging his head from the cross-ties and fluttering his nostrils. "Good boy," I told him. "You've come a long way in three months."

Anna climbed out from under the red cooler, wet towel

in hand. "They all have," she said, giving Wonder a kiss on the nose. The pony wiggled his upper lip at her. "This one, he's a complete heartthrob. He's going to make some little girl very happy."

"You'll have to ride him sometime," I said absently. "It would be nice for all of them to get used to having different riders from time to time."

"I would love that," Anna breathed. "Don't you want to ride them?"

"I do not." I dipped the sponge in the bucket and scrubbed between Dream's forelegs. I had to bend down to do it, something my back did not love. "I'm not a pony fan, personally."

As soon as I said the words, I knew they weren't true. Of course I was a pony fan. Just because I didn't ride ponies anymore, just because I hadn't made them part of my business before, didn't mean I didn't love ponies deep, deep down. It was just that Sailor had made all other ponies irrelevant. Dream and Wonder and Magic were all turning out lovely (although frankly, Magic had way too high an opinion of himself and I was wondering just how old that little stinker had been when he was gelded) but they weren't Sailor. No horse ever would be. Ivor did make a hell of an effort, when he wasn't being moody and unpredictable. (Yes, that had started up again.)

"Not a pony fan!" Anna stopped what she was doing and stared at me from around the wash-stall wall. "But ponies are *amazing*."

"Oh, Anna, ponies are trouble on four legs and you know it."

"Well..." This fact could not be denied. "But they're still so fun, and cute, and look at how precious —" She pointed at Wonder's little white head emerging from the red cooler, like a character from a Disney film. Fair enough, another fact that couldn't be denied — Wonder was an absolute doll-baby.

"Okay. He's pretty damn precious."

Anna smiled and busied herself taking Wonder out of the cross-ties and down the aisle to his stall. The pony toddled along it his red cape, looking like a cross between a super-hero and Little Red Riding Hood. Dream watched him go, his nostrils fluttering in a silent whinny. "You'll be back in your stall soon too, as soon as I get this sweat rubbed off," I told him, and went back to scrubbing. Dream took the elbow grease without complaint, shifting his weight a little when I leaned in hard enough to throw him off balance. It was amazing, I thought, that a horse could be so small that I could essentially shove him over. Years of massive warmbloods possessing all the flexibility of brick walls had made me forget such tiny wonders existed.

A little while later, Dream had been wrapped in a green cooler of similarly epic proportions to Wonder's, and I went out to the arena to watch Kennedy riding Magic. The smallest and fiercest of the ponies, Magic had a buck on him that took my breath away, and Kennedy's too, judging by the taut, strangled look her face took on when he started protesting her commands. The other ponies were about ready to start over small crossrails, already following her orders for walk, trot, canter, picking up leads, and going over trotting poles. Magic was still mastering the simple art of not being a total jerk.

Kennedy gave him a canter cue, bringing one leg back behind the girth and touching him in his ribcage, and Magic actually squealed aloud and kicked at her leg.

Kennedy kicked harder; so did he. "Stick, Kennedy!" I called, and she looked at me quickly, but didn't listen. Instead, she gave Magic a few hard thumps into the side until his hard trot broke into a canter.

"Oh, no," I said, shaking my head. "Smack him next time, Kennedy!"

"Pony problems?" Colleen slipped onto the mounting block next to me, and I made a mental note to order another bench for alongside the arena. I wiggled over to one side, giving her room to slide at least one entire butt cheek onto the plastic surface — well, two, Colleen was enviably slim — and forced a smile, though she was the last person I felt like talking to right now. Miss You Should Start A Pony Program. Well, here it was.

"He's a tough character," I admitted, instead of telling her the truth, which was that all ponies had an inherently evil streak. "But he's going to make a really nice ride once he realizes that we aren't really asking for much. He'll have a little extra panache in the ring, and judges pick up on that. I don't think he'll make a lesson pony, though. He's a one-girl horse, I think."

"Oh really." Colleen watched him canter roughly around the arena, cutting off corners right and left. He had less bend than a tank. "Maddy likes him," she went on. "I was thinking of buying him for her once Kennedy has him ready to go."

I looked at Colleen, startled, and she gave me a sidelong smile. "Unless you think we should look elsewhere?"

I didn't, of course, but I thought they should at least wait until Maddy, like, knew how to ride. She was still learning to post the trot, and her two-point canter was wobbly enough to put my heart into my throat whenever I caught sight of it, although Kennedy thought it was perfectly fine. I deferred to Kennedy with the kid's lesson program, which was expanding every week, but I seriously hoped she hadn't been talking to Colleen about buying a pony. None of us were ready — not the ponies, not the kids — for any kind of buying or leasing to go on yet.

I cleared my throat. "I think Magic would work fine for her... down the road. But obviously he's not ready for a kid yet, and definitely not a kid who is still learning."

"I'm tired of seeing Maddy on that old Douglas, though," Colleen sighed. "I'd like to see her on a pony, one I know she can show."

Maddy was still months and months away from showing. They *all* were. What was going on here? Horse show moms, heaven help us all! I remembered when I had been about to throw out Kennedy for trail riding. Those seemed like kinder, simpler times. "If you buy a pony suitable for her now, it won't be a good match for her later, when she is ready to compete. Then you'll have all that trauma of selling a pony to deal with. And believe me, you want to put that off as long as possible."

To my relief, Colleen nodded. "I understand that. But let's not put it off too long, okay? Before you do anything else with that pony, please let me know." She got up. "I'm going to tack up Bailey for our lesson. Will we ride in here?"

I had a course set up in the outdoor arena, to give Kennedy some breathing room with the mad pony, but the way the wind was gusting and the dark clouds were rolling in, I figured we'd be better off under cover. "Yeah," I said. "I'll let Kennedy know."

In the center of the ring, Kennedy pulled up the pony, who shook his little head furiously at the hold on his mouth. I marched over to her wearily, and she looked at me just before Magic jumped forward. Caught off guard, she was nearly dumped right out of the saddle. I stood still and let her wrestle the little monster back under control.

"Everything okay?" I asked eventually.

"Oh yes," she panted, wiggling the full-cheek snaffle in Magic's mouth. He'd long-since proven he couldn't have a nice plain eggbutt, and he was about two more incidents away from a twisted-wire, as far as I was concerned. Naturally, Kennedy didn't agree, and since the ponies were her responsibility, I was remaining silent... for now. "He's really not so bad tonight," she went on. "I think it's just the change in weather."

That was true. With this cold front was rolling through, everyone would be a disaster. The change in weather was almost certainly why Ivor had been practically illustrating his high school dressage skills earlier this afternoon, actually standing up and leaping on his hind legs at one point.

It was a better explanation than the one floating in the back of my mind, that I'd spoiled him with all those gallops out on the trail, and all he wanted now was to get out of the ring. But those days were over, I'd decided. I'd known I was risking injury when I'd taken him out, and I was lucky he'd only missed one show over that sore shoulder. We hadn't been out in the woods since.

We had turned over a new leaf, gotten back on track, were minding our manners.

Which couldn't be said for this hellion pony here. "How far behind the others is he? Seriously."

Kennedy lowered her eyes. "A few weeks," she admitted. "He hasn't managed to get over trotting poles without taking off or bucking." The pony crab-stepped and she kicked him straight again.

"Kennedy, you need to fix the bucking thing," I said seriously. "Or I'm going to have to do it. And I really don't want to."

"I'll fix it," she said.

"You have a stick, use it."

She looked at the riding crop in her right hand. "I don't want to hit a baby."

"He's not a baby. He's a bratty first-grader. Sometimes a first-grader needs a spanking."

"I think he's closer to a teenager."

"Well then you really better give him a couple whacks to grow on, or he's going to be too old for it to make any difference before too much longer."

Kennedy nodded reluctantly.

"Give us a canter," I urged her. "And make sure he goes straight into it. No running, no bucking. Trot, canter. Go."

She bit her lip, thinking, then gathered up the reins and gave Magic a nudge in the ribs. The pony walked off reluctantly, throwing his head up and down. She gave him another nudge, harder this time, and he broke into a choppy trot.

"Too strung-out for a good transition," I called. "Put him together. Give him a shot at getting it right for you."

Kennedy lowered her hands, widened them, gave the pony leg and some room to move forward. He considered the situation, then dropped his head and tucked his nose in, just a little bit. "Good!" I shouted. "Widen your hands a bit more, drop them below the withers. Make it easy for him to figure out where you want his head!"

She listened, widening the gap between her hands until her wrists were even with her knees, hunching over a little for balance in case Magic made a break for it. But he didn't, as I had known he wouldn't. He just wanted to feel comfortable, and he didn't know how to get that feeling by himself. He didn't know how to balance himself with a person up there. I nodded, satisfied with what I was seeing. Maybe he wasn't a pony criminal after all.

There was a gust of wind that rattled the arena, the roof creaking, and Magic startled and flicked his tail, starting to fall out of rhythm. I knew the next time something happened, he'd use it as an excuse to cause a little mayhem. "Next time," I called as the pair drew near, "next time you feel him start to spook, give him the canter cue and a little pop on the butt at the same time. Use that energy to get a good transition. He'll be happy with himself and remember to do it right more often."

She nodded tensely, opening her hands again, asking him to drop his head down in a relaxed frame. The wind picked up, a branch hit the roof, Magic's head and tail went up — and Kennedy gave him a kick and a slap with the whip at the same time.

He shot ahead like a bolt of lightning, Kennedy clinging to the reins like a beginner on a runaway, and I bit back a shout of laughter. "Now make him settle down and canter nicely!" I shouted, and she wrestled him back under control, his strides shortening, his head lowering.

"Hold that for as long as you can. The second he starts to lose it, bring him down to a trot!"

They made it all the way down the long side of the arena before Magic's balance began to wobble and he started to string out, his neck growing longer, his hind legs falling behind him. Kennedy sat down in the saddle and closed her fingers, and he broke into an ungainly, but not unacceptable, trot.

I waited for her to come down to a walk again and then gave them both a round of applause. "That was fantastic. Quit on that note."

Kennedy cut through the center of the ring so she could talk to me without shouting over the wind. "That's the nicest canter I've ever gotten from him," she said, circling the pony around me. "And the best transitions, too."

I nodded sagely. "Spare the rod and spoil the child. He just needed a little extra reminder that he actually needed to listen to you. These ponies were left to their own devices for way too long, right? Well, sometimes they want whispering, and sometimes they want shouting. Now that you've shouted, he'll be listening more closely for the whispers."

Magic tossed his head, as if to remind us he was still trouble. "We know you are, brat," I told him. "But you'll come around." I smiled up at Kennedy, who was looking a very tired version of satisfied. "I think you have a riding lesson in a few minutes."

Thirty-three

Kennedy was pretty worn out, judging by the face she made at me when I reminded her of her afternoon schedule — three riding lessons, one after another, all beginning riders from the posh school where Colleen was living up to her promise of talking up the farm at every PTA meeting. I couldn't imagine what price Colleen would exact from me in the end, but as long as Kennedy kept making the kids smile while they were struggling to learn to post trot or keep their heels down, I wasn't too worried about it. Lesson revenues were up, and the pony prospects didn't eat all that much. It was good groundwork for a new chapter at Seabreeze Equestrian Center. Diversification was in. Kennedy was just going to have to be tired.

And hell, we were all tired. There were no breaks in the show season. The trailer was perpetually loaded — those students who did not have show-specific tack were having to lug their saddles and bridles between the tack room and the rig every few days, reconsidering their decision to only own one saddle every time, mentally rehearsing the arguments they'd use with husbands to buy that second-hand Butet, that new Pessoa they'd had their eye on. Beval catalogs were thumbed into wrinkled messes, and tack vendors at the show-grounds watched benevolently as rider after rider walked through their maze of saddles, all but genuflecting at the gate, so worshipful were their gazes, so gentle their touches. Women who showed horses loved saddles the way women in sitcoms loved shoes. They fantasized about a new saddle as the end of every want and care.

Even a new saddle couldn't save us from the daily grind of driving, showing, returning, training, driving back again. After week two of HITS, we had enough horses in Ocala that I left the repeat offenders, including Ivor, at the show grounds when we drove home for the few dark days. Anna stayed behind to care for them, along with a couple of well-heeled clients who had gone in on a furnished apartment for the duration of the shows.

She watched mournfully as I drove away for the first time, wringing from me a promise that I would bring back Mason to do some low jumpers the next week. I felt so bad about making her stay there alone with seven horses, I gave in without really thinking about it. Then I had to call the office and request another stall — we hadn't reserved anyplace to put Mason. It wouldn't hurt anything but my pocketbook to bring him up for a week, I figured, and it damn sure *did* hurt that pocketbook, but Anna worked hard, and she hadn't bargained on being left alone in Ocala. I winced and let them add the stall to my bill, which was already skyrocketing into a dollar figure most people reserved for purchasing luxury cars, or very fast boats.

Kennedy, Margaret, and Tom stayed behind at the farm. Margaret because she couldn't be forced to a show by the barrel of a shotgun, Tom because he was more useful for heavy lifting than grooming show horses, and Kennedy because the kiddie riding lessons must go on.

She protested, weakly, when I announced she was not coming.

"I haven't been to a big show in years! And never one like HITS!"

"You can come when you have students ready to show," I said mercilessly, overseeing Tom and Anna as they loaded tack trunks into the rig's tack room.

"I should go along first so that I know what I'm getting them into," she said wheedlingly.

"I'll fill you in on everything you need to know."

Kennedy pouted. I ignored her. We had all been the junior trainer at some point in life. You worked with what you were given, and if you didn't like it, you kept climbing until you had what you wanted.

You didn't give up midway, as Kennedy had done, without the risk of starting over at the bottom. I didn't mind teaching her a few life lessons, even if she was helping me out tremendously with the children. That would teach her to leave the fold and get a fancy office job, that would teach her to give up showing and goof around on the trails while the rest of us toiled in the arena.

These were my less charitable thoughts, the ones I couldn't help but think when I was up to my eyeballs in show prep and riding lessons and anxious students asking ridiculous questions at every turn.

In other moods I was more generous. "If you have no lessons on Saturday afternoon, drive up and see the grand prix," I offered one morning as I was throwing things into a bag, rummaging through my office for any last-minute paperwork I might need before a weekend at the show.

Kennedy looked up from the lesson planner she'd started leaving in my office, by the phone. She was busy enough now to have an office hour once a day, coming in before she rode Sailor and the ponies so she could return calls, check lesson plans, and sort out who was going to ride what. We were running dangerously low on school horses that were suitable for the children's program. The youngest, at age five, was barely tall enough to get her legs around Douglas — they seemed to stick out comically, like a stick figure on a cartoon horse. The oldest, at thirteen, was tall enough but not quite advanced enough for Marigold, a Dutch Warmblood mare crossed with something bad-tempered and long-eared. She wasn't quite a mule, but she wasn't far off, her old owner had told me as I'd stood next to her paddock, gazing at her in quiet disbelief. I'd bought her for a school horse because she was cheap and talented, but I'd never be able to sell her a show horse — she was just too odd-looking.

Plenty of women in the barn had gotten their starts on Marigold, who had more than earned her keep, but Kennedy was sighing that Julia, one of the new kids, was constantly in danger of being run away with by the hard-hearted mare. So I'd promised that if Ivor could bring home big money, I'd buy a quiet, sensible large pony for the taller kids to learn on and show in short stirrup classes when the time came.

Those sorts of ponies didn't come cheap, which meant

I was putting off that purchase as long as possible. The lesson money was coming in, but the boarders were still trickling out. Tourists were beginning to outnumber residents in the grocery store down the highway. That was where the trail business was coming in to save the day, I kept reminding myself every time I looked at the dwindling barn roster. As soon as the show season was over, we'd work on Plan B.

"I have lessons all Saturday afternoon," Kennedy said now, looking at her planner. "Julia, Michael, Georgina."

"Michael," I observed. "A boy at last! Hang onto him. He'll be valuable down the road. How old?" Why were so many top riders and trainers men? Proportionally it made no sense. I'd take the chance that Michael had a decent shot at catapulting into stardom, based solely upon his sex. Statistics were on his side.

"Ten," Kennedy confirmed. "So I can put him on Douglas. I still have Julia, though…"

"She rides first, right? Put her on Douglas too. He needs to get a little condition on. Maybe he'll even have a little energy." This was patently impossible — Douglas hadn't had any energy in five years, and he wasn't impressed by his return from retirement.

"I can't do that. Douglas is barely hanging on. He goes around with his head on the ground as it is."

"Then lunge the crap out of Marigold. Go ride her now."

"I have to ride the ponies. If Anna were here…"

Anna was in Ocala. "It's just you."

"Can *you* ride her?"

I shook my head. "No way. I have to get up there. I have classes this evening."

"We should have bought a *made* pony," Kennedy sighed. "At least one."

I grabbed my keys and made for the door. "We had a budget. We went with the most ponies for the buck, so we can sell them to the students down the road. It'll pay off in the end. In the meantime we work with what we got. Figure out some easy stuff for Julia and Douglas so he isn't so worn out, figure out how to wear out Marigold, whatever works. I have to go. You're in charge." I paused, hand on the door. "And by in charge, I mean don't do a thing without calling me and checking first."

Kennedy's sigh saw me out the door. Welcome to the club, kid, I thought, thumping down the creaking staircase to the barn aisle. We're all mad here.

I drove like a maniac and arrived in Ocala after three o'clock. The show grounds were hopping, with horses of every shape and make and model cantering and trotting and walking and spooking and grazing and dozing and jumping. Women were everywhere, too, from toddler to senior citizen, and a decent scattering of boys and men as well, their breeches a bit more discreetly loose than the lady's skin-tight versions. Knee-high black boots, garters and jodhpur boots for the little ones. High-collared shirts and sober dark riding jackets adorned every single man, woman, and child preparing to hop on a horse or pony. Everywhere you looked, people demonstrating the look of thousands of dollars dropped for space-age technology in centuries-old camouflage.

I shrugged on my own navy-blue jacket as I was walking towards the barn where our stalls were. The coat was old and beginning to pill on the collar, but it was comfortable and felt lucky after all these years. When I was in the saddle, no one could see the sleeves were fraying at the wrist or the seams were stretching into thin pale almost-nothingness. I'd wear it until it tore off of me going over some mad maxed-out oxer, and someone would take a picture and put it in a magazine: the Veteran Trainer, Still Showing in Her Original Habit. Then I'd mosey on over to one of the fancy vendors and throw down some cash on one of the new sports jackets.

Maybe on Saturday night, after the grand prix.

Anna was waiting with a tacked-up Ivor, walking him up and down the barn aisle to warm up his muscles. Her face was creased with worry when she looked up and saw me. "I thought you weren't going to make it!"

"If I'm any later than this next time, get on him and warm him up," I told her, taking the reins and flinging them over his head. "Girth tight?"

She jumped to tighten the girth while I held Ivor, who snatched at my arm with bared teeth and pinned ears. I responded by tightening his flash noseband so that he couldn't get his mouth open. "Manners," I told him when he ground his teeth in annoyance. "Try them sometime."

"All set," Anna breathed, jumping back, and when I lifted my knee she obediently fitted her palms beneath my shin and gave me a leg-up. No mounting block, no problem — that's what working students are for. "You need me at the warm-up ring?"

"I'm good," I said. "Rub a cloth over my boots, will ya?" I reined back Ivor, who was prancing forward, his blood up and the show-ring in his sights. Anna grabbed a washcloth and dusted off my boots, restoring their dull gleam. She'd covered their scars with boot-black at the end of the last session, before I drove back to the farm.

"Perfect," I announced, loosening the reins, and she stepped back as Ivor bolted down the aisle, his head in the air, snorting through the flash noseband. I wrestled him down to a walk and he shied and spooked his way out to the warm-up ring, which was crowded with other keyed-up horses, athletes with their eyeballs popping out from a combination of good grain and not enough turn-out.

I negotiated our way over to the rail and let him trot on, not worrying too much about his high head or pricked ears. As long as he didn't take off, buck, or crash into someone else, I would accept a certain degree of silliness in the warm-up ring. It was only the second week of competition, after all, and the third time we'd been out in the rings in the afternoon, when all humanity seemed to be either a-horse or a-foot and everyone one of them was shouting something.

A mini motorcycle went howling by, its engine halfway between a squeal and a roar and the worst half of both, and someone shouted those were illegal on the show-grounds and the kid on the motorcycle gave the shouting person the finger and then a whole lot of people started yelling, and Ivor's breath came fast and hard and his heart was pounding between my legs, thudding against my perfectly polished boots. I dropped my hands to his withers and put my calves firmly against his sides, to tell him I was there and he was safe and that calm-forward-straight was his only option, and he ducked his head a little, tucking his nose politely, before trotting on like a gentleman, only his swiveling ears and his snorting breath giving away that he was watching the world very carefully.

Stallions missed very little, and Ivor was no exception,

but we had been together long enough to understand we could take care of one another. I let him trot if that was what made him happy, just making sure he had a clear path, maneuvering through the other horses on their own private trajectories, and when his breath had eased up and his ears were starting to slide back towards me, I asked him for a big bouncing canter.

God, what a pleasure he was. It was a wonder I ever rode any other horse, when I had a beast like this to carry me around the world. "We ought to run away together," I told his flicking ears. "Give up these show barn blues and just be two comrades on the road to ruin."

A loudspeaker crackled, announcing our class was beginning in five minutes. I resolved to focus. We weren't running away today. There was money on the line.

Thirty-four

At the end of April, the whirl of showing came to an abrupt end, and all of the plans we had been quietly incubating were suddenly ready to hatch. It was time to start thinking about booking our first trail ride, an idea which set my nerves on edge.

Weekday mornings were quiet, which gave us a change to get in some planning sessions and make sure our horses, tack, and trails were ready for action. I had Kennedy taking out all the trail horses, and this morning Kennedy had taken out Rainbow for a solo ride, armed with a two-way radio we'd bought especially for this venture. The radios had cost a fortune, but promised to keep us in touch even if cell phone service failed out in the scrub, something I was not willing to even consider.

"Imagine, there was a time when we just rode out in the woods and whatever happened was part of the adventure," she teased when I had finished warning her about losing one of the priceless radios.

I shot her a quelling glare. I couldn't share her sense of fun and casual lack of concern over the thousand very bad things that could happen to a horse and rider in the woods. Especially with greenies who might never have been on a horse before! What would happen if something spooked one of these so-called bomb-proof horses... no horse could be *totally* fearless... what if the whole lot of them decided to turn tail and run for the barn, leaving their clueless riders piled on the sand behind them, reins dangling as they galloped headlong along the trail... I swallowed, trying to get my lunch back where it belonged, and sought a more rational state of mind. But really, this whole venture was taking its toll on my nerves. My nights were haunted by runaway ponies, ghostly white in the moonlight, their frantic whinnies hideously familiar. If I'd been seeking the spirit of lost Sailor, sending out these trail rides was the only seance I had ever needed. I couldn't shake the feeling the phantasms left with me even in the hot yellow sunlight of spring.

I reflected that trying to save the farm by diving headfirst into the discipline which had broken my heart and cost me my pony and essentially scarred me forever might not have been the best idea I'd ever had.

Colleen wasn't helping the matter. She was determined to set the barn against the trail riding venture. I'd heard her strident voice echoing through the arena and heard her furtive whispers around every corner of the barn. In tack rooms and wash-racks and box stalls, Colleen was trying to raise up the boarders against me. I heard all about the diabolical plans I was supposedly setting into motion. I was bringing in cheap horses and cowboy saddles, I was inviting in families of tourists and half-drunk conventioneers, I was destroying the beautiful equestrian haven I had set up here and had been charging them an arm and a leg for every month for the past ten years. I was going after the cheap buck, selling pony rides like a carney, instead of investing in the community's children as I had promised her I would.

"What children?" I wanted to scream, if I hadn't been pretending I couldn't hear her nonsense. There were hardly any children around here, not compared to what she had built up to me. Kennedy was busy, but no new students were popping up these days. We had tapped out the scarce resources of the neighborhood. The fact was, around here, there was no community, and there were hardly any children. What we had were ever-more-distant subdivisions, and SUVs dropping off children and picking them up again at the prep school, whisking them away to their more collegiate pursuits of tennis and chess and computer programming. The resort villas which had sprung up around the farm were not a community; they were home only to a fancy series of transients, and their empty streets rarely showed signs of life besides a few sunburnt golfers driving their golf carts out to the custom-designed hillsides.

I *wished* I could find local kids with half the resiliency and dedication of those golfers, out swatting at balls under the merciless sun. I *wished* I could find kids just out riding their bikes who were drawn to the siren song of a stable next door. But even in the subdivisions where actual year-round residents lived, the cul-de-sacs stayed empty and the driveways stayed bare. Being a kid in Florida had somehow become an entirely indoor affair, as far as I could tell.

If I was fair, I had to admit that Colleen hadn't broken

her promise to use the PTA to drum up business for the farm. The handful of child-friendly school horses were busy, true, but thank goodness I hadn't lived up to my promise to buy new school ponies. Even though we'd spent the school money on sales ponies, I questioned whether they'd find a market here, or if they'd just end up in another barn further up the road, with more space and more kids to fight over them.

The lesson business was chugging along, but it wasn't enough. If I had decided to do things entirely Colleen's way, I would be out of options and feeling the pinch worse than ever.

At least with the trail business, I had a chance. Rodney had been true to his word, and put several resort concierges in touch with me. There would be bookings coming in the future... once I decided I was ready for them.

Whenever that might be...

I stood in the barn aisle and gazed out towards the county highway. Between me and the road, the grove of turkey oaks shivered in the breeze, their dry leaves rattling together like castanets. It was too dry. It hadn't rained since, what, March? While we were showing in Ocala, the dry weather had been a delight. Now here it was, almost May, and the grass was brown, the flowers were wilting, and all across Florida, the pine savannas and scrub were becoming a tinderbox waiting for a spark.

Anna trotted by on the new gelding she was trying out, a rangy knob-kneed Thoroughbred who had obtained local fame at his former barn after his propensity for jumping out of things was discovered — jumping out of paddocks, jumping out of pens, jumping out of his stall. He could be bought for a song if we could manage to keep him off the highway. The little-used round pen next to the paddocks had seven-foot walls, which even the flying wonder couldn't leap over, and as long as we had an extra stall guard over the top half of his stall at shows, he'd be easy enough to keep inside, so I told Anna to bring him down on a trial. Cheap athleticism was nothing to sneeze at, especially when you were a working student and couldn't afford to be choosy about your horse's looks or bad habits.

She smiled and waved as they went jogging past, leaving a choking cloud of dust in their wake. The sand washed over me and made me sneeze. The arena was so dry that every gust of wind spread a layer of sand over the neighboring grass and the entrance to the barn. I was afraid to put sprinklers on it; I'd had the well run dry in droughts before, and if I had to run a hose from the city water at the house, I'd go bankrupt in a matter of days just from watering the horses. It had been a sad day, I reflected, when they ran the sewer lines out here and introduced the concept of a water bill.

I started back inside, brushing off the sand that was settling atop my shoulders, when a flash of sunlight on metal caught my eye. I turned back, looking at the driveway. It was too early for clients.

A black car was silently sailing up the driveway.

I mentally ran through my appointment book, open on my desk in the office, wondering if a prospective boarder or student had made plans to come out today. But no, we hadn't had anyone new in weeks.

I squinted. The car came gliding into the parking area, a black Mercedes with a company logo on the side that was suddenly all too familiar.

Hannity and Roth.

I clenched my hands into fists and marched up the creaking stairs to my office. If they were here to try and strong-arm me, they'd find a professional behind a desk, ready to do battle, not a tired woman surrounded by a barnful of mouths that were becoming increasingly difficult to feed.

Tom stuck his head through the doorway, pale eyes darting about until he saw me. I wasn't easily found; I was kneeling behind the desk, frantically stuffing overdue bills, lesson calendars, and show fliers into desk drawers. It hadn't occurred to me until I'd flung open the door, but my office was currently the least professional place on the farm, not excluding the manure pile.

Tom's white eyebrows met Tom's white hair. "Grace?" he whispered. "There's a man here to see you. I told him to wait downstairs while I saw if you were free."

"Well, thank God for that." I got up from behind the desk with a little difficulty.

"It's one of them in suits from the place next door," he went on worriedly. "The ones that want to buy the farm."

I surveyed the office. Far from clean — there was dust everywhere, hay on the floor, and a pervasive odor of horse — but at least it was in some sort of order now. And there was a tidy desk to put between me and the enemy. I nodded at Tom. "Send him on up."

Tom emitted a frightened squeak, and I realized that he didn't think he'd have a future here once the man in the suit had left.

No one believed I could keep the farm going, but me.

Well, maybe Kennedy.

I felt the radio clipped to the waistband of my breeches,

and thought just for a moment of locking the door, calling Kennedy back, and not letting the developer come in until I had an ally by my side. Almost — but no. This was my fight to win. It was my promise to protect.

I'd told my grandpa I would hold this land dear, and I wasn't going to go back on that vow.

There were footsteps on the groaning stairs outside. I pulled my hair loose from its ponytail and shook the short waves out. This was no time to look like a kid obsessed with ponies.

Two sharp knocks on the door, and I shouted "Come in!"

The door opened. It was Roth, the bald one with the red face. He stretched his face into a false smile even while he was dabbing at his sweaty forehead with a white handkerchief. *City boy*, I thought viciously. *Northerner.*

"Have a seat," I said pleasantly, ignoring his offer of a hand to shake. I couldn't fathom touching that clammy white paw.

He withdrew his hand and settled down into the wobbly guest chair. "Ms Carter," he said warmly. "How nice to see you again."

I raised my eyebrows. Really, that was taking things too far. "What do you want?" I asked pointedly.

Roth seemed pleased that I wasn't going to play some sort of politeness game after all. He cleared his throat and made sure his smooth smile was pasted into place. "Ms Carter," he began in oily tones, "I'm here today to formally discuss the future of your — uh — property here."

"You mean my *farm?*" I asked, as if there might be some mistake about the location. "By property, you mean the barn where we're sitting, the arenas where horses are being worked outside, and the house my grandfather built, is that right? I'd just like to get that straight. We're talking about my successful working farm and historic house."

The sarcasm was lost on Roth. "That's right," he agreed, undeterred. "And the wooded property to the east. We would like to make you a generous offer, Ms Carter. For all of it."

Well, Colleen had said they would come with their checkbook out. It had just taken them a little longer than I had expected. They had waited until they knew I was hurting. Who had told them things were tight and business was down?

Who indeed?

I pushed the uncomfortable thought away and managed a smirk for Roth's benefit. "Oh well, you don't want much, do you? Only all of it."

He didn't even have the grace to look ashamed. "We are prepared to make the sale entirely in your favor," he went on. "With plenty of time for you to make arrangements to move the business. Your neighbors have moved up to north Florida — why wouldn't you? You could buy three, four times as much land as you have now. Or you could retire. Maybe a little place just for you up near Ocala? Have you considered the possibilities?"

I felt my face flush red. "Retire? How old you think I am?" I knew the sun and outdoor living aged a person, but Jesus Christ! Retirement? This jerk had some nerve. Suddenly I didn't feel capable of listening to another second of his nonsense. I had no stomach for this game of polite-and-nasty — I just wanted this guy to get out of my office and never come back. I leaned forward, narrowing my eyes until Roth moved back in his chair. "Mr. Roth," I intoned icily, "This property will never be for sale so long as I'm living. I don't care if I go out of business and can't afford to keep my own lights on, I will never see your bulldozers on my grandfather's land. You *can't* have everything. You *won't* destroy every last inch of this part of Florida. What makes you think you can show up, rip the heart and soul out of every good, beautiful, unique place, slap some stucco buildings on a fake hill, and call it Tuscany? You'll never get this land, and if I have anything to say about it, you'll never have anyone else's land, either."

I didn't have anything to say about it; there wasn't anyone else's land left; he already had it all, and I was nobody in the face of the great Florida real estate development machine. But still, the vitriol in my soft voice was enough to deflate the developer. Roth's stitched-on smile disappeared and a deep vertical crease between his eyes appeared in its stead. He was furious, I thought with a small thrill. I'd really pissed him off this time. I wondered what was next. Would he storm out, uttering threats, or remain calm and continue to try and reason with me?

It turned out to be a little bit of both. Roth got up and pushed the chair out of his way. "They told me you'd say something like that," he said in a voice flat with suppressed feelings. "I should have believed them, but I thought someone who had built up such an impressive business must have the sense to see when a market has changed and it's time to move on. This land has not been countryside for a long time, Ms Carter. You can't save something that's already gone. All you're doing now is wasting everyone's time. Including your own." He was at the door, his hand on the knob, when he turned to cast his final blow.

"I can convince the state that our road is absolutely

necessary for the public good. A connector between two major county roads that could cut traffic and drive-times for the area and promote growth. We can take the land that way. I'll lose residential lots and you'll lose a fortune, but if that's the way you want it..."

I picked up a paperweight, a Connemara pony of cut and polished green marble, and I flung it at him. Roth darted out and the pony hit the storm door, cracking the glass. His eyes glittered at me from outside before he turned and disappeared, and I knew I had twice the enemy I'd had before.

I slumped down in my chair and put my head in my hands, trying to hold back the terrible feeling that I was going to cry like a teenager. My sore throat and my aching ears were just a backdrop though, to the real agony — the piercing pain of knowing, beyond a doubt, that I was going to lose.

Thirty-five

Hope had been asking for a change of pace for a few days. The long winter's constant round of horse shows had gotten to him, and after the second time he refused an easy fence in the jumping arena, I decided to go easy on him. The timing was good for me, after the interview with Roth. I wanted nothing more than to disappear. Hope gave me the perfect excuse.

"He's still a baby," I explained to Anna, who was trying to pick up any hints she could to use on her new horse. "And he's about to have a meltdown, so it's my job to make sure that doesn't happen. He's getting a vacation and some trail rides to loosen him up."

What a change, me taking horses on trail rides. My nerves still ate at me out there, my mind still full of visions of white ponies and broken reins, but still… there was no time to dwell on the past, when the future was at risk. We'd spent so much time taking the trail horses out, making sure they were fit and ready for their job, that it was becoming just as familiar to me as the arena.

Anna kissed him on the nose and narrowly avoided losing her own nose when he flung his head impatiently. "I can see," she said, backing away. "Hope, have a nice long ride, okay?"

The farm was quiet today, with Kennedy off looking at a clearance sale for helmets for the trail program. Until the afternoon lessons started up around three thirty, it was just me and the grooms. I could afford to take my time out there.

"Perfect, isn't it?" I asked Hope, getting him tacked up. We'd start with a hack around the indoor. A nice walk on a loose rein, a little trot and canter to keep his brain working, and then the surprise trail ride. A shower, back in his stall for a few flakes of lunch hay — that was exactly what the silly boy wanted. He'd be asking for work again in no time.

I led him to the indoor, listening to the even rhythm of his footfalls on the pavement, and positioned him beside the mounting block. I swung into the saddle, looked through his half-mast ears at the red clay of the arena, shadowed by the roof above, and felt an enormous wave of discontent. Judging by Hope's sagging head and disinterested ears, he was feeling the same way.

Burn-out, I thought. Somehow I had avoided it all these years, but now it was hitting me and my young prospect at the same time. "Hell with it," I said aloud, and Hope's ears swung backwards to listen. "Let's live dangerously." We'd skip the warm-up in the arena. I swung the reins against his neck and shifted my seat, spinning Hope around. He turned on sluggish hooves, but when I rode him right out of the arena and through the grassy area between the barn and the railing, his head came up and his ears pricked, looking at the world around him with new eyes.

"It looks different without a fence around it, doesn't it buddy?" I asked, giving him a sliding pat on the neck without loosening my reins. I was making a major safety gaffe in taking Hope out on the trails alone — he'd already let me know he thought the outside world was a pretty scary place. But now, I thought, now when he was so bored with arena life, now when he had the show horse blues, he might just think any change of pace was a good one. Even a scary one.

"I'm heading out on the trails!" I hollered as I passed Margaret and Tom, driving the Gator back to the barn from the compost pile. "I have my phone on me. Send the posse if I'm not back in two hours."

Margaret just looked at me blankly, no doubt comparing me unfavorably to her previous employer, the competitive trail riding hero who had conquered Cougar Rock a dozen times. Tom waved and nodded and smiled as if I was a celebrity on a passing parade float. I smiled in return and turned my attention back to the trail ahead. They were both so damn weird, which was a huge part of why I loved my staff.

Hope began to prance, huffing and puffing, as we passed between the two palm trees marking the trailhead, and as the clatter of his hooves on asphalt faded to thuds on hard sand, I loosened my fingers and let him slip into an energetic working trot. My hands low and my body slightly ahead of the motion, I rode him like a green baby just starting out under saddle, never trusting where his body would be from one stride to the next. Granted, for a little while he did nothing to earn that trust, weaving from side to side and making little jerking spooks and starts in mid-stride, watching the waving palmetto fronds on either side of the trail as if they were horse-eating panthers.

Once there *had* been panthers out here, I reflected, giving his hot neck a comforting stroke without letting the rein loose. My grandfather used to tell stories about them. He said they screamed like a woman, and newcomers used to think there was some poor lady being murdered in the woods, but it was just a panther meowing. Well, I'd never seen nor heard a panther, and it wasn't likely I ever would. They were shy, and all the construction would have scared any hold-outs from the neighborhood long ago. "Nothing out here now but lizards," I told Hope soothingly, and he snorted at the notion, as if he'd never seen a lizard before.

With his long reaching stride, it wasn't long before we had reached the shell mound, and in its cool shadows I reined him back to a walk, ducking beneath the low-hanging oak tree branches. He pulled at the bit a little, then realized the foliage up here was actually edible and started snatching at the grass and brush that tangled along the trail's edges, his youthful interest in eating anything green overtaking his trepidation about being alone in the scary scary woods.

I peeked through the branches, eager to get to the clearing where I could look out over the scrub. It was a priceless spring day, a warm golden sun blazing down from a cerulean sky. That big blue Florida sky, that got even bigger and bluer in the dry, cloudless months of winter and spring, stretching over the brown-green of the scrub, could transport me back to childhood in an instant, racing out of school at two-forty-five on the dot, hopping onto my bike and skidding my way towards the barn as fast as my legs could pedal, to fit horses into every last minute of daylight before an early sunset sent me home to do my homework by the yellow light of my desk-lamp, a mighty herd of Breyer horses keeping me company.

Hope did not share my enthusiasm, being far more interested in the shreds of greenery he could fit into his mouth along with the bit, but eventually we came out into the sunlight, passing by the broken branch that had fallen down and spooked Maxine all those months ago, and I let him put his head down to tug at the sparse grass while I looked out over my domain.

The waving palmetto fronds, the distant long-leaf pines tall skinny sentinels in a sea of pale green, the white-sand road snaking through the foliage, the empty flatness of the horizon — when I was here I could pretend nothing had ever changed, that this corner of central Florida was still a rural place, where cattle and horses outnumbered humans, and a swimming hole was more common than a swimming pool. There had been a bubbling spring out there once, where we had occasionally ridden the ponies, in those first few years before I became a Serious Show Rider — we had packed lunches for the ride, which took a couple of hours in all, and rode out with our bathing suits under our jeans and t-shirts. The ponies swam, too, and a few rolled. It hadn't been so long ago, really. Change had been slow to come to our little piece of paradise. But when it had come, it had come with a vengeance. That spring was long gone... or was it? It was probably the centerpiece of some McMansion golfing community, if it hadn't dried up when canals had been dredged to drain the cypress swamps.

Still, old Florida was here, on the land I had to hold tight. I looked left and right, across my domain. Mine and old Wilcox's. But no — I remembered — Wilcox had sold out. Moved off to the Nature Coast, given up on the land he'd said he'd never give up on. I remembered when he decided to decamp to the house boat where he'd spent longer and longer vacations. "Too many people here these days," he'd said, and that was ten years ago. He was older than me, an adult when I was still riding ponies — he'd be in his seventies now. He'd had a gator hunting license, and we'd all wanted to go with him in his skiff, out on the big lake up the road, hunting killer lizards. A bunch of bloodthirsty kids. I smiled to think of it, then looked out past the cypress dome in the distance. It had been a place of safety, a shelter for Wilcox-branded cattle on hot days and during chilly rains, a shady spot to rest during long summer rides.

Now it belonged to developers.

My toes curled in my boots. That cypress dome was hundreds of years old. It rose up, smokey and ethereal against the brilliant sky, the green-feathered branches still ghostly with winter's pale gray as they reached spindly fingers towards the midday sun. In another month they would be brilliant green, shimmering with life. The bald eagles who roosted there would have youngsters to teach to hunt and to fly. Were bald eagles even endangered anymore? Could *they* save the cypress? Even if the government stopped the cypress from being destroyed, wouldn't they just clear out the land around the dome, letting the pesticides from the inevitable golf course run into the dark waters and do their dirty work for them?

Hope sidestepped, reaching for another mouthful of

dusty grass, and I turned back quickly to steady him before he slipped on the sandy embankment and sent us both tumbling down the side of the mound. Then I saw it, not to the south and the east where I had been gazing, nor to the west where the farm lay, but back to the north, in the pine savannah.

Smoke.

My heart caught in my chest, surely stopping for one reflexive moment, and my vision swam a little. I shook away the dizziness and the panic and turned around in the saddle, squinting through the half-broken live oak behind me. Through the tangles of kudzu vine and browning oak leaves, I could see it — a smudge of black idly tracing heavenwards. I looked up above the tree and the faintest blur of gray, like a half-formed cloud, was forming in the flawless sky.

"Oh, shit, shit, shit," I told Hope, who picked up his head, grass poking from his lips, and looked back at me, catching the icy fear in my voice. He straightened and turned around so quickly he nearly tumbled right over, and I snatched up the reins quickly, before he could do something stupid and leave me out here in the woods with a wildfire on my hands.

If that's what this was.

Maybe it wasn't, I thought, nudging Hope along to a spot further down the trail where I could see north. Maybe it was a camper. A hobo. The Rainbow People looking for less crowded stomping grounds south of the Ocala National Forest. Anything less threatening than a wildfire in a very, very dry season.

I thought of the rock-hard ground, of Ivor's lameness, tho dry damn winter, when had it rained last? I couldn't remember. Spring had been a succession of sunlit, golden days.

We moved past the last stand of trees, just before the path started to wind down to the palmettos again, and then I could see it through Hope's black-tipped ears: the dark smudge of smoke, rushing much more quickly heavenwards now that I could see it clearly. That was no campfire. That wasn't even the Rainbow People. That was a wildfire, blazing away in the pine savannah to the north.

I turned Hope so fast he stumbled and kicked him into a trot, regardless of the careful riding I usually treated his unspoiled little brain to, and we went skidding and sliding down the sandy path, emerging into the hot sun at the bottom and bolting into a hard gallop for home.

Almost immediately I reined back, hard, Hope half-rearing from the hold on his mouth.

At the bottom of the shell mound, a merry little fire was blazing away, looking for all the world like the site of a summer camp singalong. There should have been children dancing around it, waving marshmallows on the ends of sticks. It was that perfect, that round, that precise.

I heard a rustle and rattle in the underbrush to my right and whipped around, pulling Hope in a prancing circle, knocking my hard hat against the dangling fingers of the oak trees, just as a tiny flame peeked up over the rim of the shell mound, its orange flames licking at the base of the trees that clung to the sandy hillside. And beyond, barely visible through the thick trees, down in the palmettos — a figure running, a metal can glinting in the sunlight as it clanked against the person's legs.

The strip of fire left burning in his wake ran perfectly straight. An alarm bell went off in my head.

I'd been set up.

I shook my head, trying to pin down the rising tide of panic in my chest, and leaned over Hope's neck, peering through the branches as he pranced and sidestepped. "Be still," I hissed. "Stand up!" I had to see —

The silver canister at the running person's side, the spout of flame pouring down into the dry palmettos, the trail of fire rising up behind him.

I saw, I saw.

I pulled Hope around to the left again, facing him towards home, and stuck my heels into his sides. Beside us, the little flame burst up the side of a turkey oak, ringing the lowest branches of the tree in a shining orange halo, and my urging became quite unnecessary. Hope was more than ready to get the hell out of there. Jaw set, hands taut on the reins, I sat back against the saddle's cantle and let him slither and slide down the sandy hillside, wondering just what he'd do when he saw the fire waiting for him at the bottom of the trail.

But Hope was a jumper, and he probably thought his whole life had been leading up to this moment. At last, everything made sense to him! Before we reached the bottom of the trail he was gathering himself up, and I leaned forward and caught up with his motion just as he launched himself over the rising flames. I glanced down as we soared over the fire, which was rapidly evolving from its harmless little campfire origins to a blazing brushfire, and saw that dry tree branches, fallen from some forgotten storm and rattling with dead brown leaves, had been pulled across the trail. We were jumping a fire that had been intentionally set to trap us out here.

I processed this horror in the half-a-breath it took

Hope to clear the flames, and then we were galloping flat-out through the twisty trail just outside of the shell mound, his breath coming hard and fast with every hoofbeat. I leaned with him around the turns, holding him up with my inside leg to help him avoid a stumble, a fall, and then when we hit the straightaway I really let go. Hope went soaring across the palmetto scrub like a racehorse, his hooves drumming on the hard white sand, and I pressed my knuckles into his withers like a gallop girl at the racetrack and hoped like hell he didn't hurt himself as Ivor had done, or worse, that he didn't stumble in his panic and send me flying, to lie and wait for rescue as the wildfire roared after me.

We were nearly home before I had the courage to turn around and look, and when I did, I nearly fell right over his shoulder from the shock. Distant now, the low hump of the shell mound had become a tower of flames, black smoke pumping into the air as the orange inferno devoured the oak trees where we had been gazing at the winter scenery not ten minutes before. The inferno was spreading in a long line north, following the direction that the figure with the metal can had been running, livid fire red-gold against the faded green of the prairie.

It had barely rained in months.

This was going to be a fire for the record books. I realized, with a twist in my gut, I had no idea which way the wind was blowing. If the sea breeze from the Atlantic had anything to say about it, the fire would be knocking on our doorstep in a matter of hours.

Margaret and Tom were standing in the barn aisle, looking out at the smoke rolling into the blue sky. The pine trees towering along the property line stopped them from seeing the flames. When I reined back Hope to walk across the parking lot, they took one look at the sweat and foam rolling off him and came running.

"Is it that close?" Tom asked, clutching at Hope's reins as if he was a racehorse coming in from a hard-fought win. "You had to run?"

"It's at the shell mound," I panted, kicking my feet from the stirrups. I jumped down while Hope was still walking, landing on the balls of my feet to protect my heels and toes from the hard pavement. "We were there enjoying ourselves one minute, and then there was fire boiling up everywhere the next." I pulled the reins over Hope's head and handed them in a big cluster to Tom. "It was set intentionally," I said evenly, meeting his shocked eyes. "And professionally."

"Professionally — what do you mean?"

"You know those cans that firefighters use to set controlled burns?" Wildlife refuges and nature preserves in the scrub and pine savannas were routinely set afire — the habitats had developed with lightning-sparked fires as part of their life cycle. The drought had prevented any burns this winter, though. "He had one of those. And he set it around the shell mound, while we were on it."

"That's attempted murder," Margaret drawled. "You tellin' me someone wants you dead?"

I shook my head. "That seems really extreme." But at the same time, I wondered. How badly did those developers want that land? Or if it wasn't them — an investor?

This *was* Florida, after all. Anything was possible, no matter how macabre or bizarre the crime. A horse trainer fried out in the middle of the wilderness while on a pleasure ride? Not the craziest headline of the week, let alone the day, probably.

"Let's just call the fire department and see what's going on," I said hastily, to change the subject. I'd have plenty of time to worry if some Floridian mobster was trying to kill me once the barn and horses were safe.

"They're on their way," Tom said, leading Hope into the barn and towards the wash-stalls. "We called already."

There was a whine of a siren down the road.

"That'll be them." I turned and headed for the Gator. They'd need the gate opened up if they wanted to get in here and protect the farm.

Thirty-six

We were waiting for a rescue that wasn't going to come.

I sat on the Gator and and watched the fire trucks go past, wailing away, north towards the subdivision sitting beyond the neighboring property. The old Wilcox property. The one that couldn't be turned into million-dollar houses until I sold my land and my rights to a Native American road that had become the only hope my farm had for survival.

I sighed and put my chin on my fist, waiting. Surely there would be a fire truck left for me. Surely they weren't all going to sit up there by the tennis courts and the pool cabanas and the clubhouse, while rich people who had never been in the woods just outside their doorsteps drank iced tea and watched the smoke with a tourist's detached curiosity. Surely not.

Finally, I saw a bright red pick-up truck with red and

white lights heading up the road. Bold lettering informed me that this was the fire chief. I hopped down from the Gator and ran down to the roadside, holding up a hand. The truck slowed and pulled over. A window glided down and a round-faced man in a ball-cap blinked at me. He rubbed at his goatee and regarded me for a moment. "You okay, ma'am?" he asked eventually, as if he couldn't work out if I was crazy or not.

"There's a fire just east of my property here," I explained, trying to keep the angry edge from my voice. "None of the fire trucks have stopped here?"

"That's right, they're heading towards Eagle Preserve to protect the houses now, ma'am."

"What about my farm? I have a barn, I have thirty-some horses, I have a house, I have outbuildings —"

He heard the panic starting to creep into my voice and held up a hand. "You got horses?"

"Yes, yes, I have horses!" I waved a hand at the farm sign, which featured a jumping horse right there on it. Could he not see? "Millions of dollars in horses!"

The fire chief shook his head. "I didn't even know there was still horses out here. All right, listen. I'll send a forestry engine your way. They can get into the woods with chainsaws, cut you a firebreak. But the prevailing wind is southerly, so unless the fire cuts into the woods due north of you, you oughta be fine."

"The houses are north of the fire, so in that case they're not even in any danger," I argued.

"Lady, I gotta be sure nothing breaks out near the houses. I'm sorry. If you are in any danger we will be here. You have my word on that."

I clutched the frame of the window, not willing to let

him go. His radio squawked urgently and he looked at me with tired eyes. "Lady, please. Let me shut down this homeowner's association and I'll send some guys down here."

"You *promise* it's not going to affect me," I said urgently.

"I can't promise you that." He sighed. "But I can tell you it probably won't."

Probably. His radio squawked again, voices calling out coordinates and unit numbers, and he sighed again and picked up the microphone from its dock on the dashboard. I backed away, hands up to concede defeat, and looked back at the smoke rising above the trees as the truck pulled out, scattering gravel in its wake. *Probably.*

Tom was putting a clean and dripping-wet Hope back in his stall when I walked back into the barn. "Where's the fire truck?" he asked, sliding the stall door shut. I chose to ignore the fact that he hadn't properly dried the horse, in light of larger events.

"We're not getting one yet. Not until the homeowner's association at Eagle Preserve is satisfied their mansions aren't going to get singed." I sighed and sat down on one of the folding chairs outside the tack room. Through the eastern barn door, I could see the endless plumes of smoke, roiling into the blue sky. "We just have to wait. He said it probably won't affect us."

"He? Probably?" Margaret came out of the tack room with a coiled hose in her hand. "Who said that? And where are the sprinklers for the indoor?"

"In the storage bin by the arena. And it was the county fire chief."

"You want someone from Forestry out here anyway,"

Margaret grumbled. "Those city boys don't know nuthin' about forest fires. Now I need to find the sprinklers. You gotta keep everything wet as you can get it. I'm gonna set up all the sprinklers around the tree-lines and then I'm lettin' 'em rip."

I nodded and Margaret went marching off, looking important and satisfied with herself with the prospect of an emergency she felt she alone could handle. Margaret the wild woodswoman, I thought, following her old boss through the wilds, riding a narrow little Arab over mountains and through rivers. She could deal with natural disasters like a wildfire with the same grim-faced determination as she attacked flipping the compost pile or stacking the hay delivery.

Tom came over to stand before me, coiling and uncoiling a lead shank and looking pale beneath his dark tan. "We haven't had big fires around here in years. I didn't think there was enough woods left anymore."

"I guess you don't need much. And besides, there's a good thousand acres out there. That's enough to burn for a few days, probably."

He shook his head, looking out at the smoke. "I'm sure it will pass. When we had those big fires in '98, hardly anyone got burned out."

"I'm sure you're right," I said quietly, willing him to go away. Hardly anyone got burned out, sure, but some folks had.

The fire lit up the night, an orange glow that burned our eyes when we looked directly east, as if one of the fireworks displays from the nearby theme parks was just exploding, and exploding, and exploding without ceasing — and doing it all in near-silence. We were too far away to hear the crackling and popping of the flames, to hear the groans of trees as they snapped and succumbed, sinking to the earth in a shower of lethal embers. Ash floated down gently on the breeze and landed on our faces and in our hair, little flakes swirling and settling like dirty snow, and here and there rested the ghostly shapes of fully-formed palmetto and oak tree leaves, spirits of lost trees which dissolved into nothingness if you touched them.

The smoke spread out in a pall over the farm, flattening beneath the starry sky above and creeping over the gables of the barn and arena. We closed the barn doors and the north-facing stall windows to keep out the ash and smoke as best we could. The south-facing stalls looked out on the peace and quiet of the paddocks, empty tonight as we tried to keep everyone's lungs clean and clear, but the orange firelight gleamed against the dark tree trunks and the black-board fencing with an unrelenting reminder of the danger approaching. The horses paced their stalls and snorted, shaking their heads and striking at their doors. No one wanted to be so close to fire.

At midnight we heard the wailing of fire trucks grow closer than they had been all night, and then there was a terrible racket as the trucks blew their horns at the front gate. Tom got up and raced for the Gator, driving it at top speed down the driveway, and minutes later a massive convoy of heavy-duty fire engines and a few National Guard jeeps were lining up in the parking lot, their hoses aimed towards the smoky palmettos to the east. I got up from my folding chair, where I'd been leaning against the barn wall in uneasy observation of the glowing wilderness, and went over to find out what was happening to my farm.

A National Guardsman in camouflage came over to meet me. "We're here to protect your property, ma'am," he announced before I could say anything. "The wind is driving this thing south, but there's no telling if it might jump over this way." He looked past my shoulder, towards the mass of barn and arena huddled in the darkness beyond the flames. "You have horses in that barn?"

"More than two dozen," I said grimly. "More than I have trailer-space for."

He nodded. "Lawn sprinklers?"

"Along the tree lines." I pointed to the watery barricade Margaret had set up. "North-side, and over to the east where I border the woods."

"And the horses — you can let them loose if you have to, right?"

I swallowed. I felt that old fear rise up in my throat like a bad taste. My Sailor, running loose without me — there would be no reins dangling, this wasn't the same thing. There *was* the county highway, though... I shook my head. "I can leave them loose, but I'd rather it not come to that. The paddocks?"

He shook his head. "If we tell you to get them out, get them out, shoo them down the driveway, and shut the doors behind them. At that point, confining them in a paddock is no better than inside the barn."

I would not be sick. I would not be sick. I would not be sick. "You tell us if it comes to that."

The Guardsman nodded. His face was dark against the firelight behind him, but I could see his jaw was strong and set. He looked ready to take on Mother Nature for me. I wanted to put my trust in him, so I did — what choice did I have? But I went back and called for Tom and Margaret,

so we could get halters on the horses.
    Just in case.

Thirty-seven

"Ma'am?"

I snapped awake, and immediately started coughing. The smoke was thick in the tack room, drifting around the ceiling and swirling through the bottles on top of the highest shelves. I sat bolt upright on the folding chair, shocked I could've fallen asleep. The clock's hands pointed to the three and the five. Three o'clock in the morning, and this was still going on. *Christ.* "What's happening?"

The National Guardsman was leaning around the door frame, looking ready to bolt back down the barn aisle. "Ma'am I need you to get all the hoses in this barn and bring them out to the edge of the arena there."

I jumped up, blood roaring in my brain, and swayed a little as my vision swam. "What — is the fire here —" I stammered, and the guardsman nodded tightly.

"It's close. I have to get back out there. We sent in a

team with chainsaws to make a bigger firebreak. I might have to call them back in, though. The wind is picking up."

"The wind —" He was gone, and I was left talking to the four walls and the thousands and thousands of dollars in saddles and bridles lining them. I put an exhausted hand to my head, longing for just a moment of peace to take it all in, and then shook it off and ran out the door.

Probably, he'd said, the son of a bitch. He could shove his probably...

The barn was lit up like noontime, and the horses were all in various states of panic, pacing their stalls, kicking their doors, banging their water buckets together. Ivor slammed a fore-hoof against his door when he saw me and neighed shrilly, as if he was demanding answers. I didn't have any for him.

In the arena, Margaret and Tom were throwing bales of hay into an untidy pile in the center of the ring. As I approached, they emptied the Gator and jumped back in, wheeling it around towards me. "What are you doing?" I called. "We need the hoses!"

"We'll get 'em now," Margaret said. "I wanted some hay stowed in case we lost the hay-shed."

I opened my mouth and shut it again. The tractor was in the hay-shed, and the drag and the extra fence posts and a whole lot of flammable cans of paint and oil and varnish... at this point, the hay-shed was a very expensive bomb.

"Wouldn't take much to lose the whole building," Margaret continued, and I could only nod. "So now we got some hay to tide us over, just in case. Stay right here, we'll start connecting the hoses." She gave Tom a tap on the arm and he floored the gas pedal, roaring away in the Gator.

I turned then and saw the fire for the first time, roaring away in the slash pines that stood nearly a hundred feet tall, just beyond the covered arena's red-shingled roof.

It seemed isolated, a trail of fire that had somehow wandered away from the rest of its party. The red glow of the wildfire's main body had passed south while I had been sleeping, and I thought the light looked a bit paler. Maybe Margaret was right and we had needed to wait for the fellows from Forestry all along. They had taken their massive fire engines down the trail, their huge tires trampling down the black-ringed hoof prints Hope had left in the white sand, and the firemen were somewhere out there now, in the palmettos and the pines, doing their best to put out the fire and save not just my farm, but the hotels and houses further south. There was a big golf course just down the road that would probably help them out a lot in that quarter.

Right here, though, we had this little fire, this renegade broken lose of the mothership, and *it* was a problem for *me* to deal with. "You're not getting my barn," I announced to the flames, and I went marching forward to do battle. There was a sprinkler out there in the corner of the property, stuck in the little verge between the arena and the tree-line. I'd pick that up and spray it deeper into the woods, soak everything in sight. Wet things couldn't burn, I knew that much. I'd get the whole damn place soaking wet.

"Is the wind changing?" Tom asked a few minutes later, dragging lengths of hose through the arena. They'd connected every hose in the barn, pilfering from the wash-stalls and the aisles, end-to-end. We had one giant super-hose now, but as I watched him train the water jet alongside my pathetic little sprinkler, and saw how much brush needed to be soaked and how little we had to do it with, I felt a wave of discouragement. Had they really needed to send all the fire engines into the woods? They couldn't leave me one?

"I can't tell what the wind is doing," I complained. "It's all just smoke now." Smoke burning my eyes and my nose, obscuring the night sky, wafting behind me to cling to the ceiling of the arena, as if it was already ablaze. *Already* — no, that was the wrong word. I wouldn't use it, and the arena would never go. I spotted some embers glowing on a nearby turkey oak and set my sprinkler on it, feeling triumphant when the red sparks were extinguished immediately. *Gotcha, bastards.* I held the sprinkler by the stake that was meant to anchor it to the ground and it was spitting water all over me — I wouldn't be catching fire tonight, either. I was drenched.

Thank goodness I was. I squinted up at the inferno above me, the flames soaring through the slash pine nearest the property line, just feet away from the shriveling green St. Augustine grass which lined the arena as neatly as any suburban lawn, and aimed my feeble water jet at the lowest branches, when a burst of light made me stagger backwards, flailing as a million hot pinpricks assailed my bare skin.

The tree had exploded, the hot sap coursing through its branches unable to take another moment of the ferocious heat. There was a starburst of white and gold that danced purple and red against my closed eyelids, and it seemed to match the thousand little burns biting at my skin. I rubbed at my arms and face frantically, shaking my head from the pinpricks of heat, but they were gone in an instant, extinguished by all the water I'd been pouring over myself in my effort to spray the trees. Then there was a hand on my shoulder, pulling me backwards, away from the fire and the fight at hand. I struggled against the pressure, trying to wriggle away. Didn't they understand? "I have to fight this thing!"

"We have an engine coming." The National Guardsman's deep voice was in my ear, firm and commanding, comfortably in charge. "We need you out of the way to let it pass."

I subsided, feeling a surge of relief that the professionals would be taking over, and let him pull me back, up the little slope and under the rail of the covered arena. The smoke was billowing under the roof and the bright arena lights high above us, casting strange shadows on the clay footing. I blinked; between the slippery shadows and the glare of the blazing wildfire just outside the arena, it was hard for my burning eyes to focus. I wondered how bad it was in the barn, and thanked the heavens for the lofty ceilings. The worst of the smoke should stay high in the rafters.

Then I jumped; the National Guardsman was slapping my ass.

"What the hell?" I spun around and fixed him with a steely glare, or as steely a glare I could manage when my eyes were red and streaming from woodsmoke.

He almost smiled, the rigid corners of his mouth wobbling a little. "You had a little bit of a fire on your rear, ma'am. I took care of it for you, but you'll need new blue jeans."

I sighed. "The least of my concerns. Where the hell is the truck?"

He pointed.

Cautiously, rattling along the sloping verge between the arena and the forest, the big yellow and white fire engine was creeping towards the fire line. It looked like some hybrid between a water truck and a war tank, with fire truck tendencies just the same. The tires were massive, for crushing brush and debris under its treads on the way to the scene of some wildfire. But in this case, it was just demolishing my expensive sod.

I'd plant more, if it didn't all burn down around my ears.

The National Guardsman left my side without a word, running back towards the fire engine and shouting commands as the firemen and guards jumped out. They were unreeling their hoses and winching this and hooking up that, yelling and pulling down masks and fixing gloves. They were preparing to go to battle, I realized, to do war against the massive fire that was threatening the farm. They were fighting for my farm at last.

The guardsman started to duck under the railing and I shouted. "Hey!"

He paused, half under the arena railing, and squinted at me. "What?"

"You save my barn, I'll cook you dinner," I shouted. "Right here at the farm."

The stoic corners of his face gave way to a crinkling, sparkling grin. "You mean it?"

"I mean it." I put my hands on my hips. "But you gotta keep this roof above my head first."

He nodded, still smiling. "You got it, ma'am," he called back, and gave me a sharp salute before he ducked the rest of the way under the railing. Then he was running down the slope, shouting commands and reaching into the engine's cab for protective gear.

I just stood there a few minutes longer, dripping wet, clothes dotted with burns, a suspiciously breezy place in my posterior where I suspected my jeans had been more than just scorched. I watched the firemen dive into the woods, hoses out, axes glinting in the arena lights and the flames' glow. I heard the roars of the chainsaws from somewhere deep in the woods, saw the trees to the south begin to fall, crashing to the ground. But the fire directly in front of us was still right at the edge of the property, its flames licking the air just yards from the arena roof. I thought of the hay-pile in the center of the arena and wished that Margaret had been slightly less efficient in bringing all that combustible material into the arena. If the flames made it over to the shingles...

Another tree fell, closer this time. Hot pine needles and flaming pine cones rolled across the wet grass behind the fire engine and glowed briefly before the dripping wet ground extinguished them. There would be more, I knew. I looked around and saw Tom standing still, his hose still in hand, watching the goings-on with wide eyes. "Tom!" I shouted. "We need to keep the hose on the grass! We're not done yet!"

Not by a long shot. I went for my abandoned sprinkler and started hosing down the ground around the arena, and Tom did the same, working his way towards me. We hosed like a pair of old ladies in their garden on a Saturday morning, while the sounds grew louder and fiercer: the crashing of trees, the wailing of chainsaws, the ever-present roar, snap, and crackle of the flames, the shouting of the firemen. This is the longest night of my life, I thought, brushing water from my eyes as the sprinkler spat back at me, the plastic housings starting to separate from so much unorthodox usage. *I need it to end.*

It all just needed to end — this battle, this fight to the death, this war with nature. The dry pine trees and palmettos were just doing the work they had been put on this earth to do: to grow lean and brittle in the dry months, to go up in flames in a burst of light, the fire cleaning the undergrowth for new trees, the rock-hard pine cones splitting open with heat to release their seeds. Fire and water were always dancing in Florida, and the scrub lands needed both for life. It was my farm, and the golf courses, and the hotels, and the houses, that wanted the good without the bad.

I couldn't help that. I loved Florida, but I had to win this one.

Florida, I can't protect you if you destroy me.

I whispered the words to the angry flames, to the glowing embers floating on the air currents, to the roiling smoke bubbling over my head, to the trees and palmettos that trembled and waited for their turn to explode into a burst of orange light.

Nothing changed.

I retreated for a few minutes to the arena rail, to lean against the PVC and take the strain off my feet and my back, and also to survey what was happening over at the fire engine. Most of the firefighters had disappeared into the woods, trailing hoses behind them like fat pythons escaping into the underbrush. I looked up at the trees and noticed that for the first time, the pines closest to the arena were dark and dripping, the flames extinguished. Further into the woods, just a few more trees were left standing and still afire. The rest, for as far as I could see over the turkey oaks before my view was blocked, were either still burning, or broken-off and smoldering. Smoldering, but no longer blazing towards the heavens.

I felt a cool breeze at my back, fluttering the hairs of my messy ponytail around my neck, and then I wondered...

A figure emerged from the small tangle of men near the front of the engine and came up the hill towards me. My heart beat a little faster when I saw that it was the National Guardsman from before, coveralls pulled over his camouflage. He pulled off his helmet and wiped at the sweat on his face, leaving dark streaks of soot and black sand. "It's turning," he called. "The wind is changing. They'll keep pushing it back, but Mother Nature is going to help us from here on out."

Maybe Florida was listening.

Florida and the ranks of firefighters who knew the state's messy secrets. Good-looking guys, some of these firefighters... especially this one.

Fully aware that I was one-hundred-percent emotionally unhinged, I stood a bit straighter and ran a hand through my half-singed hair, almost certainly making it worse. Hey, how good could a girl look when she'd been fighting a forest fire for the better part of a night? "You guys are amazing," I told him earnestly. "I can't thank you enough. Maybe I'll have to invite you all to dinner," I added teasingly.

"Oh, ma'am," he said, his voice full of dismay and his eyes full of laughter. "You wouldn't."

I grinned. He started to smile in return, then his gaze flicked away, fixing somewhere over my shoulder. "What? Not more fire?" My heart sank to my shoes.

"No —" he took my arm and gently turned me. "Look through the arena, out to the west —" He pointed at the dark night sky, visible through the open walls of the arena. I followed the direction of his finger, narrowing my eyes to see what he saw.

A flash of light, a curtain of electric-blue that extended north and south from beneath a ragged-edged rolling cloud. A wall cloud. A thunderstorm. My heart began to race and goosebumps rose on my arms, just in time for the next puffing breath of cold air to race through the arena and flutter my hair.

"Oh, thank God." I closed my eyes for a moment, fingers tightly wrapped around the wet railing. "We're saved."

The guardsman nodded, the skin on his face seeming to loosen a little, as if a long-held tension was dropping away. But his words were still guarded. "It could just bring wind and lighting. Rain isn't guaranteed." There was a second flash, and a growl of thunder, to punctuate his dour lack of enthusiasm.

"But the wind is going the right way now," I pointed out. "It's turning the fire back." The breeze fluttered the wet grass at our feet, growing stronger with every second. The storm was really flying at us now, the way that Florida storms tend to do when they are big and bad and full of danger. The weather radio was probably wailing, the weather service bot itching to tell us about hail, high winds, deadly lightning, possible tornadoes. Just another spring cold front. "And there's nothing to the southeast of the woods but a golf course, so it's not as if it's going to endanger houses."

Once that golf course had been pastures, a ranch house,

and barns, but that wasn't worth thinking about now.

The guardsman nodded, still watching the storm. "Maybe you're right. It's not my policy to put much stock in anything until I know for sure, though, and with weather you can't never know for sure."

He had a country way of speaking, though he never struck me as uneducated. I liked that balance. I liked *him*, a lot, although I was willing to grant it just might be the damsel in distress talking at the moment. "What's your name?" I asked suddenly. If he was called away to work suddenly, how would I find him again? Have him over for that dinner? I was conveniently forgetting I wasn't much of a cook.

"Luke," he replied, turning towards me with another one of those rare smiles. "Luke Fowler."

"Grace Carter," I said formally. "It's a pleasure to meet you, Luke Fowler." It was a country-sounding name, too.

"The pleasure is mine, Grace Carter," Luke said warmly. "I hope you won't think I'm rude, but I have to go finish fighting this fire, so..." He inclined his head towards the blaze beyond the arena. I waved him away with the air of a queen dismissing a subject and he flashed me one more devilish grin as he went.

I stood still for a minute, gazing unseeingly towards the fire as it reached up towards the dark night sky. Well how do you like that, I was thinking. You really never do know where you'll meet a nice man.

Thirty-eight

"I hate to say this, but it looks kind of like Colleen got her way."

I glared at Kennedy. "Don't you believe it," I snapped. "Miss Colleen is about to have her ass handed to her." I turned back to the blackened ruins of the scrub. "She can't just come and burn down my woods because she got a little too spendy with her credit cards."

There was a flurry of motion out in the smoking scrub, the sunlight glinting on yellow hard hats flashing brightly between the blackened stumps of pine trees and the burnt stubs of palmetto bushes. The arson investigators were out there, along with the forestry service, Fish and Wildlife, and who knew who else. When you set fire to my land, you had better be ready to face the consequences. I'd listed every endangered species I could think of when I'd made my police report, and claimed they all lived in happy profusion out there in the scrub. Most of them did; all of them might. My goal was to put as many boots on the ground as possible. Someone would find *something* that didn't just implicate Roth and friends in the fire, but saved the land from future development — I was sure of it.

It would have been easier if I'd just put the damn land in a trust the way I'd always meant to, but I always was one for procrastinating.

Kennedy shifted beside me, kicking at a burnt pine-cone. It split into a million pieces and the seeds shifted onto the white sand at our feet. "Would you look at that," she murmured.

"Fire-dependent ecosystem," I said, parroting the Fish and Wildlife representative who had stopped by for a chat before plowing his four-wheel drive out onto the trail (which was now much easier to find, since the trees that had once sheltered it were reduced to ash and stumps). "The pine trees can't seed until their pine cones are burned up. And the palmettos will be start growing back in no time. It'll be scarred, but it'll be pretty."

"And the trail rides?"

I sighed, resigned to a delay in my plans. "It's going to take a little while before people are going to pay me to go look at these woods." All of my land's charms had been sadly diminished: the shell mound reduced to nothing but a hill with smoking crisps of oak branches scattering its charred sands; the green prairie of palmettos left twisted and blackened; the smell of wood smoke hanging in the air like a fall day in a northern clime. At least the cypress had been spared. It was the *getting* there that no one would enjoy. A trail ride through an apocalypse — I'd be marketing to a very specific demographic to sell *that*, and the zombie fans weren't really the element I wanted at my barn.

"So… what's next?"

I heard Kennedy's anxiety. She'd quit her job for this, after all. The ponies who would bring her a commission someday were still green as grass; the children's lesson program was coming along, but slowly; the farm was still teetering on the edge of bankruptcy. The fire was pushing back the trail rides for at least six months. Was this the final shove, I heard her wondering? Were we both out of luck?

A gleam of light revealed a car on the driveway. The mailman was coming. I shrugged. "Maybe there'll be a check for a million dollars in the mailman's truck."

Kennedy scowled, but I wasn't up to taking her words seriously right now. What was next? Who the hell knew? All I knew was, if I'd held onto the farm this long, there *had* to be another way to keep it going. Another way to keep diversifying the business.

The mail truck stopped and Vic, the portly mail carrier who had been delivering here for a hundred years, more or less, stepped out. He rubbed his red forehead, brushing back his sparse white strands. "Got a certified letter for ya, Grace."

I threw Kennedy a mocking smile. "What'd I tell you? Million dollars." She managed to grin in response.

Vic handed over a legal-size envelope in exchange for my scrawled signature. I scanned the return address: some firm based in Boston. "You ever heard of these guys?"

Vic shrugged. "I never hearda nobody," he said, climbing back into the truck. "I just delivers their mail."

Fair enough. I slit the envelope's seal right there in the

parking lot. If it was some development company telling me they were after the land, too, I needed to find out about it some place away from the horses. Because I was going to scream.

I read the elegantly typed letter once, then again. I was starting in a third time, my lips silently forming the words, when Kennedy lost her patience. "What does it *say?*"

"It says someone wants to pay me to run a training center for developing riders," I said, disbelievingly. " 'Adult and young riders who need special focus on certain skills in order to become competitive on an international level.' " I looked at Kennedy, the letter dropping to my side. "It's not a million dollars, but it's enough."

"It's enough?"

"To carry on." I started to laugh. "To keep the farm. We're not going anywhere."

Epilogue

I waited until Kennedy was done with her riding lesson to break the news.

She put away the last saddle while Anna started hosing down the school horses, all of them in dire need of a full bath after an afternoon's work in the heat. The covered arena wasn't quite as cool now that we'd lost so many shade trees to the fire, although it was still a better option than riding under the blazing June sun. A few kids had been threatening to give up lessons for the summer, but Kennedy was very persuasive and had managed to keep all of them committed to their saddle-time despite the heat — for now.

Still, I was glad we weren't depending completely on the kids to make ends meet. The summer rains were slowly starting to make their presence known, with rumblings in the afternoon and an occasional downpour. Once the blackened scrub was starting to sprout green again, and the smell of charred wood had been drowned once and for all, I'd call up all the hotels and let them know we were ready to start accepting clients. In the meantime, I was letting the trail horses do a little lesson-time. Sure, a spotty horse like Rainbow didn't have the glossy well-bred look that my clients were accustomed to... but he was safe, and he was quiet, and little kids didn't care about pedigrees. So the trail horses were sort-of, almost, earning their oats.

The commission from Bailey's sale would come in handy, too, once it was finished. He was at a barn in Wellington on trial right now. I only saw Colleen when she dropped off her daughter for her riding lesson. I felt for Colleen. Sure, she was a bitch and she'd been trying to save her own ass by getting bulldozers onto my property, but giving up your horse was always a harsh punishment, no matter how terrible a person you were. She was showing rare strength of character (for her) in still financing her daughter's riding, even though she'd had to put her own aspirations on hold once again.

She was also fortunate no one had yet managed to connect the arson in the woods to her or any of her friends, but I had my hopes.

So we were surviving, for now. None of it, though, not the boarding, not the lessons, not the commissions, would tip the farm back into the black with taxes through the roof, feed and bedding at astronomical highs, and show fees starting to frighten my most competitive students. The resources required to show A-circuit hunter/jumper horses was simply out of control.

Which was why this email was so interesting.

Kennedy came out of the tack room and tipped back a Diet Coke. She looked completely wiped out from yelling (mostly ignored) instructions at prep school kids for two hours straight. "Hey, Ken, check this out," I called, waving the print-out. She raised her eyebrows and came over.

"What's this?"

I handed it over and watched her eyebrows shoot up to her frizzy hair. "An eventer?"

"Yeah... you ever heard of her? Apparently they want me to work on her dressage and show-jumping. She's being sent here for three months... assuming she agrees."

"For a sponsorship? She'll agree or she's crazy." Kennedy skimmed the email again. "Jules Thornton... don't know her. But I don't know much about eventing."

Anna paused in her horse-showers. "Jules Thornton? My cousin knows her. Total diva. Got in a huge public fight with her working student last summer. Everyone was talking about it." She went back to hosing down Rainbow, who had closed his speckled eyelids in bliss.

Kennedy gave me a skeptical look. "Didn't we just get rid of a diva?"

I shrugged. "This one's going to be a working student," I reminded her. "If she gets snotty with us, we'll just give her more stalls to strip."

Anna snorted, and the rest of us broke into laughter. It was hot, and we were tired, and there were miles to go before the day was over, but things were looking up. My first development project was on her way. Even if Miss Jules Thornton tried to play the diva with me, I was getting paid to take on a working student. *That*, my friend, was diversification.

I looked around my show barn, the farm I'd built for myself and the dreams I'd made concrete on the land my grandfather had left to me, and felt that profound sense of contentment which only comes at rare, wonderful moments in life. We all got the blues once in a while. All it took was a little kick in the pants, though to shake things up and change things up. We were on a new path now.

"Boss? You need to ride Donner now if you're going to have time for Gayle's lesson before we feed supper. He's tacked and ready to go."

I snapped myself out of my daydreams and made for the tack room to grab my hard hat. There were horses to ride, a hint of rain in the air, and a thousand things to be thankful for. I'd count them over while I was trotting around the arena.

After all, things always looked better from the back of a good horse.

About the Author

Natalie Keller Reinert grew up with horses: first riding hunters, then discovering her true love, eventing, with a green off-track Thoroughbred named Amarillo. But never one to turn down an experience, she has also started and galloped racehorses, groomed for Olympians, rode on mounted patrol in NYC, and so much more. Today, Reinert lives in Florida with her family, where she spends most of her time writing.

For more information and to keep up with new projects, visit NatalieKReinert.com. You can also follow Reinert on Twitter at @nataliekreinert and on Facebook at facebook.com/NatalieKellerReinert.

CPSIA information can be obtained at www.ICGtesting.com
Printed in the USA
LVOW11s1138140816

500334LV00008B/555/P